IN THE NAME OF LOVE

Why does a twenty-three-year-old graduate student feel guilty if she forgets to call her parents twice a week? What can a twenty-eight-year-old businessman do when he can't make a decision without consulting his father? How can the adult child of adoring parents ever live up to their high expectations? Why is the spouse of an overparented adult child never quite good enough? Why do parents become obsessed with their childrens' lives to the exclusion of their own?

The answers to these and many other questions are found in—

WHEN PARENTS LOVE TOO MUCH

LAURIE ASHNER is a writer, teacher, and educational therapist.

MITCH MEYERSON is a psychotherapist specializing in the treatment of dysfunctional family relationships.

WHEN PARENTS LOVE TOO MUCH

WHAT HAPPENS WHEN PARENTS WON'T LET GO

LAURIE ASHNER & MITCH MEYERSON

AVON BOOKS ◢ NEW YORK

AVON BOOKS
A division of
The Hearst Corporation
105 Madison Avenue
New York, New York 10016

Copyright © 1990 by Laurie Ashner and Mitch Meyerson
Published by arrangement with the author
Library of Congress Catalog Card Number: 89-48252
ISBN: 0-380-70813-2

Published in hardcover by William Morrow and Company, Inc.; for
information address Permissions Department, William Morrow and
Company, Inc., 105 Madison Avenue, New York, New York 10016.

The William Morrow and Company edition contains the following Library of Congress Cataloging in Publication Data:

Ashner, Laurie.
  When parents love too much: what happens when parents won't let
go/Laurie Ashner and Mitch Meyerson.

  p. cm.
  Includes bibliographical references.
1. Child rearing—United States. 2. Parental overprotection—United
States. I. Meyerson, Mitch. II. Title.
HQ769.A795 1990
649′.1—dc20   89-48252

First Avon Books Printing: May 1991

AVON TRADEMARK REG. U.S. PAT. OFF. AND IN OTHER COUNTRIES, MARCA
REGISTRADA, HECHO EN U.S.A.

Printed in the U.S.A.

RA 10 9 8 7 6 5 4 3 2 1

To Sylvia Schwab,
who loved me just enough!
—L.A.

To my parents,
who always supported my dreams
—M.M.

PREFACE

This is not a book about blaming parents. In fact, it was parents who encouraged us to write it and who shared their stories of love and concern for their children, so all-encompassing and absorbing that it became painful and self-defeating.

In a world where so many children are abused and abandoned, devoted parents who love so much that they will do anything for their children appear ideal. But parents who love too much share a daily experience of hurt, anxiety, and emotional pain that comes from a habitual way of thinking about and behaving toward their children.

For parents who love too much, worry is a constant companion. Concern over their children's lives and troubles can become so torturous that they cannot eat, sleep, or think about anything else.

Nothing is too difficult to do if it will help the child. Expectations are so high that continual frustration with their children is inevitable. Frightened that their children may flounder unless they navigate and steer them through their daily activities, they become frantic guides. They see their children's responsibilities as their own. Friends, interests, and even the spouse is neglected so that they can be available to the child at every moment. They give until they are empty and aching inside, but it is still not enough to stop the constant worry or help their children change into all they believe they can be.

Children who grow up in homes where dedicated and well-meaning parents "overparent" because they care about their children so deeply become adults who know they are loved. But they also live with a burden of anxiety, guilt, and dependency that can be emotionally crippling. The adult children who speak out in this book reveal a history of high parental expectations coupled with over-protective love that had far-reaching costs for all involved.

No one sets out deliberately to love his or her children in a way that is ultimately self-defeating and destructive. How does it happen?

The patterns of loving too much are acquired unconsciously during a parent's own childhood. In every parent who loves too much, there are memories of someone in the past who failed to provide the acceptance or love that he or she needed desperately.

If you are a parent who loves too much, you may have grown up in an alcoholic, violent, or chaotic home where the people you depended on were unable to meet your emotional or physical needs. Or perhaps the people you depended on were indifferent or preoccupied with their own troubles. They ignored you, or demanded so much from you that nothing was ever good enough. Or maybe they loved you, but only when you repressed your own feelings or frantically tried to please them in any way you knew.

All of this caused you pain and disappointment. Still, you kept trying to get the love you were denied, going to the same dry well over and over again. You became dutiful and responsible. You learned to take control in situations where everyone around you seemed out of control. You learned to put your own needs last. You became a giver, hoping that others would give you the love or acceptance you needed in return.

Whatever you did, it was never enough. In the end, you left childhood feeling that *you* were not enough. A desire was born to never, ever, allow your own children to feel the same way.

When we love our children too much, we don't usually suspect that it's because of our own needs, rather than theirs. This is hardest to understand, especially if we are parents of a child who is in trouble. We provide love, money, attention, understanding, and help in a way that is almost obsessive. We devote our lives to making our children happy by solving their problems. The pain when we don't succeed can be unbearable. We want to put an end to the awful feeling of not being good enough—good enough to be *loved*—by being enough as parents. It's no wonder that nothing less than being perfect parents with perfect children will do.

An obsession with other people's lives and problems to the extent that we seldom deal with our own has been termed codependency. Codependency is a compulsion to help and control others, and do for them what they could be doing for themselves. Parents who love too much are codependent people whose own needs go unmet as they focus all of their energy on their children's lives and troubles.

If you are an adult child who was loved too much, you may not recognize your parents in this description. Outwardly, your parents may seem to be a tower of strength. They may share very little of their own past with you. Because of their devotion, you know that you are loved. You can count many advantages of growing up with so much attention and protection and it makes you feel terribly guilty to question your childhood at all.

Still, you never feel that you are good enough. Your parents expect so much of you and their constant advice and overprotection frustrates and unnerves you, even as it makes you feel safe. The fact that you've been given so much feeds your guilt, especially when you think about how little you've been able to give your parents in return. You're extremely self-critical and so perfectionistic that you can't bring yourself to really *do* anything, because your performance might be less than phenomenal. So much love and attention flowed freely in your direction that you're amazed that it's so difficult to find love and intimacy outside of your family.

You are not alone. Hundreds of adult children and parents shared their stories for this book. Although the case histories included are composite portraits and do not represent any particular individuals, the heart of the stories has been kept intact.

This book is not about blaming you or your parents for what you feel today. It's about recognizing and understanding the patterns that result from loving and being loved too much that lead to a legacy of emotional pain, bitterness, and dependency for both parents and adult children. It's about changing these patterns, and gaining the freedom to live your own lives.

ACKNOWLEDGMENTS

Many people contributed to the publication of this book and we are grateful to each of them:

Susan Schulman, our agent, for believing in this project from the beginning and guiding it through to completion

Marcie Tilkin, for reading and enthusiastically supporting our work

Nancy Block, for her unfailing encouragement and support

Anita Loneiro, who convinced us that this book needed to be written

Jay and Pat Levinson, for providing a vision and the inspiration to go for it

Dr. Michael Franz Basch, Dr. Ann Jernberg, and Dr. Joseph Walsh, for their wisdom and insight into parent/child relationships

Mark Langgut, Rick Tivers, and Alice Graubart, for their editorial skill and helpful feedback

And all of the people who agreed to be interviewed for this book and shared their most intimate experiences.

CONTENTS

I

The Children Who Were Loved Too Much

CHAPTER 1

THE SILVER PLATTER

"You deserve the best of everything."

"My parents think the world of me. They'd do anything for me. The truth is, they do too much. People think that if you grew up in a nice home, with parents who love you as much as mine loved me, you never have a problem. Well, I've got more trouble in my life than anything else. I can't be in a relationship without screwing it up. I feel guilty about everything, and nothing I do ever seems good enough."

—Jeff, age 26

In the beginning, giving in seems easier than fighting back. Our parents only want what's best for us. They just want to help.

Their constant phone calls confirm this: "How come you never call me?" they ask. "I've been so worried about you. Why don't you come over more often?" They're interested. They're concerned. They need us.

Their advice falls over us in an endless stream. We squirm under it for hours, every time we visit.

Envelopes full of newspaper clippings arrive in our mail. The headlines read, THE DEADLY VIRUS YOUR DOCTOR MAY OVERLOOK, or SINGLE GIRL MURDERED IN UPTOWN APARTMENT. Scrawled at the bottom, in bold letters, our parents' concern: "Are you taking care of yourself? You look too thin. You're wearing yourself out at that job. Why don't you relax more? Why don't you meet someone nice and get married? Why do you want to live alone, in that dirty city, where people get murdered?''

In a world where so many children are orphaned, abused, and mistreated, we feel ungrateful and ashamed because our biggest problem is that our parents love us too much.

Nothing takes too much time or is too much trouble if it will help us. If they could, they'd shield us from all pain and hurt. If we'd just listen to them, they'd solve all our problems.

Since babyhood we've been told how much we mean to our parents, how important our accomplishments are to them. Their pride in us is enormous. Their expectations of us are even greater. We feel their judgments, subtle yet pervasive. We deserve only the best. How can we settle so easily for less?

Although our parents love us, they don't necessarily provide a home that brims with understanding, acceptance, or even visible affection. For some of us, bitter words, angry sulks, or anxious exasperation sum up our day-to-day experience with our parents. But always, as their children, we're in the spotlight. Our lives become a stage on which the drama of our parents' hopes and dreams is played.

If we allow it, our parents stay firmly enmeshed in our lives. We drown in the outpouring of their attention, concern, and anxiety. Gripped by guilt, we choke on resentment when we can't be all the things they expect us to be. Bickering across the dinner table, we struggle to free ourselves. "Love me," we want to say, "but don't love me so much!"

Kate's story is a case in point. "My mother is driving me crazy," she admits. "I'm going through the hardest time of my life, and she's making it worse."

Recently, Kate's husband, Jim, told her he wanted a divorce. "Since I told my mother, I haven't had a moment's peace. She calls me all day long with warnings like, 'Don't let him take anything out of your house!,' and

'Make sure you get everything you're entitled to!' She phones Jim at his office to lecture him about his responsibilities to his family.

"I've told her to stop calling, to let me handle Jim on my own. She'll stop for maybe a day or two, then she starts up again. She's terrified that I might make a decision on my own, without her input."

Kate, the youngest of three children, has always been her mother's favorite child. "You have to understand my mother," Kate sighs. "She simply believes I can do no wrong. She has more in common with my brother, who's interested in books and music like she is. She does more with my sister, who's always in trouble and needs her for something. But I've always known from the way she looks at me and talks to me, that I'm *it* as far as she's concerned. I guess that's why my divorce bothers her so much."

Kate married Jim when she was twenty-one. "My parents gave us a huge wedding, with all the trimmings. The thing is, they couldn't really afford it. My dress alone cost close to a thousand dollars. I know my father had to take out loans to pay for it, although he denied it.

"Actually, Jim and I wanted a small wedding with just our immediate families, but my parents wouldn't hear of it. They kept saying that they had waited for this day all their lives, and that we shouldn't deny them the happiness of walking down the aisle in front of all their friends and relatives. So we gave in. In the end, I was glad we did it their way. But Jim never really forgave them."

As time passed, tension grew between Jim and Kate's mother. "Jim called my mother 'The Director.' He complained that she was always interfering. My mother and I have always been close. Not that we don't fight all the time, but I've always discussed everything with her. Jim couldn't understand it. He'd tell me not to share all of our intimate stuff with her, to keep certain things to myself. But, really, my mother means well. She only wants what's best for me."

After an uncomfortable pause, Kate admits, "I know my mother interferes in my life. It's just that I've never been strong enough to stand up to her. I can only remember standing up to her once. When I was eighteen and applying to colleges, she insisted that I apply to Brown University. It was important to her that I go to a 'prestige' college. Well, I refused to apply to Brown. I knew it was a really hard school. My grades in high school were never that great. I always avoided the difficult classes. If a teacher was too hard, I made my parents complain and get me switched out of the class. When I had a hard assignment, they'd sit down at the kitchen table and do it with me. So even though my grades looked good on paper, I didn't kid myself. I was pretty sure I'd flunk out of Brown.

"My mother thought differently. To her, I was a genius. She had this 'shrine' in the kitchen of my report cards and papers I'd written and dozens of pictures of me hanging on the wall. If one of my friends wanted a Coke or something from the kitchen, I'd run to get it. I thought I'd die if anyone saw all of that stuff hanging there.

"Anyway, I told my mother there was no way I was applying to Brown. One afternoon a letter came in the mail for me from Brown University. 'We are pleased to inform you that your application for admission has been accepted.' I was livid. My mother applied for me, and signed my name on the application, wrote my personal essay, and everything."

The fight over colleges was the first battle that Kate won. But the school Kate chose for herself wasn't all that she'd hoped it would be. Knowing how her mother felt about the school made her feel too guilty to enjoy it, as if enjoying it would be too much of a slap in the face to her mother. Worse, Kate was lonely and homesick, spending most of her freshman year alone in her dorm room, ordering pizzas and lying in letters to her parents about all the friends she was making.

"I've never made friends very easily," Kate says. "My mother could never accept that. It's just that I'm shy. I hate parties, and parties was what my college was all about. As a child, if I wasn't invited to someone's birthday party, my mother would phone the kid's mother and wangle an invitation for me. I'd be so humiliated, but she'd force me to go. I've avoided parties ever since."

Sophomore year was worse. Kate went through three roommates that year, unable to get along with any of them. "By April, no one was speaking to me.

"I never admitted any of this to my parents. How could they understand? They always told me how beautiful I was, how wonderful. They refused to listen to anything else.

"It all exploded inside of me one night. 'This is your wonderful, beautiful daughter calling,' I sobbed into the phone. 'You keep telling me how terrific I am. Well, how come everyone hates me, except you?'

"My mother blamed it all on the college I'd chosen. I got a lot of I-told-you-so's. My grades went from bad to worse. There was no one there to help me. I felt life was pretty unfair. Finally, at the end of sophomore year, I dropped out."

Kate returned home, feeling guilty and afraid to face her mother. "I felt like I was this huge disappointment to my parents. They'd expected me to shine at college. I knew my failure was killing my mother. What would she tell her friends?"

Kate enrolled in a community college, where she met Jim. "It was so easy to be with Jim at first," Kate recalls. "We never argued about anything. He seemed interested in everything I was thinking and feeling. He was always asking me questions about myself, like I was the most fascinating person in the world.

"We married the day after I graduated. From the beginning, Jim felt hurt that I trusted my mother's advice more than his. He said I did much more to make my parents happy than I ever did for him.

"I was never the type of wife who had to crawl inside her husband's head and understand everything about him. Jim would complain that I wasn't interested in his career. To tell you the truth, when Jim would tell me stories about what was happening in his office, I'd get bored.

"At the start, I ran to my parents every time Jim and I had a fight. I knew I'd get sympathy. No matter how much I knew I'd provoked him, fifteen minutes at my parents' house convinced me that I was right and he was wrong."

Jim felt that he had to perform for Kate's parents and

that nothing he ever accomplished was good enough. The mistrust Jim and Kate's mother felt for each other stayed hidden beneath the growing tension until Kate became pregnant with her daughter, Cara. "My parents bought me a full layette, a bedroom set, a roomful of toys for the baby—and all sorts of things I didn't really need. Jim got really mad. I couldn't understand what he was so angry at me for. I didn't ask my parents for all those things. They just did it on their own, like they always do. He said he'd like to buy some things for our baby, and that my parents had ruined it for him. I didn't have the heart to tell Mom to take all of that stuff back. We kept it, and it was a real sore point between the two of us.

"When I was in my eighth month with Cara, Jim was laid off from his job. He walked around depressed for days, constantly talking about how scared he was and how he felt like a failure. One morning he actually started to cry. I was so uncomfortable. I was all wrapped up in my pregnancy. To be honest, I was having a hard time trying to hide the fact that I was pretty angry that he'd gotten laid off. I just wanted him to stop talking about it. When I tried to change the subject, he stormed out of the house.

"After Cara was born, I spent more time with my mother than ever. Cara would cry for hours at a time. I wouldn't trust myself to do the right thing, so I'd call my mother, who would rush over.

"When Cara was about a year old, she ran a very high fever. I got hysterical; even though our pediatrician told me not to worry, that all babies run high fevers. Mom drove us to the emergency room that afternoon. She didn't trust the doctor, either.

"We were at the hospital for hours. Neither of us thought to call Jim. When I got home, he was there, pacing the floor. He'd tried to call me all day, and panicked when he couldn't reach me. He couldn't get over the fact that I hadn't phoned him. 'Would you have known what to do?' I demanded. He stared at me in disbelief and hardly spoke to me for the few next weeks.

"When Cara was five, my mother began this campaign to convince me that Cara should go to a private school, instead of our neighborhood school. I knew Jim would hate that. Behind his back, Mom and I took Cara for an interview with the private school's principal. Of course, Cara couldn't keep the secret. She told Jim all about the nice lady she met at the nice school. Jim exploded. After that, we did nothing but fight.

"Things went from bad to worse. Jim called me a spoiled brat, still tied to Mother's apron strings. I accused him of being a lousy father, more interested in saving money than in Cara's education. One night Jim packed a suitcase and left, saying that he'd had enough of me and my mother.

"Today, Jim says that I never really loved him, that I just wanted him to love me," Kate confides. "He blames my mother for most of our troubles, but I don't think it's true. She really just wants to help. I know she cares more about me than anyone ever will. But her love is beginning to feel like a weight around my neck. She's tried all my life to protect me. I can't be angry with her, even though she's driving me crazy these days. I owe her too much."

Kate's early experiences were typical of a child who grows up in a home where the drama of the children's lives becomes the parent's obsession. Nothing was more compelling to Kate's mother than her children's problems. She sought to navigate and steer Kate through the troubled waters of her responsibilities, terrified that Kate would flounder without her help and advice.

When Kate's mother enmeshed herself in her daughter's life, she did it out of love and the desire to be a caring parent. However, Kate's mother *overparented*, and loved Kate too much.

What is too much love? Let's look more closely at characteristics of parents such as Kate's that differentiate them from parents who love in healthier ways:

- A parent who loves gives time, attention, and affection to the child and provides for his emotional and physical needs. A parent who loves too much enmeshes himself in the child's life, and sees the child as an extension of himself.

- A parent who loves is determined to be the best parent he or she can be, while recognizing that it's impossible to be perfect. A parent who loves too much "overparents" and overprotects the child in an effort to dispel anxiety over being a "good" parent, or to make up for his or her own childhood deprivation.

- A parent who loves encourages independence and growth while setting appropriate limits, thus providing a safe environment for the child to explore and promoting his autonomy. A parent who loves too much discourages the child's independence, seeks to control the child's thoughts and actions, and unconsciously wishes to mold the child into the image of his highest expectations of himself.

- A parent who loves accepts that the child has strengths and weaknesses. He or she provides a nonjudgmental atmosphere in which self-esteem is fostered. A parent who loves too much unconsciously judges the child who can't live up to his rigid expectations. He does *for* the child, rather than *with* him, fearing that the child will fail without his help.

- A parent who loves communicates with the child in a direct, open, and honest way, creating an atmosphere of safety and trust. A parent who loves too much often creates insecurity and mistrust by communicating indirectly with the child, seeking, unconsciously, to manipulate or control.

- A parent who loves listens to the child and gives out of a desire to meet the child's emotional or material needs. A parent who loves too much unconsciously gives to meet his or her own unmet desires and unfulfilled hopes, with little regard to what the child truly needs.

- A parent who loves encourages the child's internal strengths and qualities. A parent who loves too much is more concerned with externals, and anxiously compares his child to others.

People who overparent their children may be rich or poor. They may be single, married, or widowed. They may work sixty-four-hour weeks, or rarely leave home. The capacity for overparenting is not a function of wealth. Nor does it have as much to do with time spent in the physical presence of the children as the hours spent mulling, brooding, and worrying about them. Overparenting is not necessarily spoiling children, although that can be one outcome. It's an intense emotional overinvolvement coupled with a need to control the child. It encourages a mutual dependency that is powerful as well as painful.

Sometimes overparenting is reserved for one child in a family. It may be the firstborn. It can also be the baby. Sometimes it's the child who shows special talent, but it is just as likely to be the "problem" child who shows little ability at all. Which child is singled out has more to do with the parents' needs than the child's.

Kate's mother had many of the characteristics of a parent who loves too much. She bestowed the "gifts" of time, attention, and material things with little regard to what Kate truly needed or wanted. She sought control of Kate's life, invalidating her daughter's wishes and encouraging her dependence. She gave Kate such a high assessment of herself that Kate's life became a series of disappointments when others couldn't love or acknowledge her the way her parents did.

A parent's love forms the basis of a child's early self-esteem. Without our parents' care, interest, and approval, we grow up with feelings of emptiness and worthlessness where our self-love should be. It would therefore seem logical that the more love we receive from our parents—the more attention, concern, and protection—the greater our sense of self-worth. For Kate, the opposite proved to be true. Like most children who were loved too much, the anxious direction Kate received throughout her life from her mother did little to bolster her self-esteem. In fact, her self-worth became tied to her mother's approval. Kate felt safest when she was pleasing her mother. The more her mother controlled her, the more passive she became.

Nothing in her history with her parents prepared her to

contribute emotionally to relationships, or to take some responsibility for maintaining them. In light of Kate's early experiences, it is no surprise that she and Jim encountered problems early in their relationship. When Kate met Jim, all she had to bring to their relationship were her somewhat sketchy notions, gleaned from her parents, of what it meant to love or be loved in return. Kate's overpowering feelings of anxiety when Jim cried in her presence and her unwillingness to meet his needs are evidence of her emotional absence from their relationship. Kate was looking for a provider in Jim, someone who would care for her without asking for much in return. Kate sees now that although she married Jim and had his child, she was never really intimate with him. Kate's dependence on her mother and the closeness of their relationship left little room for Jim.

Not all children submit to their parents' control as willingly as Kate did. Many rebel, only to give in and return each time the guilt becomes too great. But whether they rebel or submit, each pays a heavy cost for being overparented.

When our parents see us as a mirror, seeking to "mold" us into the image of their highest expectations; when they enmesh themselves in the day-to-day drama of our lives, fighting our battles for us and shielding us from pain; when they give us more attention than we could ever need or desire; when they make our responsibilities their own, we get a mixed message with mixed results. We learn to feel special and deserving of attention, but we don't learn to identify and ask for what we need. We learn to take direction from others, but we become afraid to use initiative or trust our own instincts. We learn how to manipulate to receive attention, but we do not know how to give clear and direct messages to people. We understand how to "look good" in relationships, but we are too fearful to open ourselves to true intimacy.

From our beginnings, we reach adulthood with a particular style of behavior and a certain set of beliefs about ourselves. The following characteristics become typical of adult children who, like Kate, were overparented. If you grew up surrounded by smothering attention, overconcern, or unrealistically high expectations, these characteristics may be true of you, also:

You Have Problems with Intimacy and Relationships

Our relationships with others are confounded by two extremes: neediness, or an unconscious desire to distance people who come close. In either case, we enter adulthood with the feeling that other people's needs for closeness (or our own) are overwhelming.

We desire intimacy, yet we fear it. We learn from our parents that with love comes high expectations for performance. What if we can't be all a lover expects? If we let someone become close to us, and we fail to be all that they want us to be, won't we be rejected? And if we are what they desire, won't we be smothered?

We begin to push other people out of our lives by becoming overly needy and dependent, or by distancing them with aloofness or arrogance. Whatever our tactic, the result is the same: We crave intimacy, but we're too fearful to let ourselves truly experience it.

You Thrive on Approval from Others

Adult children who were overparented often become "people-pleasers," sensitive to the needs of others and preoccupied with "looking good."

As children, we measured our self-worth by how much approval we received from our parents. Approval rarely, if ever, came from within. Our self-esteem became dependent on praise and recognition from parents. With little or no "sense of self"—awareness of who we were inside without our accomplishments and talents to define us—we transferred this dependence onto others in our lives.

We're constantly waiting for others to make us feel

good, and living for other people's approval is a dangerous way to go. Much of the time we won't get the approval we thrive on. Most people just don't care about us as much as our mother or father did. This is reality, and it never stops frustrating us.

You Have a Pervasive Sense of Guilt, Even When You're Not Responsible

"I feel guilty about everything!" is a frequent statement of children who were overparented. Such children realize in the early years that their parents will go out of their way to provide for them. Some of this giving is in material offerings of money, clothes, food, and shelter. Much more is in the form of attention—an eternal vigilance that quickly becomes smothering. The child develops a sense of debt toward parents who love him so enormously.

If this was our experience, the only way we know how to pay back our parents for their love is to be a good little boy or girl. We feel we should never be angry at our parents, who have done so much for us. We learn to suppress any negative feelings, as they might hurt our parents. We feel we have to achieve things for them, please them, and make them proud of us. When we can't, we feel enormous guilt.

You Feel That Life Is Unfair

Early in childhood, the child who was overparented discovers that the world doesn't share all of the admiration and confidence in his or her talents that was routinely bestowed at home. Disappointment and insecurity follow.

Few of us are able to live up to the high hopes and expectations of our parents. Unfortunately, we grow doubtful about any of our accomplishments. Our parents told us that we were capable of so much, that we only had to reach out and grab all life had to offer. When the world isn't every wonderful thing our parents promised us it would be, life seems unfair.

You Have Difficulty Putting Trust in Other People

Trust is a troublesome issue for children of parents who loved too much. We either trust no one, or become hopelessly naive to the true motives of others, believing anything we're told until we're bitterly disappointed.

Why is trust such an issue for us? Our basic sense of trust or mistrust is shaped in early childhood. We make conscious and unconscious decisions about whether our world is a safe place for us.

Mothers and fathers who overparent their children are generally driven by anxiety about their child's well-being. If parents seek too much control or make all the decisions for their child, he or she receives the indirect message, My decisions are not good enough . . . I cannot trust myself. If his parents overprotect him and fill his ears with warnings about how other people and things in the environment can hurt him, he or she grows to believe, I cannot trust others.

This pervasive feeling of insecurity is at the core of our personalities, staying with us as we grow up. Our trust may be further shaken when we begin to interact with our peers. In our early childhood years, our parents let us know that we were special and deserving of constant attention. As we meet people outside of our family, we sadly realize that the rest of the world does not always share this view. Whom, then, can we trust? This basic core of mistrust is projected out into the world to create an even more threatening environment. We mistrust people and opportunities, fearing criticism, rejection, and physical harm.

You Need to Feel in Control

Feeling "in control" is extremely important. Because adult children who were overparented have a long experience of being controlled by their parents, they often become rigidly controlled in an effort to fend others off.

As young children, we are totally dependent on our parents. In normal development, we are allowed to stretch ourselves and test our power in new situations. We have some success and some failure. We learn from our mistakes.

Overprotective parents, however, do not let us take risks. Seeking to protect us, they get overly involved in the moment-to-moment drama of our lives. To buffer us from any potential harm, they steer us away from the challenges of life where we might fail or be frustrated.

As a result, we can grow up feeling helpless. As a defense, we need to feel in control, and can become very controlling of others ourselves. Often we exert our control in a passive, withholding manner. We withdraw, avoid, reject, or rebel against people who have authority over us. The lack of confidence most of us have in our bosses, our children's teachers, or the government is a reflection of this. It's difficult for us to be "team players." We're much better working independently, where we're completely in control.

Because letting go of control has always meant being smothered, dominated, and overprotected, we "expect" the same response from others in our lives. The rigid and controlling personality style we may adopt gives us the illusion of assertiveness and strength, but also creates distance and conflict in our relationships.

You Have Difficulty Following a Project Through from Beginning to End

Children who were overwhelmed by the unrealistic expectations of their parents often become dreamers with excellent schemes, plans, and intentions that are never carried out. Somehow we never finish anything we start.

This is understandable. Growing up with special attention and special favors is a blessing and a curse. On one hand, we feel protection and comfort from our parents. On the other, we learn that we will be rescued from any consequence if we do not follow through.

Our parents completed homework assignments, buffered our arguments, found us jobs, made us friends, and "pulled strings" to help us. It's no mystery that we came to expect that things would magically be taken care of for us. We start projects and wait for this genie who never comes anymore. You can tell an adult child who was overparented from his files, drawers, and notebooks brimming with unfinished poems, lists of things to do, ideas, and plans that will never be carried out.

Procrastination became our downfall when we internalized a message that we could not accomplish anything very well on our own and needed to be constantly protected. Or it happened when we internalized such high expectations that any task began to seem like a setup for failure. Today, we play it safe. We avoid the three R's— risk, rejection, and responsibility—by rarely finishing what we start.

You Have a Tendency to Be Self-Critical

"I beat myself up emotionally every time I make a mistake," says one adult who was overparented. Adults who were loved too much as children are their own worst critics. They constantly feel judged by others, most often by their parents. Nothing they achieve is ever good enough.

Why, after having been given so much, and praised so often, are we so self-critical? As children, we were in the spotlight. We believed that the hopes and dreams of our parents lay in our hands.

In early childhood, we internalize a lot of "should" messages from our parents: We should be a doctor or a lawyer. We should get high grades in school. We should be popular. We should be happy all the time. Soon we don't need our parents to tell us what we should be—and at the same time, all of the things we're not. We develop a voice in our own heads called the "inner critic." The voice perpetuates a constant refrain of painful negative back talk.

As adults, we excel at embellishing the critical messages we received as children:

"You can't do that, let me do it for you" becomes "I'll fail if I do it by myself."

"I love you when you're a good girl" becomes "I will only be loved if I'm successful. I have to look perfect and be perfect in everything I do or I'm a failure."

A thriving inner critic, nurtured on negative thoughts, subverts our self-esteem, feeds our depression, and leads us to avoid people and opportunities.

You Have Subconscious Feelings of "Entitlement"

First to return a less than perfect meal in a restaurant, to complain about poor service, to request a better seat, the child who was loved too much enters adulthood with the feeling, often subconscious, that he or she is entitled only to the best.

We commanded special treatment as children, and we soon came to expect it. When privileges, possessions, and attention are handed to us on a silver platter, we start to believe that this is the way life works.

We enter into relationships, unconsciously expecting others to treat us in this same manner. We set ourselves up for grave disappointment. When we walk into a room and no one notices us, we're surprised. When we're feeling sad and no one asks us what's wrong, we feel cheated. When we don't get the job we want or the salary we demand, we feel indignant.

As our disappointment grows, we look for relationships that will take care of us the way our parents did. We may choose an overly nurturing and self-depriving spouse to fit our expectations. These unequal relationships often end up in resentment and conflict.

You Have Difficulty Having Fun
or Appreciating the Moment

"Why get excited?" the adult child asks. When we were children, suppressing emotions and acting "in control" won approval. Outbursts of emotion were threatening or embarrassing to parents.

Now, we're afraid of our emotions and expect to be criticized for them. Now, a feeling of joylessness and a hesitancy to lose oneself in the fun of the moment persists even in the best times. Life is a serious business. Adult children who were overparented tend to live life intellectually, analyzing themselves and others.

You Have Trouble Making Decisions

"I can't even choose my own clothes," one woman confided. "I go to my mother and ask her opinion. I think when you do this in your thirties, it's pretty sad."

Decision making, even about the most basic things, causes anxiety and insecurity in the child who was overparented. The "blessing" of others is sought, even when the best option is clear.

Parents who love too much in an attempt to be protective and caring, tend to help by making decisions for the child. This form of caring too much can be costly.

When our own efforts at making decisions are sabotaged by our parents' zealous desire to help us, we learn indirectly that our own decisions don't really matter. We never learn to trust our own intuition and judgment.

If this was our experience as children, we become very ambivalent adults. We look around for someone to rescue us by taking responsibility for our decisions. We often seek out a husband or wife who will play our parents' part. As a consequence, we can find ourselves in the role of a child in our adult relationships.

You Fear Success

Children who were overparented become adults who are underemployed. They get a "late start" in life after a period of drifting. So often, they sabotage their own success. "The higher you climb, the farther you fall" is their rationalization for the opportunities they failed to take. Their biggest fear is that if they succeed, others will demand a sequel and they'll be unable to write one.

That others will have expectations of us is a reality of life. But for people who have spent a lifetime jumping across the hurdles of enormous parental expectations, the slightest suggestion that they do more becomes a heavy load to bear.

Another reason to fear success is that it means taking responsibility for yourself. If you were overparented, along with all of the love you received was a message that you would always be taken care of. It's easy to give into the pull of being forever protected by your family.

Success requires risk, and more often, independence. Becoming independent and successful can be like flying on a trapeze without a net. If we leave our parents' safety net, and separate emotionally from them, we fear we'll fall on our face. When did we ever learn to pick ourselves up, unaided? Better to stay off that shaky trapeze to begin with, and away from the risks of success.

You are Susceptible to Developing Eating Disorders

Bulimia, anorexia, and obesity are common among people who were overparented. This predisposition to developing eating disorders stems from a pattern of using food to meet emotional needs.

When our parents enmesh themselves in our lives, we grow up with little emotional "space" of our own. Our boundaries are not respected. We never achieve a real sense of autonomy or independence. We don't know what is ours, or what isn't ours.

Overprotection and anxious attention can become so intense and intrusive that we feel violated. Sometimes our parents' expectations of us became unendurable. Disrespected, with our real needs invalidated, we grow up with an enormous need to be heard, to be validated.

Life becomes an invention to avoid the anxiety of being close to others. One of the ways we calm our fears is to become emotionally obsessed with food. An absorption with food is one means of wresting control from domineering parents. It can also be an attempt to build a shell and hide. When we become overweight, or lose so much weight that people become anxious looking at us, others are kept at a distance.

You Love Your Parents Too Much

Reading this book may make you feel uncomfortable. It may trigger anger, anxiety, and the need to protect your parents. You may want to justify them, cover for them, defend them, explain them, and forgive them, because you love them and what you read smacks of criticism of them.

Let's look at this urge to defend our parents more closely for a moment. We tend to see our parents as weak, fragile, depressed, confused, or unhappy. Why do we cling to this picture of our parents? True, they're unhappy at times. Obviously, they aren't always perfect in everything they do. But they're hardly as weak or needy as we see them. These are people who have managed households for twenty years or more, held jobs, raised children, made friends, planned vacations, gotten out of bed each morning and survived more than we can begin to understand. By anyone else's standards, they would be considered strong, competent, and vital. Still, we see them as defenseless, and jump to protect them.

If questioning your relationship with your parents makes you feel guilty and upset, consider this: You can reevaluate your relationship with your parents without ending it. You can question why, when you don't live up to your parents' expectations, you become angry and miserable, and still love your parents deeply. You can explore why you feel so anxious when you go against "family rules," and still preserve your close ties with your mother and father. You can come to terms with your guilt and constant need for your parents' approval, without being disloyal. You can learn to love them back, without loving them so much that you lose who you are. You can give them the freedom to do likewise.

The first step will be seeing your parents more accurately. They are stronger than you think. You have been a big participant in your own overparenting and are equally responsible. The dependence is mutual. Your parents have been as troubled by loving you too much as you've been by loving them too much in return.

It takes two to make a relationship, but it only takes one to make the relationship begin to change. Our parents are strong enough to survive it when we explore our relationship with them, and what it's meant to both of us.

You may not see yourself in all of these characteristics. But if you can identify with many, rest assured that you are not alone. Most of us who were loved too much as children share these traits to some degree.

Surviving childhood, even in the best of families, is a difficult and demanding task. Sometimes parents' best intentions can indirectly undermine the strength and security they were hoping to nurture in the children they love so much. Sometimes our own need can bind us to them, long after we should be relying on ourselves. This is when we need support in order to change. Only by fully exploring how and why we were loved too much, can we begin to recover and change.

This book is not an invitation to be ungrateful or to blame our parents who have given us so much. It's not about blaming ourselves. It's about self-acceptance, understanding, and change, for all of us.

CHAPTER 2

THE PAMPERED/DEPRIVED CHILD

"We gave you everything."

> "Every month checks come in the mail from my dad. I send them back, but they keep coming. My friends think I'm crazy for not taking his money. It's hard to explain, but there are too many strings attached to everything he gives me. He'll give me anything in the world that I want—except freedom to be myself."
>
> —Karen, age 21, secretary

There are no words in the English language more loaded with ambivalence, charged with obligation, or colored with a troubling sense of resentment than the words "thank you" when we say them to our parents. Mumbling, "Thanks, Mom and Dad," with our feet shuffling and our eyes drifting away, we feel as vulnerable as a five-year-old.

Why should this be? We're well aware of what we owe them. No one seems more deserving of our appreciation than our parents, who loved us so much. To them, love was synonymous with "giving." What they didn't have, they couldn't give us, but nothing stopped them from seeing to it that we had everything they felt we needed.

We may search far into the world without ever finding anyone again who will so willingly do and provide for us.

Still, it's hard to say, "Thanks." Are we spoiled and un-grateful? Or were we given too much?

While most parents give time, attention, and material things to their children, parents who love too much give too much. What is too much giving? Tracy, a thirty-four-year-old high school teacher, tells a story that exemplifies what life is like for a child who is surrounded by unselfish providers who love and give too much:

"My mother really didn't have very much in her life," Tracy begins. "She wasn't the type of person who got involved in charities or lunched with the girls. Her 'thing' was us.

"If I was bored, she'd drop what she was doing to take me to the zoo, or shopping, or to a movie. She never said, 'Why don't you call a friend?,' or 'Tracy, I'm busy now. Can't you find something to do?'

"She hated the thought of leaving us with baby-sitters, so my brother, Mark, and I went everywhere with her and Dad. They never made plans on a Saturday night without asking us what we were doing first, and trying to include us. They never took a vacation without us.

"All of our friends turned our house into their hangout. We made a mess, and my mother cleaned it up. It's not that she didn't yell about it. She did. But it had no effect. My mother can't stay angry at anyone for more than two minutes. She'd yell at us and apologize for yelling at the same time.

"Does this sound like the perfect childhood?" Tracy laughs, and then grows thoughtful. "On the outside, it was. You know, you can be a pretty spoiled kid even without a lot of money. We were never rich, but we were comfortable, and I never went without anything I needed.

"What's funny is that I never asked for anything. It was my mother who would say, 'You're going to high school next year, so you need some new clothes,' or 'You should have those jeans all of the kids are wearing.' She was the one who really needed new clothes, but used to say, 'I never go anywhere. Why do I need new clothes?' "

Tracy grew to depend completely on her mother, and she wasn't disappointed. Always, her mother cared. "I was a quiet kid, and this really worried her. At dinnertime the four of us would sit around the table eating, and my brother, Mark, would clown around, while I'd sit there, quietly picking at the food on my plate. Then I'd feel my mother's eyes on me. 'What's wrong, Tracey? Why aren't you eating?'

"I'd say, 'Nothing's wrong,' and then she'd ask me again, a hundred times, until I'd scream, 'NOTHING'S WRONG! WHY CAN'T YOU LEAVE ME ALONE?' and go running off to my room.

"Soon she'd be at my door. I knew she'd come. No child was allowed to feel unhappy in our house. She'd sit down on my bed and keep at it until she got out of me whatever had me all upset. Then she'd tell me how wrong my teachers were, how wrong my friends were, how wrong my boyfriend was. Anyone I was angry with was wrong. She meant it, too. Nothing was ever my fault. I'll tell you one thing—she always made me feel better.

"Years later, when I was in therapy, I used to get quiet and look down at the floor and expect the therapist to pull out of me what was wrong. Then I'd expect him to tell me how right I was, and how wrong everybody else was. When he wouldn't, I'd be furious.

"My mother always said, 'Tracy, you know your dad and I would give you the moon if we thought it would make you happy.' They would have, too. No one in my life ever put as much energy into trying to make me happy as my mother. I'll give you a great example. One day I was bored, and I started whining about how much I wanted a part-time job after school. I went to one store and filled out an application, and then I gave up and complained some more. It was my mother who ended up walking into all of the neighborhood shops talking about what a talented daughter she had. Finally, she found someone in a camera shop who would hire me."

With an embarrassed smile, Tracy recalls, "My job lasted about a month. It was boring dusting off camera lenses and sorting packages of prints, so one day, when I was scheduled to work, I just didn't show up. That was it. That's how I handled a lot of things. I'd just fade out and let them figure out what happened to me. Or I'd have my mother call.''

When Tracy graduated from college, she continued to live at home. Her parents never encouraged her to leave, and actually discouraged her whenever she mentioned it. ''I got a job teaching high school, and the pay wasn't great, but I loved having my summers off. The principal, who expected me to stay late to coach sports and sit on teachers' committees after school, hated me. They were only paying me until three o'clock, and as far as I was concerned, that was the time to hit the door.

''I wasn't rushing home to anything great, though. Most of the time I felt like I was going stir-crazy. I wasn't meeting any men, or at least no one I would consider getting involved with. Even my best friends started being too busy to get together with me. I complained that they never called me, and they said, 'Why don't you call us, once in a while, instead of always expecting us to call you and make the plans?' But I was never good at making plans. Before I knew it, the weekend would come around, and I'd end up sitting around watching TV.

''I was twenty-five and feeling like my life hadn't really started. I was always exhausted, yet I wasn't really doing much of anything. I started thinking that if I moved out of my parents' home and into the city, things would change.

''One weekend I took the train downtown and walked around, trying to find an apartment I could afford. Doing something like this without my mother's help was hard, but I wouldn't let her go with me. This was going to be my big stab at independence, right? Well, by the end of the day, I was worn out. All of the apartments started to look the same. I got so confused, I finally just rented a place.

''I admit that it was an awful apartment—a real cockroach haven. There was cracked plaster hanging from the ceiling and a big orange rust stain in the bathroom sink. But I was tired of looking, so I handed over the security deposit and signed the lease.

''The next day my parents went to see the new apartment and went crazy. My mother said, 'You can't live like this!' I screamed back, 'This is what I can afford!'

"My father ushered both of us, hysterical by now, into the car. He drove around the city, and pulled up outside this classy looking high-rise building in the glitzy part of town.

"I walked in and thought, Gee, this is great. It even had an indoor pool and sundeck. I could really see myself living in a place like that.

"I knew it had to cost more than I could afford, but I didn't say a word. My parents said, 'This is where you should live.' So I moved in, and they gave me a check each month to help cover it. It's almost funny. Here I was, trying to strike out on my own, and I ended up, at twenty-five, getting an allowance from my parents instead."

Tracy neared her thirtieth birthday, and found herself visiting her doctor regularly, complaining of constant exhaustion and stomach ailments. He found no physical cause, and recommended psychotherapy. Tracy was furious. "I found another doctor immediately. To me, therapy was for people who had been abused or had emotional problems. I couldn't believe that anyone would think I needed therapy."

It was her brother, Mark, who finally convinced Tracy to see a therapist. "We were close, and he knew me better than I would have believed. From the outside, I look like I've got a lot of good things going in my life. I have a nice apartment, and a decent job. I function and I survive, but I'm really just going through the motions. I'm depressed all the time. Nothing really interests me. Everything seems like the same old thing.

"It's hard to admit, but I'm lonely. I'm unhappy, yet I don't know what it would take to make me happy. People ask me what I'm good at, and I don't know. I complain about my life, but I can't seem to change it.

"I know I'm a big disappointment to my parents. After all they invested in me, the least I could do is be happy. It kills them that I'm depressed all the time and in therapy, even though they're paying for it. They call me on the phone with all sorts of suggestions. I can see them, sitting together at home worrying about my problems and saying, 'How can we get something good happening for Tracy in her life?'

"Their last idea was that we open a fast-food franchise together, as a family. They were ready to invest their life savings in it. My father said, 'You'll be the boss, Tracy. We won't interfere. We just want to see you happy.' But I couldn't do it. I just don't have the energy right now."

It seems difficult to understand how Tracy, a child who basked in the attention of two parents who tried every way they knew to make her happy, grew into the depressed and exhausted adult who eventually sought therapy.

Tracy's parents indulged her, believing that freedom from need and frustration would create a strong foundation for the child they loved. What went wrong?

To Tracy's mother, being a loving parent meant an endless cycle of cooking, cleaning, chauffeuring, organizing, listening, pampering, and indulging a child. To a certain extent, it does. But Tracy's parents gave too much.

Tracy learned the rules of the game early. With the slightest look of distress, or sometimes with no look at all, her mother and father would instinctively rush to her rescue. She was unhappy, and they tried to solve her problems. She needed a job or an apartment, and they provided them. Her parents took her responsibilities and made them their own.

In grade school, when children learn the most profound lessons from their mistakes, Tracy returned home each day to her mother's convincing arguments that her errors or frustrations were the fault of others. Tracy's mother couldn't stand to see her upset, and attempted to rationalize away Tracy's pain as a way of loving and protecting her.

What did all of this giving do for Tracy? Bored, restless, and expectant, she spent most of her life waiting for something to happen to make her happy. She came to believe that there was no reason to take control or responsibility for her own life.

Because Tracy was so used to someone anticipating her needs, she drifted along, tired and yawning, without any real ambition or energy to do more than take what she was given.

She had the security of knowing that she could always depend on her parents, for which she was grateful. She could rely on being rescued from her own decisions. Like so many children who were given too much, she learned to trade freedom and a sense of accomplishment for the easier route dependence on her parents could provide.

But the result of this dependence was a core of self-doubt. Tracy began to avoid all tasks that might expose her as inadequate. She became immobilized when she had to make a decision. She couldn't set a goal, find a more fulfilling job, or even call a friend with a suggestion for how to plan the evening.

The exhausted passivity with which Tracy confronted life was really fear rather than physical fatigue. It was a defense to cope with her growing feelings of inadequacy.

Tracy is the epitome of the pampered/deprived child—a phenomenon that most parents who give too much unwittingly help create. Excessive doses of love, attention, money, time—anything her parents possessed and could give her—deprived Tracy of something very basic: a sense of competency, self-esteem, the drive to initiate, to persevere, to rely on herself. Tracy was never able to gather the resources that would enable her to gain a sense of accomplishment or mastery over her life. Her parents, with the best of intentions, stood in her way.

Giving and extending oneself to nurture a child is a parent's responsibility. But, parents are giving too much when they continually anticipate the needs and wishes of their child so that the child receives as a matter of course what he doesn't need and hasn't even asked for. We're talking here about a child who is well past infancy—a state of total dependency when such "mind reading" is appropriate. Parents who give too much continue to anticipate and grant their child's wishes automatically, long past the time when it's necessary or desirable.

The growing child in such a home is hit daily with an avalanche of material goods and services that his parents have determined he "needs." He never demands his mother's or father's attention. He doesn't have to. He doesn't beg, or bargain with them for toys, clothes, or spending money. He barely has to ask. Few limits are set, and few desires are denied. His parents say yes when they really mean no and do for him what he is capable of doing for himself.

Parents who give too much often feel that they know their child's needs better than anyone else, especially the child himself. Such parents know best—and best is making sure the child doesn't risk things that might cause him to fail or feel frustrated. A steady stream of help and guidance goes beyond suggestions to where the child's own thoughts are seldom encouraged, regarded, or respected.

Such parents believe that the more they give and guide, the more they are "loving," and the happier the children should be as a result. Love is the food they prepare, the money they shell out, the nights at the kitchen table doing their children's homework with them, and the material things they surprise their children with. It's anything they can do to smooth their children's path.

But with all they give, do their children ever get what they really need? Those of us who grew up in a fashion similar to Tracy don't always know the answer to this. We know our parents loved us. We know we had food, shelter, attention, and contact with our parents. We see ourselves as having had happy childhoods because our parents gave us so much.

But to reach our full potential, we require some things we never got. We needed all of the following:

- Acceptance and validation of who we really are
- Respect and tolerance of our real thoughts and feelings
- Freedom to explore and make our own decisions
- Nurturing of our strengths and acceptance of our limitations
- Support of our creativity
- A sense of accomplishment
- A feeling that we make a contribution
- A feeling of mastery or control over our lives
- The opportunity to share our feelings of loss, grief, or anger

It's possible that our parents could have given us "everything," yet deprived us of these things. This is the essence of the pampered/deprived child.

There is a time for our parents to nurture us and pamper us. In the first few years of life, we wouldn't have survived if we were forced to rely on ourselves. But as we grow older, our parents' task becomes encouraging our independence and reducing our need of them. By continuing to pamper us, our parents indirectly taught us many things: to rely on other people's talents rather than our own; to be passive rather than active; to look anxious or depressed so that someone will come and rescue us. As one man put it, "When the going got tough, my parents got going."

The development of self-esteem is directly related to our mastery of tasks and our resulting feelings of competency. Michael Franz Basch, noted psychiatrist and author of *Understanding Psychotherapy*, writes, "True self-esteem, a genuine sense of one's self as worthy of nurture and protection, capable of growth and development stems from the experience of competence . . . no one can give another the experience of competence: one must achieve that for oneself."

Competence grows from the experience of having sufficient ability to accomplish what we set out to do. Parents who love too much, in an attempt to make life easier for their children, inadvertently sabotage their children's opportunities for gaining this sense of competence. As they rescue their children by taking control and providing solutions, they also deprive their children of the necessary tools and experiences to build a sense of mastery over their world.

Our childhood experience contributes greatly to how our lives develop and to the person we are today. Competence in childhood grows into adult self-confidence. Unfortunately, the experience of succeeding on our own merits without our "helpers" was a rare one for us, so the road to self-confidence is a difficult, if not impossible one. Having few resources to deal with frustration due to a history of being rescued from it by our parents, we become adults who avoid challenges. We wander through life, looking to others for direction, excitement, material things, guidance, and advice. Even when we do accomplish a lot—and many children who were overparented *do* succeed—we never feel it's enough. We need the approval and blessings of others to make us feel good about ourselves.

Given our history, it's not surprising that we tend to confuse "love" with another person's desire to help or control us, because this is what we're used to. We seek out people who will willingly assume the responsibilities of our lives. These, we think, are the people who truly "love" us.

But what is love, really? M. Scott Peck, in *The Road Less Traveled*, defines love as the will to extend one's self for the purpose of nurturing one's own or another's spiritual growth. What is compelling about this definition is its emphasis on growth as an outcome of what we give to another. But not all giving furthers growth, Peck asserts. Sometimes what truly nurtures another's spiritual growth is withholding what we could easily provide, especially when the person we love is capable of achieving what he needs himself. Judicious giving is what Peck calls it, and it includes making a thoughtful and sometimes painful decision not to give when giving will inhibit growth and foster dependency.

We never learned to define love in this way. It was too painful for our parents to withhold from us and watch us become frustrated or unhappy, even if this was in our best interests. The road we traveled ended in dependence on our parents—on their approval, attention, opinions, and, sometimes their economic support.

People who were deprived as children wonder how anyone could ever complain about being given too much: "What are these people whining about? I would have been thrilled to have parents who loved me like that!"

Children who were loved too much know better. There was no question that our parents loved us. But there was more than love behind much of the giving that went on.

Sometimes all of this giving had little to do with us or our needs at all.

We're not talking here about parents who give appropriately out of affectionate concern or those who give for the simple joy they get in return for the love they extend to their children. We're talking about parents who give and give until they're worn out and exhausted; who often hear their own children say, "Please! No more!" but don't stop; who worry and feel uncomfortable with the fact that they give too much. Such a parent gives too much because he *needs* to. He's unconsciously driven by his unmet needs to the exclusion of everything else.

When someone gives and gives to us, we sometimes become uncomfortable with it because we sense that all of this giving is calculated to make us feel obligated. Often, children sense a hidden agenda behind all they're given, a tacit agreement that they do, or even be things, in exchange. Consider Tony's story:

"My parents' divorce was a bitter one," Tony begins. "My mother swore that if Dad ever left her, he'd never see me or my sister again. Dad threatened to get a court order and bring the police with him if he had to, but no one was going to keep him away from his children."

Things settled down eventually, and Tony and his sister, Lori, saw their father every other weekend. "It's funny, but I don't remember having tons of clothes or toys before my parents divorced," Tony says. "We certainly weren't deprived, but we weren't spoiled, either. I definitely don't remember ever going, as a family, to a restaurant, unless it was some fast-food place. But all of that changed after my father moved out. Every time we went to see Dad, he took us out to dinner at some expensive restaurant. Can you imagine it? A five-year-old and a seven-year-old dining in some of the finest restaurants in town. He really wasted his money. We always ordered hamburgers, because that was all we'd eat.

"Dad had presents waiting for us every time we came over. They weren't junky little toys, either, but things like stereo equipment and TV sets. My mother had a fit every time we brought this stuff home."

Like many children whose parents get divorced, Tony hoped that his mother and father would get back together. When his mother remarried, it ruined everything he was secretly praying for. Soon his parents became locked in a competition over who could give the children more.

"When Dad would take us on a vacation at Christmas, Mom would start planning a longer, better trip for spring. If Dad took us to the circus, Mom would take us to the ice show. Both of them gave us money. Lori and I never asked for anything. We just got it."

With a thoughtful look, Tony admits, "All of the things my parents bought us were supposed to make up for the divorce, I guess. They didn't. I'd open an incredible pile of gifts for my birthday and start to think, Gee, this is really terrific. Then I'd turn and see my mother watching me. There would be something in her eyes that I really can't explain. I'd want to say thanks and mean it, but something in my mouth tasted so bitter.

"It's funny, but both of my parents at one time or another gave me a lecture about the value of a dollar and how I shouldn't take everything I had for granted. My dad would talk about how he had to work for his living since he was twelve years old. They'd both say all of this, then they'd shower me with money.

"Maybe my parents were insecure that we'd love one or the other of them more, but how was I supposed to understand that? Where we lived, most kids had to argue with their parents to get five extra bucks to go to a movie. I never told my friends about how things were for me, although I bet they could see it. I took a job every summer not because I needed one, but because I wanted to be like everyone else."

As Tony grew older, he quarreled frequently with his parents. "It's hard to say what we argued about. We just stopped getting along. Everything they did irritated me. One night after a huge fight with my father over something stupid, he showed up with a new leather jacket for me. 'That's your solution to everything!' I screamed, and ran into the house.

"I wanted respect. He offered a leather jacket. After

that, he called me an unappreciative little brat. He started
to ignore me, which was fine with me.

"My sister, Lori, didn't concern herself with any of
this. She thought I was nuts. She milked my parents for
all they were worth. I remember one big fight between
Mom and Dad, when Dad bought Lori a car for her 'sweet
sixteen.' 'She's too young to have her own car!' Mom
yelled at him. 'You don't really care what happens to her.
It's easy for you, because you don't really have the responsibility for raising these kids.'

"That really hurt my dad, and I felt kind of sorry for
him. But the truth was that Mom had been planning for
months to buy Lori a car for her sixteenth birthday. Dad
just beat her to it.

"You know what my sister is today? A whining, complaining nag. She's never had a job. She's never been able
to hold on to a boyfriend for longer than a month. Lori
thinks of herself first, and everyone else last. She manip-
ulates my parents into doing everything for her. If she
can't get what she wants from Mom, she gets it from Dad.
No one seems to see what it's doing to her. If they did, I
doubt they'd care. And I'm the spoiled, ungrateful one.
But, I won't take their money. My sister's welcome to all
of it.''

On the surface, it appears that Tony and Lori's parents
gave them so much in order to provide for their needs and
ease their lives after the divorce. And it appears that it was
''love'' that drove them to insure that neither of their children went without anything they needed even though the
family would no longer be together under one roof.

A closer look, however, reveals a host of hidden agendas and manipulative games that provided not for the children's needs but for the parents'.

When feelings of loss and abandonment surface, as they
do during a divorce, they disrupt our equilibrium and ex-
acerbate feelings of guilt and self-criticism. We attempt to
regain control by enlisting any resources available. In the
case of Tony's parents, the resource they chose was money.
Tony's father treated Tony and Lori to expensive dinners

and bought them presents not because his children needed or even desired them, but to overcompensate for his feelings of insecurity and helplessness. He understandably feared losing his close ties to his children when he no longer lived with them. His ex-wife's remarriage intensified these fears, adding to them the fear of being replaced by another man who would live daily with his children and undeniably exert influence over them. He fought back with gifts, dinners, vacations, and spending money.

Tony's mother, threatened by her ex-husband's attempts to win his children's allegiance, attempted to "outbid" him. Every gift became a jab at her ex-husband's ego.

It was not the conscious intent of either of Tony's parents to use or exploit their children in their battle with each other. All people seek to meet their unmet needs automatically in whatever way they can. Tony's parents gave too much because they needed to ensure that they wouldn't be forgotten or replaced after the divorce. Both of them suffered from feelings of abandonment and insecurity. Their children's appreciation of the gifts they gave them made them feel adequate and necessary.

Tony couldn't comprehend the hidden agenda behind his parents' gifts and became suspicious of them. All the money and material things he was given embarrassed him because he could sense his parents' need to hurt each other. He could also sense their desperation. Tony felt inadequate because he could give neither of them what they needed. The result was a deep feeling of bitterness. His combination of passive-aggressive and direct assaults was a way of punishing his parents for all the pain that he endured.

The difference between the way Tony and Lori reacted to their parents' largess is significant, however. Lori took what she was given and asked for more. She accepted and basked in all the attention, but the implications for her were just as far-reaching.

The experience of growing up in a family that showed love through gifts of money and material things taught Lori that happiness was the pursuit and acquisition of things. Security became a function of how much she could attain.

In families where great emphasis is put on acquiring possessions, many children begin to determine self-worth with the quantity and quality of things they own. The child with the designer blue jeans "feels" more worthwhile than his friend with the department-store specials. "We love you, so we give you these things" translates into an erroneous belief that love is shown by the quantity of material things we can provide and that happiness comes from what we own. Emptiness within the family is remedied by purchasing more "toys." As a long-term result, children who were pampered in this manner grow into adults who look for security and happiness outside of themselves. Whenever they feel insecure on the inside, they try to control the feeling by attaining possessions.

Lori and Tony were different, but both found it difficult to be grateful to their parents, and to say, "Thanks." This is so often the case when children are given too much. These children aren't spoiled so much as angry, because what they feel is that they are being manipulated by what they are given, rather than respected and valued for who they really are.

While Tony and Lori's parents gave to get revenge on each other and "buy" loyalty from their children, there are many other reasons why parents give too much. Giving, helping, and obsessing about their children can fulfill a host of parental needs. Some of the most pervasive ones follow:

Giving to bolster self-esteem. A person who is insecure and never feels good enough may try to compensate by proving he or she is "enough" as a father or mother. "I'm a good person, see how much I do for my children" is what many parents are unconsciously trying to demonstrate by giving too much.

Giving to overcompensate for early deprivation. "I don't want my children to have to suffer the way I suffered" is a statement many parents make. Sometimes the child grows up feeling tremendous guilt for the opposite reason—that he never suffered, or even made an effort for that matter, and feels undeserving of all he got.

Giving to alleviate guilt and discomfort. Sometimes a child's frustrations lead parents to recall their own failures and pain. They had few resources to deal with their discomfort then, but they can prevent the same frustrations in the child by doing for him what he might be capable of doing for himself with a little extra effort. On an unconscious level, the parents feel, You inherited your weaknesses and fallibilities from me, and it's harder to accept them in you than in myself. I feel guilty every time you hurt. I feel guilty every time I make a mistake with you. Let me make it up to you.

Giving to fill the emptiness inside. Giving too much runs rampant in marriages that have failed to fulfill either partner's needs but continue to remain intact "for the sake of the children." Usually, one spouse feels abandoned by the other and gives an absurd amount to the child, believing on an unconscious level that this might prevent the child from also abandoning him. Focusing his or her life on the children deflects the spotlight away from the marriage.

Giving to make up for the absence of the other parent. One parent may be alcoholic, abusive, selfish, ill, or indifferent to the child. The other parent feels guilty and fears that the child will grow up with emotional problems if this lack isn't compensated for. In trying to make up for what's missing, he or she goes overboard, giving too much. The child feels the loss of the other parent anyway, and now it's compounded with a guilty feeling toward the parent who gave so much, because it really didn't help prevent the pain.

Giving to make up for the parents' own absence. Parents who are deeply involved in their careers and seldom home often fall into this trap. To make up for their constant absence, they buy their children presents, overindulge them, or submit to any of their wishes, no matter how outrageous they are. Guilt is a powerful motivator for too much giving, because giving alleviates feelings of selfishness.

Giving to change the child's behavior. Whenever the child is angry or upset, the parent who loves too much steps in with the equivalent of a pacifier—money, the car, the promise of a new outfit, permission to stay out all night—anything that will stop the impending commotion. Emotional outbursts are very threatening to the parent's need for control. The child learns to change his behavior for a bribe. At worst, he learns to manipulate for further bribes, and as a result is given too much.

It is clear that parents who give too much often do so because of their own unmet needs. When we first sense these needs, it's a very uncomfortable realization. The fantasy of superhuman parents who are infallible and have no needs of their own is comforting to cling to. We resent our parents' neediness, and feel overwhelmed when they seek to fill their emotional needs through us. At the same time, we strive to give them whatever it is we think they need because we love them and depend on them to love us in return.

We feel inadequate because nothing we do is ever enough to make our parents feel complete or fulfill their emotional needs. We can't undo their pain. We can't make up for the losses and disappointments they've suffered, but we keep trying. Nothing we do is ever enough. We may even abandon our true selves and behave in whatever way we sense our parents need us to behave in order to fulfill their needs.

Listen to several adults recall what they received from their parents and what they sensed their parents needed from them in return.

Ted: "Because my father wanted me to be a doctor, there was always money for medical school. What I really wanted was to be an artist. At least five of my art teachers tried to have a serious talk with my parents about the talent I had. But there was never money for art lessons or materials. They were saving for my future, the one they'd picked out for me, and I was going to have it no matter what.

"Today, I'm a doctor, and there's a part of me that's grateful to my parents for pushing me into this profession. There's also a part of me that can be making the rounds of the hospital, looking every inch 'the Doctor,' and at the same time wondering, Who am I really?"

Sharon: "I was down at college and I had a big argument over the phone with my father over a guy I was dating. He kept making fun of him because he was short and overweight, which was so petty of him that it made me crazy. I knew he was goading me to get a reaction, so I finally just let him talk, without saying anything. When he could tell I was angry, he said, 'Listen, I have a check for you.' Not 'I'm sorry,' or 'Why are you so quiet?,' just 'Here's some money.' I was so mad by this time that I said, 'Forget it. Don't send me anything. I don't want it.'

"He sent the check anyway, so I sent it back. You would think he'd just give up, but when my cousin came home for the weekend, he made a special effort to see him and gave the money to him. My cousin walked over to the dorm with it, and I had to laugh. I was trapped. What was I going to do, tell my cousin to keep the money so that our whole family could get into an argument? I took it, and at the same time, I forgave him no matter what he had said, or how much it hurt.

"I go over to see him these days, and he hugs me and calls me 'Daddy's little girl.' Inside, I'm ready to explode. He has no idea who I really am. But how could he? I'm the one who keeps selling out."

Joel: "When I saved up the money for a car, my dad and I shopped all of the used car dealerships in town. Finally, I found a convertible with a great stereo that I could afford. We went back to look at it about four times, until finally I said, 'That's the one I want.'

"My father was in the room with the salesman, and he called me in to sign the papers. I don't know why, but after I signed, I started to read them. They didn't look right. I looked at my dad and said, 'Is this the right car? The one I picked out?' He was almost blushing. 'It's a good car, a reliable car.' But was it the right car? I wanted to know. 'It's the one you should have. Why did you keep asking me to go with you to look at cars if you weren't going to take my advice?'

"He wasn't even paying for it, and he conned me into buying a different car, one I didn't even want, out of guilt because he'd spent so much time looking with me. I drove this car that he picked out, that I hated, that didn't even have a stereo, for over two years. It was reliable, all right. Too reliable. I couldn't even have a good excuse to get rid of it.

"My father got his own way out of all of this—something he really needs to have. What I got is two years of anger at myself for not being strong enough to stand up to him—or to do without his help in the first place."

What becomes clear in these stories is how thin the line is between "giving" and "controlling." Each of these stories illustrates some of the different ways in which parents give to their children in order to control them, shape them, and mold them to meet their own needs. The children became what their parents needed them to be. They complied with the family rules, and were rewarded with someone who worried about them, helped them, guided them, advised them, and gave them everything. They wanted to take care of these people who gave them so much—even if that meant they never took care of themselves.

The outcome of a childhood of pampered/deprivation is a passive expectancy that other people will provide for us coupled with an expectancy that when they do, we'll have to meet a multitude of their needs, which may mean compromising ourselves. The result is a host of contradictions in our lives:

We feel entitled to have people do for us and care for us. When they do, we feel uncomfortable, obligated, smothered, and compelled to push them away. We find them just too needy.

We believe we are special and sometimes even better than others. We also feel inadequate and become some of the most self-critical people on the face of the earth.

We hate it when people try to control us. When we can't control others, we feel out of control.

We push people away be becoming overly dependent on them. We push other people away by becoming aloof and arrogant.

We rationalize and defend ourselves for continuing to take so much from our parents. We feel enormous guilt about it.

We feel devoted to our parents. When we're with them, we fight, bicker, get upset, withdraw.

We resent it when our parents overprotect us. We overprotect them.

We don't feel that we should need help to solve our problems, because we aren't supposed to have any. We need help to put the facade of the "perfect" family behind us.

We're not crazy for feeling torn in two directions. These contradictions are the outcome of being overparented—of being given too much. They're why we never feel at peace with ourselves. But when we begin to explore the patterns of our own lives and how they developed, we gain the awareness to change those patterns.

CHAPTER 3

LOOKING GOOD

"Smile for Mommy and Daddy!"

"My mother and sister were having a screaming match at the table and really going at it. My mom was yelling so loudly she was turning purple. Right then, the phone rang. She picked it up, and without missing a beat, said, 'Oh hello, Mary. How are you? No, I wasn't busy. I was just thinking about you.' Her voice was as sweet as sugar. I just stared at her. I mean, how could she change so quickly like that? She taught us that no matter what you really feel, you never let anyone outside the family know."

—Jill, age 21, student

Michael grew up in a museum. "We had couches no one was allowed to sit on, drapes we weren't suppose to touch. Half the house was encased in thick plastic covers. It was a real picture of comfort." He laughs.

In Michael's home, no one was trusted near any of the household furnishings. Everything was just for "show." "The big walnut dining room table was only used once a year, for Christmas dinner, when we had guests over. It was the only time we used the 'good' china and the 'good' silverware. Every other night we squeezed into the stuffy kitchen, eating in shifts off chipped plates and drinking out of glasses that used to be jam and jelly jars."

Nothing in Michael's home was ever clean enough for his mother. "Mud tracked into the house was the kind of thing that would make her cry," he remembers. "Even my dad got hollered at if he put a glass down on one of my mother's end tables. Things like a thumbprint on a kitchen cabinet, or a soap stain on a bathroom tile, made her crazy.

"I was amazed when I started school and visited my friends' houses. Other people actually wore shoes inside their homes and walked around in them, right over the freshly vacuumed carpets and waxed floors. You'd never do that at my house."

One might ask, What's so terrible about a clean, well-organized, nice-looking home? Nothing. But, our parents' compulsion to keep everything "looking good" seldom stops at the polished floors and immaculate kitchen cabinets.

Perhaps nothing is more important to a parent who loves too much than how his family, especially his children, look to others. When Michael's father took on an entire school district in a battle that continued long past his son's high school days, Michael learned just how vital "looking good" to peers, neighbors, teachers, and other relatives was to his parents.

"Mom and Dad wanted me to be the most popular kid on the block," Michael recalls. "Everyone was supposed to love me. If there were thirty birthday parties in the second grade and I was invited to twenty-nine, they were devastated about the one I wasn't asked to. They'd want to know what I did to that one kid to make him hate me so much."

And popularity wasn't enough. Michael's parents made it clear from his first day of kindergarten that superior grades in school were essential. "Neither of my parents went to college. Both of them grew up during the Depression, and they never had that option. I didn't know it until I was twenty-three and my uncle let the secret out, but my mother never completed high school. She dropped out and took a job as a bookkeeper when she was sixteen. I guess both of my parents wanted their kids to have the chances they never had. They began talking to me about college long before I was even in high school. The pressure was tremendous.''

But Michael wasn't exactly a model student. His parents hired a succession of tutors when he began to have trouble in school during the fourth grade. ''It was nothing too serious, just that I was a slow reader. To tell the truth, I never really liked to read. I had trouble sitting still in school. I was much more interested in Little League and hanging out with my friends. Although I was shaping up to be a pretty good athlete, that wasn't enough for my parents. They thought I should be number one in my class, too. After I started having trouble reading, a tutor came to the house every day after school and forced me to sit and read out loud for an hour and a half. My mother sat there and listened until one of my tutors said that her presence was making me nervous.''

Although Michael's reading ability improved, his parents continued to hire tutors for him, because they wanted to help him avoid future problems in school. But the saga of Michael's school troubles continued. ''It turned out to be pretty easy to get my tutors to do my homework for me. I used the fact that my parents were putting pressure on me as an excuse. 'If I don't get an ''A'' on this assignment, they'll never let me out of the house again,' I'd whine. After meeting my pushy parents, most of my tutors believed me. It was easy to charm them over to my side. Maybe I was sure I'd fail if I tried to do the work by myself. I don't know. But my parents would have died if they'd known who was really earning all of those terrific grades.''

By the time Michael reached high school, he had a strong academic record. Little of it was based on his own efforts. ''I told my parents that I froze up on tests and couldn't concentrate. That was supposed to explain my lousy scores when someone wasn't sitting next to me, helping me. The truth was, I never cracked a book the whole time I was in high school.

''My parents took me to a psychiatrist who tried to help me get over my 'test anxiety.' My father met with the high school guidance counselor to get special privileges for me. I got a lot of extra help. Everything was great, until my junior year.''

That year, Michael's English teacher handed back a term paper to him. "See me" was written in large red letters on top, where the grade should have been. "This isn't your work," she maintained, despite Michael's frantic arguments.

The next morning, Michael's parents came to school and met with the teacher. "She showed them a stack of papers I'd written in class. They were all pretty awful. My father still insisted that I'd done the term paper myself. I sat there feeling like a fool. Of course I didn't write it. I'd never written any of the papers I'd handed in throughout high school, but there was no way I was going to admit that. So I swore up and down that the paper was completely my work. I said the other stuff I'd done in class was lousy because the teacher made me nervous.''

The teacher wouldn't budge. Michael's father was furious. "I ended up feeling sorry for the teacher. My father came on so strong that he made her cry. I wanted to crawl under the table, I was so embarrassed. Then he met with the principal. When he got nowhere with her, he met with the superintendent. Because my grade would be affected for the whole semester if the teacher didn't give in, my parents wouldn't quit. They hired a lawyer and took their case to the school board.

"In the town I lived in, my parents' case was big news. When reporters began calling my house and my father started giving them interviews, I thought I'd die.''

Late at night, Michael tossed and turned with his guilt. "I just couldn't tell my dad what really happened. He kept saying how he had so much faith in me. How could I start telling the truth when my whole life had been one lie after another?''

Michael's parents went on to sue the school district, over his objections. They waited for their day in court with a patience that knew no limits.

When Michael was a freshman in college, his aunt finally persuaded his parents to drop the case. "I have no idea what magic she worked on my dad,'' Michael sighs wearily. ''The lawsuit was a big hobby for him. He probably would have taken his case to the Supreme Court if he could have.''

When Michael's parents took on the school district to battle an injustice they felt had been done to their son, they did it out of love. They had great hopes for Michael's success. They spent time, energy, and money to insure that he'd achieve it.

But Michael's parents loved him too much. Their expectations of him had more to do with their dreams than Michael's abilities. What began as a desire to support their child through his troubles at school escalated into an obsession.

Michael grew up in an arena where he wasn't allowed to fail. When his parents were confronted with Michael's relatively minor difficulties in reading, they quickly shielded him from frustration and disappointment by providing him with a circle of ''helpers'' to constantly guide him and protect him from failing.

But who were Michael's parents really trying to protect? Though it appears on the surface that everything they did was for Michael, his parents were actually intensely driven by their own needs. Their compulsion to help keep Michael ''looking good'' was very much a product of their insecurities over being good parents. If Michael could be number one in his class, then they would be number-one parents. Underneath their tremendous investment in Michael's school success was their fear that if he failed, they would be judged as bad parents. Michael must be perfect in all ways, so that these feared negative judgments would be fended off.

Michael's popularity, grades, and athletic achievements became his parents' accomplishments. Unconsciously, they saw Michael as an extension of themselves. They had little empathy for their son's feelings and needs because they were so driven by their own. An example of this was their determination to take Michael's conflict with his teacher to court, over his objections. If they realized that their actions were humiliating their son, this was second-ary. More important was fulfilling their own dreams through Michael.

Michael grew up with pressure that was tremendous. He was never encouraged to solve his own problems be-cause his parents quickly became enmeshed in any diffi-culty he had. Whenever he failed, they sent in the rescue squad. Although Michael's parents had good intentions in wanting their son to overcome his reading problem, their rescue attempts sabotaged Michael's independence and re-inforced his dependency. Unconsciously, his parents sought to encourage Michael's dependence on others for help, and thereby protect him from the dangerous risks of allowing his average ability to jeopardize their dreams of college and future professional achievement.

Youngsters quickly learn to adapt to their environments. Michael sensed his parents' fear of his independence, and consequently expected to fail if he tried to do his school-work on his own. Rather than take the risk of failing and disappointing his parents, he became an expert manipu-lator. He conned others into doing his work for him, as he passively looked on. It was Michael's way of adapting to the rigid family system. He did what most children do when their success is their parent's obsession. He found a creative solution to the problem of having to "look good" all of the time, and survived.

Although Michael succeeded in giving his parents the success in school they'd asked for, he couldn't fool him-self. His strategies may have helped him regain control from his controlling parents, but all of his life he lived with the fear of being found out. His self-esteem suffered deeply as he realized what a sham his academic record was. The term paper with "See me" scrawled across the top was his catastrophic expectation come to life.

It's very conceivable that Michael's parents had a sus-picion, from the beginning, that the term paper that be-came such an issue had been ghostwritten. Why, then, would they hold so stubbornly to their position, to the point of initiating a lawsuit to prove that Michael was falsely accused of cheating?

Denial was as much a habit for Michael's parents as manipulation and lies were for Michael. Admit the truth and they'd usher in harsh reality. Not only wasn't Michael a scholar, but he was a young man who was very capable of deception. His teachers, his classmates, the neighbors, friends—everyone would know. They would probably look pretty inadequate as parents for producing such a spectacle.

In their eyes, this was unacceptable. Better to deny everything than to admit that their son was just as "average," fallible, and imperfect as they were. Only as long as the denial continued could they be content.

Michael's parents were able to continue their denial because their son zealously sought ways to protect them from the truth. What does such a parent do, however, when his child's failures stare him so blatantly in the face that they can't be denied? Susan's story is a case in point.

"My uncle tells a story about my mother that would be hilarious if it had happened in another family," Susan laughs softly. "I was about three months old when she read some article about gifted children in a magazine. It said that as infants, gifted children rolled over in their cribs by themselves months before other babies. Well, I wasn't turning over or showing any other signs of being particularly gifted. My uncle swears that after reading that article, my mother spent half an hour, every day, turning me over and over again, thinking she would teach me to do it by myself."

Susan grew up under an avalanche of her mother's high expectations. She recalls being compared to other children, and pressured to surpass them. But nothing annoyed Susan more as a child than being constantly compared to her cousin Melissa. "My mother was always in major competition with my aunt," Susan confides. "Everything my cousin Melissa had, I had to have. We were the same age and attended the same school. I was constantly being dragged off to ballet lessons, piano lessons, baton-twirling lessons—you name it—because Melissa was taking them. My mother would come to watch and coach me from the sidelines. I was terrible at everything, a real klutz. Melissa, of course, was terrific, which was a real downer for my mother.''

Susan's mother tried to push Melissa and Susan together, but, predictably, they hated each other. "I couldn't make my mother see that I was never going to be like Melissa. First of all, Melissa was petite and delicate-looking, while I was tall and big-boned. Melissa was always talking and laughing, never serious about anything. I was quiet and shy. Melissa had tons of friends, and was the most popular kid in our class. I had a couple of friends, but none of us fit into Melissa's crowd. In sixth grade, when we started to go to boy-and-girl parties, the guys would fight to dance with Melissa and her friends. None of them would even talk to me. Next to Melissa, I was a social zero. I'm sure I was an embarrassment to her.''

Although Susan had many personal strengths, they faded in comparison to Melissa's popularity, at least in her mother's eyes. "I was a much better student than Melissa was, because she was always goofing off. My mother was happy about my grades, but she could never understand why I wasn't more popular. She harped on me all of the time. She'd tell me how I had so much more to offer than Melissa. She'd wring her hands over me, and give me loads of advice, like, 'You need to smile more. How do you expect people to notice you if you never smile? Take your hair out of your eyes. Tuck in your shirt. Why don't you speak up? No one can hear you. And try not to look so bored all of the time.' ''

Susan's mother would try to orchestrate her daughter's social life for her. "Once I caught her in the kitchen discussing who might be a good boyfriend for me with a couple of girls who had come over to study with me. I was only in eighth grade, but already she was worried. I was mortified, and I thought I'd kill her. I swore I'd never speak to her again, but I couldn't stay mad at her. How could I stay mad, with her telling me everything she did was for me, because she wanted to make me happy? I knew it was true. I let it go, like I did a hundred other things she did to interfere.''

Susan's mother hoped fervently that things would change for Susan when she started high school. They did, but not in the way her mother expected. "In high school, there were a lot more kids. I became friends with a group of girls I really liked. They might not have been the most popular girls in the school, but I felt comfortable and accepted with them. My mother hated them all. She blamed them for what she referred to as my 'downfall.' I'd always been an 'A' student, and now my grades were 'B's and 'C's. I stopped dressing the way my mother insisted on, and went to school in sloppy blue jeans and sweatshirts like the rest of my friends. I stopped trying to be a part of Melissa's crowd. I came home and ate whatever was loose in the refrigerator, and started to gain weight. This was the last straw for my mother. She couldn't stand it. She started talking to my father about moving out of the neighborhood and into the suburbs. She said that the school I was going to was ruining me for life. By June of my freshman year, we were packing."

The summer before the family moved, Susan's mother embarked on a complete makeover of her daughter, determined that Susan's experience in the suburbs would be different than it had been in the city. "This was my mother's big chance," Susan says, grinning. "She took me shopping, saying, 'The sky's the limit!,' while I walked around choosing a closetful of new clothes. She took me to a doctor for a diet that would help me lose all of the weight I'd gained. She paid for the top stylist in town to cut and style my hair."

All summer long, her mother's advice was a steady stream. Susan, happy to be getting away from the specter of Melissa, decided to listen to her mother. "I started to get into the idea that I could make myself over and start this new high school as a totally different person. I thought, Maybe my mother's right after all."

Susan began her sophomore year at her new high school with high hopes. But, the larger building, impersonal teachers, and classrooms full of strange faces intimidated her. She was lonelier than she'd ever been, too shy to reach out to others. Susan walked the hallways of her new school alone, with the knowledge that nothing had really changed for her after all of her parents' efforts. "I'll admit I was really depressed about the way things turned out," Susan says, shaking her head slowly. "You know, for a while there, I really believed things would change for me. But, you see, I might have looked perfect on the outside, but I was a mess inside. I was well into my twenties before I realized that it was okay to be who I was, and that I didn't have to be everything my mother wanted me to be. Until then, I was miserable."

Susan struggled between independence and compliance throughout most of her childhood. She was continually bombarded with strong and direct messages that she wasn't good enough the way she was. Her mother tried to "package" Susan according to her high expectations. She had little empathy for her daughter's true feelings, or for the growing shyness that was a reaction to being constantly compared to her popular cousin Melissa.

Predictably, Susan rebelled when she reached adolescence. She expressed her growing inner rage through passive-aggressive behavior, such as gaining weight, studying less, and dressing in the sloppy manner she knew would irritate her mother.

Susan's failure to be what her mother needed her to be became so blatant that it upset the entire family system. Her growing independence threatened her mother's tremendous need for control over her—a need rooted in a fragile self-concept based to a large extent on her daughter's accomplishments.

Susan's mother regained control by forcing the family to move to a new neighborhood. She rationalized that it was all for Susan's good, but she was really opting to "fix" Susan and make her look good again, rather than accept her for who she was. However, the family packed its troubles along with the household goods. Nothing really changed for Susan in her new neighborhood. Susan learned that living by her mother's "shoulds" was a costly endeavor.

Though the details differ from story to story, both Michael and Susan shared a common experience: Both were raised in arenas where they weren't allowed to fail, or even to have a problem. Because they knew that "looking good" was so important to their parents, they tried very hard to comply.

To parents like Michael's and Susan's, it's crucial that their children achieve and perform. It's essential that they "look good." It's true that most parents enjoy their children's accomplishments and encourage their children's success. But if our parents love us too much, our successes and failures become a cause of great anxiety.

If we aren't admired by others, they're upset. If our talents go unnoticed, they're overly concerned. They want to "fix" whatever is wrong, and make us "look good" again. It's a mutual family conspiracy. We're keepers of the family secrets, hiding what we really think and feel. Smile for Mommy and Daddy. "Look good" for us.

As children, we learn that when we don't "show well," we make our parents unhappy. "You can't do that!" our parents scold. "How would it look?" Or, "Don't say those things! What will other people think?" When we're giggling and laughing, we're told to settle down and stop acting so silly.

We argue for our independence, and they look at us in surprise. "Be who you want to be," they tell us, "but do you have to broadcast it to the rest of the world? We love you just the way you are; but does Aunt Sally really have to know that you failed math?" So much for unconditional love and support.

As children, we tend to mold our personalities to adapt to our environment. If our environment is supportive, nurturing, and flexible, we are freed to express our own individuality. If our environment is rigid, demanding, and conditional, however, we are forced to shape our behavior to fit the needs of others. We substitute our true self for a false self that is more acceptable to our parents, whose love and approval we need desperately. In essence we compromise who we really are, and become what our parents need us to be.

The false self is a disguise, a masquerade. Yet it is very convincing. It fools many people. It fools us.

A false self can take many different shapes: "the victim," "the quiet one," "the crazy one," "the rebel," "the critic." For the child who was overparented, "Mr. or Mrs. Perfect" is a common adaptation of the false self, followed closely by a depressed and frustrated "Mr. or Mrs. Misunderstood." All of our masks have one thing in common: They attempt to cover up parts of ourselves that we feel are unacceptable.

To understand ourselves, it's necessary to understand our past. Where did we learn to dislike parts of ourselves? How did we develop a "false self" to protect ourselves? To answer these questions, we must look back into the first years of life.

From the time a child is born until about age three, he goes from a stage in which he perceives no boundaries between himself and his mother to where he recognizes himself as separate and whole, with talents and personality traits uniquely his own. This is called separation and individuation, and is both a physical and emotional process.

Parents can enhance or impede this process. If a child is given acceptance and support, at least much of the time, he will feel safe in sharing his true self with the world. He learns, "It is okay to be me," and "I am loved for who I am."

However, when parents love too much, they feel great anxiety over the separation process. The child's needs conflict with the parent's needs. The parent's need for control is threatened by the child's spontaneity or individuality. The parent has a constant compulsion to stop this undesirable behavior and exert his greater control. As a result, the emerging sense of self is threatened.

Obviously, the fact that our behavior can be shaped and controlled by others is sometimes a good thing. All of our impulses as young children are not healthy or in our own best interests. However, the power our parents have to shape our behavior so that we become civilized and able to live in society is the same power that can be misused to rob us of autonomy and force us to respond to demands based on very unrealistic expectations.

The most powerful and destructive tool for shaping a child's behavior lies in the withdrawal of love. The most potent fear in any human being is the fear of abandonment. In our early years, abandonment is equivalent to death. The withdrawal of love can be experienced as abandonment. A child will do anything in order to avoid this, even compromise who he is. As a defense against this fear, he will attempt to comply with his parents' expectations of him. If he is told never to cry, he will try not to cry. If he is told never to talk back to his parents, he will learn to suppress his feelings. If he feels more love when he brings home straight 'A's, makes the team, or plays a piece of music without a mistake, he will learn he has to perform to be loved.

Although we may realize that we are something separate from our mothers at age three, separation and individuation continue throughout a lifetime. Our sense of self is either strengthened or weakened by our experiences. Natural emotions and impulses will be repressed if we are forced to respond to others who need us to act in certain ways. If we were appreciated most for our special talents and abilities rather than for our simple humanity, we learn to deny parts of ourselves that don't "show well" enough to win any applause. We learn to "look good."

"Looking good" is not a show of self-confidence. It's a defense—a mask that hides who we truly are and what we really feel—that has its roots in the internalized wishes and demands of our parents. When we put on the mask as adults, we're defending ourselves against deep hurt—a pain reminiscent of the first hurt we felt in childhood at not being fully accepted by people we needed and loved deeply. Adults today can vividly describe the incidents in their past where the need for a "false self" their parents would accept came across with an impact they never forgot:

Kevin: "We were never allowed to wear jeans when we were kids. According to my mother, they weren't proper. We argued about every piece of clothing I put on. I'd come downstairs, dressed for Thanksgiving dinner, and she'd look at me and say, 'Oh, Kevin, you've got to run and change your clothes. Those pants are from hunger! You don't want to embarrass me in front of Aunt Judy, do you?' When I got older, I'd refuse, and my father would get into the act. 'Come on, Kevin. Just do it for me. You don't want to make your mother ill, do you?' It was so absurd. My clothes were really going to make her ill. But in the end, I wore what she wanted."

Joe: "I was on Spring Break and I decided to visit my father at the office. He gave me a tour, introducing me to all of his staff. 'This is my son, Joey,' he said, 'who's working on his master's degree.' He kept saying that, over and over again, to everyone we met. This might not seem like a big thing to most people, but you've got to understand my father. It was never okay to be just Joey. I had to be 'Joey the——.' I had to be achieving or creating something. Otherwise I wasn't adequate."

Sandy: "My parents wouldn't allow me to write that I had epilepsy on school health forms. I had a very mild case that was controlled by medicine, but even so, they didn't want anyone to know. They said everyone would treat me differently. I think they were protecting themselves, or ashamed that they had created a 'damaged' child or something. I always wonder what would have happened if I had a seizure in school. Who would have known what was wrong with me? It's hard to believe that my parents would take a risk like that, but they did."

Kim: "You wouldn't believe what went on at my house when I decided I wanted to get a job rather than go to college. I broke the news to my mother first. She locked herself in the bedroom, and I heard her telling my father later. It was like she was saying, 'Oh, Stanley, our daughter's dead. What did we do to deserve this?' For two years after that, I'd hear her tell her friends that I was applying to different colleges. I found myself telling my family and friends the same thing, when I knew darn well that I was never going back to school again.''

All of these adults learned how important "looking good" was to their parents as children. By the time they were able to tie their shoes, zip their jackets, and write their names neatly in their notebooks, they'd learned how to keep their fallibility hidden from others. Their self-esteem became dependent on their performance. If they *did* good, they *were* good.

When they couldn't be good, they enlisted their survival strategies: avoidance, withholding, lying, placating, and covering up true feelings. This was how they protected themselves.

"But my parents never really pressured me," you may be thinking. "I was a naturally good child. If anyone put pressure on me, it was *me*. My parents just told me to do the best I could."

We may not, in fact, be able to recall any direct words or "looking good" messages we got from our parents. But words aren't always necessary.

Perhaps your parents told you how all they ever really wanted in life was children, what a wonderful miracle it was when they had you, and how you were the most important person in the world to them. It may seem like you're getting quite a compliment, but what a burden it poses for you. What if you fail to bring them all the happiness your birth was supposed to produce for them? Being your parents' main source of joy is an awesome responsibility.

We can sense, even as very young children, when our accomplishments are our parents' sustenance, even if they tell us nothing at all. Perhaps you took your first steps, stumbled, and looked up to see anxious determination on your father's face. Maybe there was a sudden cold, detached look on your mother's face whenever you couldn't do as she wished, which became your most powerful motivator. When you yelled, "Leave me alone, I can do this by myself!," your parents still stared anxiously over your shoulder, afraid that you'd fail to do it right. Our experience of ourselves is reflected back to us through our parents, much like looking in a mirror. We introject their judgments. If we looked into their eyes and saw anxiety over how good we were, how well we stacked up to other children, or how closely we fulfilled their hopes, we concluded that there was something to be very anxious about. We concluded that if we did "bad" things, we were bad people. We did not understand that we could be good, loving people who occasionally make mistakes or fail to please others around us.

Given our history, it's no surprise that many of us develop an insatiable need for praise, recognition, and approval. Our true selves are starving for it. We keep looking into the "mirror" of other people's faces to reassure us that we are okay. Our parents' anxiety is inside of us, internalized, and worse for wear. Life become a serious, stressful business.

When our parents' happiness seems dependent on our accomplishments, we become masters at hiding our shortcomings from them. We become adept at giving noncommittal answers to a host of probing questions. "Looking good" becomes a survival strategy. One woman recalls darting into an alley, almost getting hit by a truck, when she saw her mother walking down the street toward her. "The week before, I'd gone skiing with my friends and broken my arm," she explains. "I'd been avoiding my mother since I'd returned—not an easy thing to do. She would have gone nuts if she'd seen my arm in a cast. I would have been dragged off to every specialist in the city. I think I would have preferred getting hit by a truck to dealing with my mother's anxiety and judgments."

"Looking good" carries over to most of our relationships. We react the same way to other "parental figures" we encounter in our lives. We can't face our teacher, our boss, our mother-in-law, or anyone else who appears to be in authority with the awful truth that we're imperfect, fallible human beings. Children who were loved too much become adults who:

- Feel hurt but hide it
- Choke back normal feelings of anger and resentment
- Say everything's fine, when it isn't
- Never ask for help when they need it (except maybe from their family)
- Feel like they always have to be perfect, or right
- Become very critical about their bodies, hairstyles, health, or physical features
- Become immobilized by a fear of making mistakes
- Fear that others will sense their vulnerability
- Believe that if the real person inside them is exposed to others, he'll be rejected

"Looking good" also had its payoffs, however. Children who were overparented often find themselves in the creative arts, flawlessly performing for others, with their hearts in their throats and a look of calm detachment on their faces. They're great teachers and lecturers, and even better salespeople. Who could represent a product better than someone who's learned so well to minimize the flaws and put the best features forward?

Think of the woman who interviews for the job she barely qualified for, and clinches it with a strong show of confidence even though she's shaking in her boots. Or consider the man who sits in the meeting looking so intelligent and concerned that everyone else is impressed, never realizing that his mind is a million miles away and he hasn't heard a thing that's going on.

Children who learned to hide their fallibility from the rest of the world find the business world much simpler than life at home. Their parents' glances were much more penetrating. They convince others of their skills and abilities with a studied artistry that is the envy of all. The mask on their faces reads, "Everything's fine here; everything's under control."

No one would ever suspect how much more of us there is behind our mask of confidence and control, how hard we work at it. The effort of it all can cause stress and a host of psychosomatic symptoms. Adults whose success was their parents' obsession often wonder why they have constant headaches, backaches, insomnia, high blood pressure, and chronic fatigue. These are all direct results of the anxiety they've internalized over how good they look to others along with the desire to protect their parents from disappointment in them.

The desire to protect our parents by "looking good" is such a part of us that we tend to pressure ourselves with far greater expectations than our parents ever really had of us. We learn to hold back our feelings and to reveal only what is expected of us. Some of us turn to alcohol and drugs for the help they seem to give us in escaping our feelings. We experience life like warriors, with our protective armor in place.

It's in our personal lives that we suffer most for all of our "looking good." Consider Kathy's story. Tall and blond, with soft hazel eyes and a confident smile, Kathy, at thirty-six, looks more like a model than the successful doctor she is. "I can't understand it," she muses with an uncomfortable laugh. "My friends tell me I have everything going for me. My practice is doing great, and I really love my work. I spent years in medical school, and more years paying off my student loans. Now, I can relax and afford pretty much what I want. This should be the happiest time in my life, but I'm miserable.

"What I really want," Kathy admits, "is a husband and a couple of kids. But I just can't seem to connect with anyone. I meet tons of men. I've gotten fixed up so much that last week, when a friend offered to set me up with a man she knew, I had to laugh because another friend had fixed me up with the same guy a week ago. But nothing ever seems to work out."

What puzzles Kathy most is that the men she cares about leave just when the relationship appears to be meaningful to them both. "I date a guy for a while and think that everything's great. I start believing that this is the one. Next thing I know, he tells me that he isn't ready for a relationship. Six months later, I hear he's getting married to someone else."

Ron is a man who dated Kathy. He says, "She's a great lady. She's a lot of fun and incredibly smart. Kathy really has it all together. But something just wasn't happening with us.''

What was missing for Ron? "I just never felt she was really there when we were together. Maybe I was intimidated, I don't know. But I never really understood what she wanted with me. She certainly didn't need me."

With a self-conscious smile, Ron explains, "It's not that I want some weak little woman depending on me for everything. I'd get bored. But I like to be asked for advice once in a while. Most men do. I like to think that other people make mistakes every now and then. I love to see a woman with her hair messed up and her shoes kicked off. Kathy was too perfect. We didn't hook up. Maybe this sounds silly, but I never thought of Kathy as someone I could cuddle with."

What Ron couldn't see in Kathy was her vulnerability. Kathy, who "looked so good" and had so much to offer a partner, hid her feelings deep inside of her.

Kathy's past explained why. "My mother was a very depressed woman. I'm not talking about bad moods or a little sadness. She had the kind of depression that you hospitalize people for."

Kathy's mother was, in fact, hospitalized several times when Kathy was a child. "My father would take me aside on the day my mother was coming home and say, 'Kathy, I don't want you ever to cry in front of Mommy. Now that she's coming home, we all have to try to make her happy and not bother her with our problems.' "

In effect, Kathy's father censored Kathy's emotions. She learned never to cry, never to show her feelings, no matter how sad she felt. Because her excellent work at school was something that made her mother very happy, Kathy worked hard. She escaped into her studies, and reveled in her parents' praise. Although she felt loved by her mother and father, she felt empty inside and afraid to fail lest her parents stop loving her.

Kathy became a calm, capable, responsible child, who was never overtaken by unexpected emotions. She was, at thirty-six, a successful, competent doctor. But her friends and lovers felt they could never really be close to her.

That's the problem with looking good. It's the antithesis of intimacy. We tend to believe that others will love us if we present them with a flawless "package" of achievements. Worse, we expect others to be flawless, too, or at least bent on self-improvement. We project our parents' "looking good" message onto our friends and lovers. We expect the same perfectionism out of others that we are driven to ourselves.

"There's always that something about someone," one man said, when asked why he never married. "It's almost always that one thing you just can't live with." We're quick to find our lover's Achilles' heel, and become disenchanted. The recruiting goes on as we dismiss the applicants.

We need love so badly. Why can't we ever find the right person? We have so much to offer. Why is it that when we find someone who seems perfect, they're gone, in spite of all our talents and attributes?

What we fail to realize is what really makes one person lovable to another. Although we find it hard to believe, it's the run in our stocking, the chronic mismanagement of our checkbooks, the way we break out in hives when we have to speak in front of a group of people that makes us vulnerable, and therefore lovable.

Instead, we continue our "looking good" and end up puzzled by questions that, at first, seem unanswerable. "Why is it that no matter how much I earn or achieve, how many people praise or compliment me, I still feel so empty inside? Why do I always feel as if something's missing in my life?"

Whenever we receive admiration and praise for our accomplishments—and we set things up so that we receive a lot—we feel a void inside. We feel as if these acknowledgments have little to do with who we really are. They're merely applause for the show we've starred in all of our lives. We long to be recognized for our true selves, our deepest thoughts, feelings, and fears. We long to be validated for who we are, not praised for what we do.

Let's look at how praise and validation differ for a moment. Praise is an acknowledgment of our behavior based on other people's expectations or society's norms that dictate how we should be. The value system imposed is based exclusively on our behavior, not on our inner selves.

Validation, however, is an acknowledgment of our inner experience or "true self" by another. The experience includes support of our thoughts, feelings, fears, and dreams.

If we grew up praised for "looking good," rather than validated for who we really were, our self-esteem became based solely on our achievements. We began to believe that we must excel brilliantly in everything we undertake or lose the admiration of others, which is what we know of as love. We need to achieve and earn praise in order to feel secure. "Looking good" becomes a defensive overcompensation hiding our imperfections, which we mistakenly believe make us "unlovable."

Again and again, we repeat the childhood drama of trying to become the child our parents praise. Even though we may be "looking good" to the rest of the world, if we aren't pleasing our parents, we never feel comfortable about it. We can be dentists when our parents wanted doctors; accountants when our parents wanted lawyers; parents of two when our parents wanted three. Part of us wants to scream, "Isn't anything ever enough for you?" Still, we're silent. We love them too much to take a stand as our true selves and let them know by how much we've been hurt.

Few people share our parents' expectations of us. Fewer still could live up to them. Most would gladly love us in spite of our imperfections. Admiration isn't love, and the more perfect we appear to others, the more unavailable for love we seem.

If you were a child who was loved too much, chances are you were never truly allowed to experience your feelings and emotions. You grew up feeling your parents' need for you to "look good." You developed what your parents needed, because that's how you insured their love for you. You've had a lot of praise when you succeeded, but never enough validation of who you really are.

To others, you may appear a little aloof as you hide your feelings, believing unconsciously that it "looks bad" to show real emotion. Look at the list of normal human feelings that follow. Which do you hold back because you fear that you won't "look good" if you let yourself feel it?

Anger	Anxiety	Bitchiness
Caring	Competitiveness	Dependency
Discouragement	Disgust	Distrust
Envy	Eagerness	Fury
Giving	Hesitancy	Hopelessness
Hostility	Inadequacy	Impatience
Loneliness	Loss	Neediness
Openness	Love	Panic
Playfulness	Pride	Rage
Sensuality	Sexuality	Smallness
Self-consciousness	Self-concern	Silliness
Tenderness	Weakness	Worry

These feelings make you vulnerable. You believe—again, unconsciously—that vulnerability is a weakness and that keeping what you feel under wraps is a strength. You remember what happened when you were angry, resentful, lazy, jealous, messy, alone, or scared in front of your parents, and it isn't a happy memory.

We are, each of us, all of these things, because we're human. But to insure your parents' love, you become a convenient child—responsible, capable, understanding, and well behaved. In other words, you tried to "look good."

You can only hope to end the emptiness inside when you make a decision to exchange "looking good" for letting go. You must stop feeling that you will only be accepted if you're successful, competent, and controlled. You have to stop asking, "How would it look?" and ask, "How would it feel?" You need to believe that if you expose the real person inside of you, including your flaws, you'll be accepted.

This is a process that takes time. Although you cannot expect overnight to exchange "looking good" for other behaviors, you can become more self-aware. You can allow others to peek behind your mask. Only then will you learn that you will be accepted for all parts of yourself, even your very human imperfections.

CHAPTER 4

ENTITLEMENT: PRINCEHOOD AND PRINCESSHOOD

"We want you to have all the things we never had."

"Inside there's a feeling that people should do things for me, pay special attention to me, appreciate me, drop what they're doing to make me happy when I'm upset. They should be able to read my mind."

—Linda, age 34, teacher

From a distance, Steve can pass for Richard Gere if you squint a little. Dark and medium height, with a trim, athletic body, he has a powerful yet reserved look about him. A sort of tenseness, a turned-in-upon-himself air, surrounds him. People who might otherwise approach him often mistake it for arrogance and pass without lingering.

"That's part of the problem," Steve admits with a grin so suddenly open and friendly that the previous image evaporates. "I'm really a nice guy. But, basically, I'm pretty shy."

Shyness disguised as arrogance is far from an asset in the people-oriented career that Steve steeps himself in ten hours a day. Two years ago, Steve was scuffling, wondering what he was going to do with his life. Next month, he'll open his third restaurant, and his net worth will approach more than a million dollars. Plans for two more restaurants are in the works.

"I'd drifted around a lot trying different careers," Steve begins. "I sold insurance for a while. Then, a few years ago, I took the real estate exam, thinking I'd make a great broker. But you had to be a salesman first, and I wasn't making big money at it, so I quit.

"Those were my more stable ventures. I also drove a limousine for a while, which would have killed my parents if they'd known. I think my parents would rather see me live off of them for the rest of my life than have me drive for a living, or work someplace flipping burgers or something like that. I always got the impression from my father that there was a message there, that I was better than others and above certain jobs. I know that sounds awful, and it's nothing that he ever said out loud, but I heard it just the same. Even so, if a guy I went to high school with hadn't come up to me with the idea for a restaurant and the know-how to pull it off, I'd be driving that limo right now."

Steve was in a record store, leafing through the oldies section in search of a Rascals' cut, when he looked up and recognized Neal. "We hadn't seen each other in years. We weren't great friends or anything in high school, but it was such a kick to run into each other that we went out for coffee to talk about old times. He started talking about his dream of getting into the restaurant business. He'd been doing some research and had a location in mind. Listening to him, it sounded like a terrific deal."

Neal admitted to Steve that he was twenty thousand dollars short of what he needed to get started. He was looking for a partner, he said, with a good credit rating and access to some cash. Did Steve want in?

Steve did. The next night, he took the idea home to his parents. "Let's face it, the deal wasn't going to happen without my dad. I think I had about twenty-eight bucks in the bank at the time. The only credit I ever had was with him. But to be honest, I didn't feel embarrassed going to my father for the cash. You see, my brothers had been there plenty of times before. Dad gave my younger brother the down payment on his house, and bailed my older brother out about once a year when he ran out of money. I figured it was my turn.''

So Steve showed up at his father's door, with no real numbers or specific details to present but with the firm conviction that this restaurant was what he wanted to do with his life. His father listened intently, but finally remarked, ''What do you know about the restaurant business? And what do you know about this Neal, whom you haven't seen in years?''

The truth was, nothing. His father looked at him with the same expression he wore when Steve was eleven years old and left his new bicycle out in the rain. That was Steve's cue to start begging.

''You have to understand my dad,'' Steve explains. ''He's a partner in one of the largest law firms in the city. Another of the partners is an alderman, so he's got connections all over the place. Everything to him is numbers and logic when it comes to business deals. But he's not ruthless or anything. Everybody loves him and talks about what a great guy he is. My mother never lets any of us forget how hard he's worked to give us all the advantages. I knew he'd help me out if I begged him, told him how much I needed him in what could be my one big break. Believe me, no wanted me to succeed more than he did.''

Steve's father agreed to look into the deal. For the next two weeks, Neal came over every night, and listened avidly as Steve's father discussed loans, licensing, management, and partnership agreements. ''It was Neal and my father who did most of the talking. I tried to stay with it and pay attention, but in the middle of my father's complicated explanations about things like credit lines and cash-flow statements, my eyes would glaze over. Then my mother would come and put in her two cents' worth. A couple of times, I actually fell asleep in the chair while they all hashed over the details.''

His father's ''take charge'' attitude was nothing new to Steve. ''Actually, it brought back old times.'' He laughs. ''For some reason, it reminded me of a Thanksgiving, years ago, when he was showing me how to carve the turkey in the kitchen, a man's job in our house. I was making a mess out of it, not carving it anything like the way he showed me. 'That's not how you do it,' he said, grabbing the knife out of my hands. 'Let me do it.'

"It was like that with everything we did together. I'd start to struggle, and then he'd do it for me. Today, I'm thirty-three years old, and I still don't know how to carve a turkey. I have no great desire to learn, either."

In another home, the father and mother might have assisted their son the first time he struggled with something new. Then they'd say kindly but firmly, "Now, you're on your own. You can do it yourself." The child would gain confidence as his ability to meet new challenges increased. But in Steve's home, a child's frustration called the parents to the rescue.

Although it was far from his intent, Steve's father taught him to demand little of himself. Steve's experiences with his mother reinforced this. Each morning he was greeted with a barrage of reminders to brush his teeth, wash his hair, eat his eggs, take his vitamin, wear his jacket, grab his lunch box, listen to his teacher, do his homework. "She couldn't help it," Steve says. "She didn't believe I'd do anything without her reminding me."

With his mother standing anxiously over his shoulder, directing him so that he wouldn't make a mistake, Steve grew quiet and reserved. He also grew lazy. One scene stands out for him: "I was sitting in my room, struggling over a term paper due the next day on the history of the Civil War. Actually, I think I was copying it out of an encyclopedia. My mother came in to help, because God forbid I should feel frustrated over anything. Anyway, in fifteen minutes, I was downstairs watching TV, and she was upstairs typing away. My mother did more term papers than anyone else in our house."

Steve was an awful student, which frustrated his mother, who constantly nagged him about it. "But, I had a saving grace," Steve says with a winsome grin. "I was cute. Seriously. She got the biggest bang out of the way people stopped her on the street when I was little, just to look at me and tell her how cute I was. She still talks about it.

Not to sound conceited, but I was the best-looking one in the family. Although she made a great point of saying that she loved all her children equally, everyone saw through it. To her, I was special, because of my good looks more than anything else. This wasn't a bad thing. I was glad I could make her proud of something.

"But she was always worried that something was going to happen to me. She wouldn't let me play hockey or even touch football. You know what I think? I think she was afraid I'd fall on my face—literally—and ruin it."

Steve admits that part of him bought into his mother's image of him as a special child. Friendships with other children didn't come easily to him, especially in his teens. "I'd have an argument with someone, and that would be it. I'd think, Why should I have to put up with this guy's bull? I'd tell myself he was a jerk and never talk to him again. The only person I was ever really buddies with was my next-door neighbor, Mike, who pretty much tagged along with me and did whatever I wanted to do. With him, I had great times."

When Steve graduated from a two-year program at the community college, he got an apartment with Mike. For three years, they were roommates, while Steve drifted in and out of the insurance business, the real estate business, the limo business, always disappointed with the salary he commanded. "I would have starved if it hadn't been for my parents' occasional handouts. But nothing seemed to happen for me until I met Neal in the record store and decided to open a restaurant."

It was Steve's father whose name went on the lease for the new restaurant. His personal signature guaranteed the bank notes, and his money allowed Steve to be a full partner from the start. His connections speeded up the transfer of the liquor license that made it possible for Steve and Neal to open.

The doors opened in the spring. "We knew we'd made it after the second month. People came in and just kept coming. Neal had known all along what he was doing, and only needed an injection of money from someone like my father. And as for Dad, it's a wonder that his law practice survived with the amount of hours he put in at the restaurant after the opening.

"For me, it seemed like a lot of headaches, and a lot of drudgery at first. I tried to pass my share off on Neal. I stuck him with the holidays and extra shifts when a manager quit on us. With my father's name on practically everything we owned, I knew he really couldn't kick too much."

But then, Steve began to change. Although it meant hard work and long hours, running a restaurant was more responsibility than he had ever experienced in his family. It was responsibility he began to crave, because it provided him with a sense of accomplishment for the first time in his life.

"The way all of our employees went to Neal whenever they had a question started to bug me. Granted, at first I didn't know the answers. I'd check out every decision I made with my father. But after a year or so, I'd learned a lot, and was just as capable as Neal was."

Soon his father's constant advice started to grate on his nerves. They argued frequently. Steve insisted that he knew what he was doing, and wanted to be left alone to do it. But still his father remained underfoot, overseeing things and coaching Steve from the sidelines.

In a couple of years, Steve and Neal were firmly established in a highly profitable business and planning their next venture. But at night, long after the restaurant closed, Steve would toss and turn, depressed and unable to sleep. "Maybe it was finally finding out that I was good at something and being successful at it that made me so aware that there was no one there to share it with. I mean, my parents were thrilled, but the fact that I had so few relationships with anyone else was staring me in the face. Over the years, I'd invested about as much in friendship as I had in anything else."

The turning point for Steve was the night his second restaurant held its grand opening. "We threw this huge party—very classy—with a pretty well-heeled crowd. Neal had tons of friends there, while I had my parents and a few other people that I'd call acquaintances rather than friends. I was in a bad mood all night because so many of the people I'd invited didn't show up. I told myself most of them were jealous of my success, but still it pissed me off. I didn't even have a date for my own party. I stood there that night pretty much alone, thinking that I'd worked hard for once in my life and I deserved the success. But there were so few old friends and no old enemies to see it.''

As he sat with his parents and watched Neal surrounded by a crowd of his friends, Steve thought sadly of Mike. Their friendship had ended a couple of years earlier, after an argument that almost came to blows. It had started over a girl.

Mike and Steve were sharing an apartment at the time, when one afternoon Mike's friend Joanne had come to the door. Steve, who had a day off from the restaurant, answered and invited her in. ''Mike had been carrying a torch for this girl for years, but I had never paid much attention to her. That afternoon, though, we got to talking. Mike didn't show up, and we got hungry waiting for him, so we went out for something to eat.''

Lunch turned to dinner, one thing led to another, and Steve ended up taking Joanne back to her place, where he spent the night.

''It meant nothing to me at all. To tell you the truth, one night with her was plenty, and I was glad to be on my way the next morning. But I guess she made more out of our night together than I did, because she started calling me every day and dropping around the apartment. I didn't mention it to Mike. I mean, it wasn't like she was his steady girlfriend or anything, so that made it none of his business.''

One day Mike came home earlier than he usually did. Steve was sitting on the couch, watching the game and having a beer, when he looked up to see Mike glaring at him. ''His face was all red, like he'd run all the way home or something. 'You've been seeing Joanne,' he said. It was a statement, not a question, so I couldn't really deny it. 'Hey, nothing's going on,' I said. 'It's all in her head.'

''Mike walked into his room, yelling, 'That's just what

I thought you'd say!' over his shoulder. I ran after him, shouting, 'Look, man, it's not like I did anything. For chrissakes, she came to me!'

"He didn't answer, and when I saw that he was packing, I really lost it. 'You can't just leave me with the lease, you know,' I shouted. I couldn't help it. It was the first thing I thought of. Ever since I got a little money, it seemed like everyone was trying to suck off me, and take some kind of advantage. I threatened to get a lawyer. 'Go for it,' he shouted, and ran off down the stairs. I yelled something like, 'Forget you, man,' after him, but he never even looked back at me.

"All this fuss wasn't about some silly girl, I thought at the time. It's because he's jealous. I've got a restaurant, and he's got nothing.

"Well, we never spoke again. But, you know, if I knew where he was today, I'd call him. I'd go to him on my knees even, to apologize. The two of us went back a lot of years.

"All those crazy times growing up next door to each other," Steve sighs. "And you know what? Mike would have been genuinely happy for me today."

Steve felt depressed and lonely at a time in his life when he might have been happiest. A common symptom of children who were loved too much is that no matter what they accomplish, they don't experience much joy as adults. "Joylessness" is actually a low-grade depression, an anger turned inward as they grapple with finding an answer to the question, Why don't people appreciate me? Why, with everything I have, am I so unhappy?

Steve's depression cloaked growing feelings of rage and resentment that remained outside of his awareness. Where was the happiness he was supposed to feel when he finally made it? he wondered. Where were all the people who were supposed to congratulate him on his success and seek out his company? Where was the fun he was supposed to be having? Hadn't he earned it? Wasn't he entitled to it?

From pampered/deprived children, we grow into "entitled" adults. Psychiatrist J. Murray first coined the term "entitlement" in describing people who expect all things to come to them. Various theorists have since explored the roots of psychological entitlement—these unconscious, projected expectations that the world will pay attention to us, rescue us, appreciate us, forgive us, and love us. For the most part, they stem from the reality of our experience with our parents.

Steve felt entitled to a great many things. He felt entitled to use his father's services, money, and connections to get started in business. He felt entitled to be left alone to do it on his own once he was assured of success. He felt entitled to work shorter hours and with less effort than his partner, Neal. He felt entitled to betray his best friend without reprisal, when he slept with a girl he had no real interest in but whom his friend was in love with. He felt entitled to a large turnout at his opening-night party, and the types of friendships that are the outgrowth only of mutual caring and acceptance.

How did Steve get the idea that he was deserving of all these things? Steve's attitudes, feelings, and behavior are typical of a child who was overparented.

The root of entitlement is having others do for us, cater to us, overinflate us, and indulge us to the point where we come to expect it. Steve's mother and father saw it as their duty to solve their children's problems with whatever resources they had at their disposal. And when it came to Steve's problems, whether they involved carving a turkey or opening a restaurant, they didn't just provide the solution—they *became* the solution.

Most of what Steve did to get his needs met in his family was play the role of helpless. It always worked. Together, his parents drove home the message that he was a special child, and expected to accomplish great things. No one, however, ever told him he really had to *do* anything to accomplish these things. In fact, when he tried to do something, one of his parents grabbed it out of his hands and did it for him.

The coupling of the conflicting messages "You're special and therefore should accomplish great things in your life" and "To do things right, you need my help" becomes a firm foundation for a lifetime spent feeling entitled to a lot, without having to do much to get it.

What occurred when Steve decided he wanted to be a partner in a restaurant was a classic example of these types of conflicting messages. Steve sought out his father's assistance immediately. What's interesting here is that although Steve's father was a skillful lawyer and could decipher leases and agreements full of legalese for Steve, he knew as little about the day-to-day details of running a restaurant as his son did. Yet, Steve, so used to depending on his father, delegated these decisions to him also, much in the way an executive might delegate chores to an eager assistant.

With his father, mother, and partner enthusiastically working out the details of opening the restaurant, Steve's input became superfluous. Discussion raged around him, determining his future, while he slept in a chair. Most of his life he had been a passive observer, shifting his responsibility for making decisions to others around him who seemed so much stronger. Now, making decisions scared him, and sleep was a good escape.

Why would Steve's parents devote so much time and energy to Steve's problems to the point of becoming experts in their son's restaurant business? One obvious answer is that they loved their son and wanted to help him succeed. A less obvious answer is that Steve's parents needed him to depend on them.

Consider that when Steve no longer wanted his father's help, his father wouldn't leave the restaurant, and continued to give him advice and suggestions that Steve now resented. Subconsciously, Steve's father "needed" a son who would bring him problems to solve. Both of Steve's parents were actually *drawn* to problems. This attraction is characteristic of most parents who love too much, and it makes perfect sense in terms of their own childhood history.

No one becomes a parent who loves too much by accident. Typically, parents like Steve's grew up in families where their emotional needs for affection, love, and acceptance were denied or insufficiently met. Their own parents may have been indifferent, demanding, alcoholic, or physically or emotionally abusive. They survived by adopting a particular role in their families: the responsible one, the problem-solver, the peacemaker. This role gave them a sense of control and self-worth. By being "helpful" and taking over responsibilities not really their own they sought to get the love they desperately needed from people who could never really give it.

Unfortunately, these survival tactics were a forerunner of a lifetime of codependency—an obsession with making things "right" for everyone they care about, through too much selflessness, love, and control. As adults with children of their own, they continue to replay the familiar childhood role of caretaker and rescuer that they've become adept at. Overparenting their children is unavoidable, because their identities have become wrapped up in this role of problem-solver and helper. Without a problem to solve or someone to assist they feel anxious, out of control, and useless. In the end, the need to be needed is everything. When it's time to let go, parents who love too much can't.

The experience of having the people we love drop everything to rush in to solve our problems and free us from any discomfort has far-reaching ramifications. With all Steve was given, he never got what he really needed: motivation to gain a sense of competency through experience and an incentive to do things on his own. Instead, a lifetime of having his smallest problem become his parents' obsession left him with a feeling of grandiosity.

Most of us would call grandiosity conceit when we see it in others. Outwardly, the grandiose person appears to feel superior to others, and very full of himself. But underneath is despair.

Alice Miller, in *Drama of the Gifted Child,* indicates that grandiosity is often a way people fight off depression caused by feelings of inadequacy:

The person who is "grandiose" is admired everywhere and needs this admiration; indeed, he cannot live without it. He must excel brilliantly in everything he undertakes, which he surely is capable of doing (otherwise he does not attempt it). He, too, admires himself—for his qualities: his beauty, cleverness, talents—and for his success and achievements. Woe betide if one of these fails him, for then the catastrophe of severe depression is imminent.

Feelings of entitlement are defenses against feelings of inferiority and shame. To avoid these feelings, we pretend just the opposite. We overinflate ourselves to convince others that we are okay and that they should give us the praise and admiration we need. A host of projected expectations are then foisted on an unsympathetic world. Steve, who believed that he was entitled to special treatment from others, with him providing little in return, eventually found that such expectations led to frustration and depression when the world didn't pay attention to him, appreciate him, forgive him, or love him as his parents did.

Feelings of entitlement such as Steve's exist to some extent in many adult children who were overparented. They may not feel especially "entitled," but the nagging feeling that they deserve much more than they're getting out of life is evident in their quick disillusionment with their friends, intimate relationships, and work.

People who unconsciously feel entitled do many of the following things, and drive their friends, lovers, and co-workers crazy in the process:

- Listen with half an ear to other people's problems, waiting to interject their own
- List a multitude of things other people should be and ways they should act before they'd seriously consider them as friends or lovers
- Walk away leaving tasks unfinished or inaccurate, reasoning that other people are paid to pick up where they left off
- Play "poor," and expect others to buy them or their children things or pick up their tab
- Judge dates or even marriage partners by how much money they make, or how much they're willing to spend

- Grab the check in restaurants not to pay it, but to add up what everyone else owes, lest they be cheated
- Play "helpless" or "too busy" when they're faced with mundane tasks they think are foisted on them unjustly, such as cleaning the ring around the bathtub, emptying the dishwasher, or placing a new roll of toilet paper on the roller
- Blind themselves to dust on end tables, dishes piling up in the sink, and rotting artifacts in the refrigerator, assuming that the people they live with will eventually clean them up
- Give a host of excuses, albeit good ones, for not being able to work overtime, on Saturdays, or on extra projects
- Blame others for not helping them whenever they want
- Look sad, so others will ask them what's wrong
- Consistently arrive late, so others have to wait for them
- Yell impatiently for others to help them find the things that they can't locate in their drawers, closets, and cabinets, claiming that they've searched for hours when they've barely even looked
- Grab the aisle seat on airplanes and in theaters because they have "long legs" or claustrophobia and are therefore always entitled to better seating than the person they're with
- Command a table for four in restaurants when they're only with one other person
- Borrow things and forget to return them
- Accidently break or ruin something they've borrowed from a friend, and then feel resentful when they have to pay for it
- Create a list of reasons why they should be mad at the person who's angry with them
- Request a single room at college, a seminar, or a business trip, even if they have to trump up a medical excuse to get one, because they just can't sleep in the same room with strangers

The list could go on. Children who were loved too much are masters of assertiveness, but standing up for their rights is hardly the point. The point is that they unconsciously jockey themselves into the best position without even realizing it, and then feel hurt and outraged when others, feeling taken advantage of, bring this to their attention.

If you recognize yourself as a child who was overparented, you may see yourself in some of these attitudes and behaviors. You may find that you have unconscious expectations that others should be stronger, give you more, and be overly sensitive to your needs. You may feel frustrated because other people so often let you down. You may feel that you're endlessly searching for the "right" relationship, the perfect job, or friends who will really understand you. You may not feel especially "entitled," but perhaps lonely, vaguely disappointed with your life today and unable to put your finger on what's missing.

Others tell you that you expect too much out of life, that you set your sights too high. But the belief that all of your fantasies will come true, that things will always work out for you and that you deserve it automatically, is part of the baggage you carried out of your parents' home into your own, causing frustration when reality doesn't match these expectations.

You may wonder where you got this feeling of being entitled, especially if you grew up in a home where the family budget was tight and you went without many material things. This feeling of being "privileged" to special consideration and special attention of others isn't restricted to wealthy, or "spoiled," children. It doesn't take money to raise children who feel entitled. It happened to us if our parents waited on us, rescued us, overprotected us, controlled us, and became enmeshed in our smallest problems.

This, again, is the essence of the pampered/deprived child, who gets much of what he wants but little that he needs. Convinced that any childhood trauma will cause a lifetime of trouble, parents who love too much vow to protect their child. The child will have an easier life than they did, and never know frustration, sickness, loss, want, or unhappiness if they can help it. From the time he is an infant, he becomes the center of their lives—"His Majesty the Baby," as Freud referred to this phenomenon.

He or she grows up being told of the talents, intelligence, beauty, and charm mother and father see in him or her, all overestimated because of their own needs. The message "You're so special" becomes "I'm so special." And "You're so much better than others" becomes "I'm so much better," in a process that psychologists refer to as an internalization. The overall message, "You mean everything to us and we pamper you because you deserve special treatment," is internalized through constant repetition, and then projected onto the rest of the world.

We become adults who always want more than we have. Wanting so much should drive us to achieve more, or try harder. Too often our entitlement feelings cause us to sabotage our own success.

When we grow up "entitled" and expectant, something very destructive is in progress. The experience will have long-term effects on our thinking skills, our capacity for intimacy, and our ability to maintain friendships. Let's look at each of these consequences separately, beginning with the way entitlement gets in the way of our thinking ability. The reluctance observed in many overparented adults to use their cognitive abilities, especially their analytic skills, stems from an early reliance on parents who always had ready solutions when they began to struggle. Such adults learn to ask others, rather than to think for themselves.

One woman realized this was true for her when she told her boss she'd like to be considered for a promotion and her boss told her frankly that she saw little evidence of supervisory skills. "I'd always be the first one begging for more creative assignments, but when I got one and it came time to put the pen to the paper, I'd panic," the woman admits. "I'd end up delegating big chunks of the project to other people in the department, telling them I was too busy with more important things. At times, I even convinced myself. But nothing was further from the truth. I alienated a lot of people by taking credit for projects I did very little actual work on. But since it was my project to begin with, I still thought I deserved the credit.''

A lifetime as a ''special'' child convinces us that everything we undertake must be ''special'' or perfect. This is immobilizing. ''I didn't try and I failed'' is a lot easier to take than ''I tried as hard as I could, and I failed.''

Entitlement is a means of rationalizing a way out of taking responsibility. Responsibility triggers feelings of fear and inadequacy. As a result, many people who were overparented give only what's absolutely required of them, and no more. They aren't overly concerned if what they hand in to their teachers or, later, their bosses, is perfectly accurate or not if they can get away with it. They do what they are asked to, or what they believe they're ''paid'' to do, and that's as far as they think they need to go. They avoid tasks that challenge their ability to think and analyze.

Analytic abilities get rusty from disuse. For the adult who was overparented in childhood, tax forms, mortgage agreements, insurance policies, and even simple directions are confounding. Filling out forms or writing reports are agonizing experiences, often put off. Most hand in paperwork that makes the people they hand it in to cringe. All of this symptomatic of a feeling of entitlement to some answer that exists outside of themselves.

We need to recognize our dependence on others to think for us, which is at the core of our feelings of entitlement. Our parents were the decision makers, the direction readers, in our lives. They took care of the mundane details and responsibilities of our lives, and they still do, if we ask. When we were frustrated and things seemed too hard, we turned to them, and they responded to us. Many times they grabbed our responsibilities out of our hands, did it for us, and then turned to us and told us what a great job we did. Little wonder that we reach adulthood with shaky confidence in ourselves and a terror that deciding for ourselves might expose us as inadequate.

This is not to say that we lack intelligence or are doomed to a lifetime of failure. We have a knack of collecting people around us who have what we lack. One very suc-

cessful man, overparented in childhood by a very domineering father, admitted the secret of his success. "I have
no real talent, except in finding other people who have
real talent and convincing them to work for me." All was
well until any of these people decided they wanted a star-
ring role or bigger percentage in what they helped him
create. Then he balked, arguing and defending his entitlement.

The tendency to wait for things and people to come to
us, to think for us, subverts our confidence and trust in
ourselves. If we don't use our brains and skills to direct
our lives, we remain trapped in childhood, where parents,
teachers, and others compensated for our reluctance to use
our brains by thinking for us.

Feelings of entitlement also get in the way of our personal relationships. Over time we recognize that our relationships are short-lived, seldom lasting past the initial
flash of excitement in the first few weeks.

Valerie, an attractive redhead in her midthirties, exemplifies how entitlement can be the culprit in destroying a
relationship. Valerie became despondent after a relationship she hoped would end in commitment fizzled and died.
"I look back and realize that Gary was the one. At the
time, though, all I could see was his faults."

Valerie admits that no man had ever treated her as well
as Gary did. "He could be so sweet sometimes. He'd bring
me flowers, pick me up at work, listen to my problems."

Other things about Gary disturbed Valerie. For one
thing, he watched a lot of football games on weekends,
when Valerie wanted him to play tennis with her. Another
is that he'd talk about his job a lot, which Valerie found
boring. He was solid, responsible, and dependable, but
what Valerie wanted in a man was excitement.

"I've always wanted a man who could surprise me, the
type who would plan romantic picnics, or take me away
for a special weekend," Valerie confides.

Did Valerie ever suggest any of these things to Gary?
"I think if you have to tell a man how to be romantic,
then that takes the joy out of it. If someone really loves

you, they should know what would make you happy. Besides, I wanted a man who would take control of the relationship, show me new things, instead of the other way around.''

Valerie's birthday was a turning point in her relationship with Gary. She spent the evening sulking, silent and bored. ''The week before, Gary asked me what I wanted to do for my birthday, and I said, 'Surprise me.' Well, he took me to this Thai restaurant. What I was hoping for was some romantic French restaurant. You know, a place with dim lights and expensive bottles of wine. And do you know what he bought me? A briefcase. Oh, it was beautiful and very expensive, but you couldn't really call it a personal gift at all.''

After than evening, little that Gary did seemed right to Valerie. They'd argue frequently. Gary would always be the one to patch things over and apologize when, stubbornly, Valerie would go days without returning his calls.

One weekend Valerie needed to borrow a car to go to visit her sister in a nearby town. Gary lent her his. ''I brought it back to his place late Sunday night, and the next morning he called me, furious. I'd returned the car with an empty tank of gas. It was just an oversight, really, no big deal. But Gary said that he had overslept, and having to stop at the gas station on the way to work made him late for an important meeting. He said that all I ever thought of was myself. He acted like I was some kind of criminal or something. I said I was sorry, but he kept yelling and I ended up hanging up on him.

''On such a silly note, the whole thing ended. I just refused to call him, thinking he should apologize for the way he had gone off at me. I kept thinking about all the things about him that bothered me, little things like the way that he wasn't tall enough, and that he was starting to get a potbelly, and that his friends weren't very exciting.''

Valerie admits that she was raised in a home where her parents gave her everything. She and her sister were the center, and everything revolved around them. ''My parents had always been critical of Gary. When I told them I was fighting with him, they pointed out to me that he was immature for not accepting my apology. A stubborn man who would stay angry about such a little thing wasn't good husband material according to my mother.''

The silence between Gary and Valerie lasted two and a half weeks, when Valerie finally called with the excuse that she had left some of her things in his apartment and wanted them back. When she went to his apartment that night, Gary told her that he had met someone else. ''He said that he just couldn't handle the way nothing he did was ever right. He said he's had time to think about the way he'd gone out of his way to try to make me happy, but nothing was ever good enough. He wished me luck finding someone who could make me happy, because he sure couldn't.''

At first, Valerie was philosophical about their breakup, feeling that Gary probably wasn't the right one for her after all. But a month later, after a number of disastrous dates with other men, Valerie realized she missed Gary more than she would have thought possible. Loneliness, depression over losing Gary, and the feeling that she'd never find the right person and get married drew Valerie to examine her expectations of relationships.

Valerie, like many other people who were loved too much, brought a list of ''entitlements'' into her relationships. She felt entitled to be taken care of in a relationship by a man. He should always be available to her. She should be wined and dined. He shouldn't have any career problems or other troubles. He should place his own need to watch football second to her need to play tennis.

Because saying she was sorry was difficult for Valerie, she felt entitled to total forgiveness after an apology. A man who truly loved her should make allowances for her self-centeredness and never grow angry at her. She felt entitled to have her mind read by people who cared about her. Gary should be able to know intuitively what she wanted and provide it. The act of communicating with him would violate her feeling of entitlement. And, finally, she felt the entitlement of not having to look at her own responsibility for the problems in their relationship.

In essence, Valerie, who was desperately seeking love, distanced anyone who came too close with her entitlement feelings and rigid expectations. Like many children who were loved too much, she never had do to anything to retain the onslaught of attention she received from her parents. Valerie realized that most of her wishes were anticipated in childhood by her father, who pampered her by way of demonstrating his love. Now, she yearned for a man who would anticipate her needs without her having to ask and "surprise" her with exciting adventures to alleviate her boredom as her father had done. Because few men could read her mind, she grew quickly discontented.

As adult children who were overparented, we often imagine that we have within ourselves a tremendous wealth of love and devotion that we would share if we ever found that special person who would finally be "The One." These "gifts" inside of us can only be relinquished to the person who can enthusiastically and consistently gratify our needs. For us as for Sleeping Beauty, the right person (or princess) will come along and awaken our love and passion.

Nothing is a better escape hatch from intimacy than entitlement feelings such as these, since no one can really fulfill the high expectations we bring into relationships. We begin each relationship with hope that finally this will be "The One," but soon we're tuned into the other person's faults. The person isn't the prince or princess we hoped for, but just another human being who's too critical, too weak, too poor, too heavy, or too needy. The faults become the focus more than the person.

Again this stems from childhood. The result of being consistently focused on and rescued by our parents is the development of a grandiose, "entitled" sense of self. We begin to believe that our needs come first, and that we're more important than others.

We get a sense of power from the way our parents always focused their attention on us and tried to meet our needs without our having to ask. We begin to think that if we wish for something, it will happen, with little effort on our part. Such expectations almost always backfire on us.

Wishful thinking and expecting others to read our minds are very passive behaviors, and quite unrealistic.

Friendship is another area where our entitlement feelings run rampant. Jack, a twenty-five-year-old car salesman, exemplifies the problems we can have with our high expectations and critical attitude toward our friends.

Jack spends a lot of his time alone. "The friends I had in college are all married now, and into their own thing. I just can't get vitally interested in their babies or their new lawns or garages."

As for his friends at work, Jack seldom initiates getting together with them on weekends. He feels they should call him, and they seldom do. At times, Jack allows himself to admit that he's lonely. He has one close friend, Ryan, whom he spends occasional Saturday nights with, but lately he feels that this relationship is ending, too. "Ryan is pretty boring when you get right down to it. All he cares about is his music or women. He thinks he's Eddie Van Halen, but I've heard him play, and he's pretty pathetic. We go out to dinner and I'm trying to talk to him, but his eyes are roaming around the room looking at all the women. How can you have a conversation with someone like that?"

Jack sees himself as a victim. He can't seem to find the type of friends who share his interest and fulfill his needs.

What do people say about Jack? People who meet him see him as arrogant. They complain that he's defensive, always ready to argue with whatever anyone says. "Jack always has to be right," a man who knows him well explains. "He has to win every argument. No one ever feels heard by him. I think he enjoys making other people feel stupid. And he's always complaining about something. He thinks everyone should cater to him, go where he wants to go, talk about things that interest him, like cars."

People like Jack, intent on winning every argument, win the battle and lose the war all of the time. Such behavior always has the effect of keeping others at a distance. Friendship has to be a two-way street. It requires patience with others, acceptance of their limitations, and empathy toward their needs.

Jack brought none of these qualities into his relationships with others. He grew up in a home where he wasn't encouraged to develop much empathy for others. Empathy can be defined as putting ourselves in another person's shoes and gaining an appreciation for how they think and feel. Jack, the only son, was firmly centered in the spotlight in his family. The focus was on what he felt, what he thought, and most of all, what he needed.

In therapy, Jack and the other members of his support group were asked to make a list of what exactly was wrong with all of their friends. It was quite a list:

- They're never there when I need them
- They're insensitive
- They act stupid
- They have to have their own way
- They talk too much
- They never want to go anyplace new or different
- They brag about their jobs
- They brag about their relationships
- They brag about their money
- They brag about their children
- They whine about not being able to have children
- They think they know everything
- They can never get a date
- They throw boring parties

The list could have gone on, but everyone in the room was laughing too hard by that time to continue. How in the world had they all acquired such awful friends?

If we grew up in a similar fashion to Jack, we're quick to perceive other people's personal failings or weaknesses. These are our friends, yet we find fault with them on the basis of their financial troubles, unemployment, dating habits, illnesses, infertility—every aspect of their lives. Most of all, we find fault with the way they treat us. Unconsciously, we feel entitled to friends who are stronger, more giving, and more sensitive than we are, who can gratify our needs. We give up on people very quickly. We hope for more exciting friends, people who will truly understand us, yet we don't go out and seek them, but wait passively for them to find us. In the meantime, we may remain essentially alone.

Group therapists use a technique with people who feel entitled in their relationship with others. For several weeks, the person is assigned the role of "king" or "queen" by the therapist. The other members of the group bring the person small presents at the beginning of each session. However, no one is allowed to talk directly to the "king" or "queen." He or she is required to sit at a distance from the others and is not allowed to be a participating member of the group. While the conversation goes on, the "king" or "queen" is never allowed to speak or join in.

At first, people have a lot of fun with this assignment. There is much laughter and arrogance as the "king" or "queen" sits alone on his or her throne. But after several sessions, the picture changes. The person begins to resent not being allowed to participate, to speak to others. Most people who have participated in this exercise admit to feeling loneliness and ask to be taken off their "assignment" and be part of the group again.

Through the exercise, people begin to feel the cost of their aloofness and entitlement in a way that is not always so obvious in real life. Entitlement distances us from other people in subtle ways. It leads to isolation from others, much in the way the "king" is separated from the others in the group who bestow gifts on him but never relate to him on the same level as they relate to everyone else. Entitlement limits our ability to love because love demands that we remove the boundaries between us and another and act as equals.

Understanding the connection between our entitlement and the lack of intimacy in our lives is crucial to breaking the cycle that leads to loneliness and joylessness. Whether it's a life crisis, the loss of someone we now realize we love, or just another empty Saturday night that forces us to reconsider our expectations of others, we're apt to experience a fair amount of emotional pain in the early stages of change. It's hard to give up the defense our parents gave us, that the frustrations in our lives result from the imperfections of others.

Entitlement is a habit. In attempting to confront it, you may be trying to undo a pattern that you've lived with for thirty or forty years. Even with insight into your behavior, it can be hard to break, because insight alone isn't curative. However, giving up feelings of entitlement opens the door to intimacy, healthier and lasting relationships, and the joy of giving.

Remember Steve, the restaurateur who felt depressed and lonely in the midst of all his success? Today, he is in a committed relationship with a woman that gives every indication of being lasting and fulfilling for them both. He has come a long way from the lonely self-absorption of entitlement, and is finding both reward and challenges in maintaining a healthy, intimate relationship.

He's the first to admit that it hasn't been easy. ''By the time I met Kris, I'd started to take a hard look at what my part had been in a lot of relationships I had that didn't work out. There had been a couple of women in the past that I realized had been really terrific to me. I let those relationships slide and spent all my time looking for someone better to come along, when I could have been happy.

''When I met Kris one night in the restaurant, she was so beautiful and smart that I told myself I wasn't going to screw this one up.''

A year of therapy had given Steve a heightened awareness of his entitlement feelings and how he was distancing people who came close to him. But in the beginning of his relationship with Kris, Steve found that even with insight, breaking a lifetime pattern of behavior was difficult, and had to be attempted one day at a time.

''Kris is very warm and giving, but she's also a very assertive lady,'' he acknowledges. ''Where the other women in my life gave in to me, Kris fought for what she wanted.

''I've learned a lot from our relationship. A lot of times Kris comes home from work and needs to tell me about something that happened that day. She tends to get into a lot of details. A couple of times she caught me drifting off and not listening to her, even though I was shaking my head and nodding. She really blew up at me.

"But for the first time, I'm really trying with little things like this. Before, if a woman got mad at me, I'd just tell myself she was too sensitive. Now, I realize that if I want Kris to listen to me, then I have to listen to her. This may not sound very profound to a lot of people, but it's something that was very hard for me to see. I think it will always be difficult for me to be interested in the mundane details of other people's lives, even people I love. I never had that experience as a kid, because I was always in the spotlight.

"With Kris, I learned that giving to another person could actually be satisfying. I surprise her with presents all of the time—just little things, but it makes me as happy as it makes her. I never had the slightest notion that giving was getting until Kris and I got together.

"Kris isn't perfect," Steve admits. "She can get angry, and resentful. She can also be pretty sloppy around my house. But instead of walking out on her when we argue, or getting all defensive if she accuses me of being selfish, I listen and try to work things out.

"My feelings that other people should focus on me, listen to me, and do things for me will probably never go away entirely," Steve confides. "It gets easier to give instead of take, but the idea that I should be first on the receiving end doesn't simply disappear. I have to watch it all of the time. It's still a big pull to try to see if I can manipulate her to do things for me, like seeing only the movies I want to see, or spending our time with my friends instead of hers. But instead of feeling resentful when I give in to her, I look at the big picture of this relationship, how much Kris adds to my life."

For Steve, it's well worth the cost of compromise.

CHAPTER 5

STAR SEARCH

"You can do better."

"I'm not looking for that much. Just someone who's intelligent. Independent. Pretty. Thin. Exciting. A good dresser. It wouldn't hurt if she had some money, either."
                    —Tom, age 39, marketing consultant

At 9 A.M on a Saturday morning in December, Carole slams the door of her locker and adjusts her leotard. Glancing in the mirror, she straightens her headband, and starts for the exercise studio where a high-impact aerobics class is beginning.

The health club is the city's most exclusive. The quarter-mile track boasts a special injury-reducing surface that cost a fortune to create. Expensive Nautilus equipment shines in the weight rooms, and the pool, divided into four wide lanes for laps, is Olympic size.

Already this morning the club is crowded. Men and women, visible everywhere through the floor-to-ceiling glass, work out together with little self-consciousness. This is a place to see and be seen. No one here is fat. Everywhere are toned muscles, flat stomachs, and shining health.

Carole dieted for months before she joined the club. She gives up a host of other things she would love to be able to afford in order to pay steep monthly membership dues. But she isn't here to achieve a perfect body. She's here this morning looking for something she's beginning to think she'll never find: a relationship with a man that will last. Since early morning is the time most men come to the club to exercise, Carole, never an early riser, sets her alarm for 6 A.M. and struggles out of bed and into her sweats.

What's depressing her this cold December morning is the prospect of another New Year's Eve without someone special. Yesterday, Carole turned thirty-one. Over brunch in the club's restaurant, she picks at her Caesar salad and muses, "I passed the single-life-is-terrific phase of my life a long time ago. I can survive on my own, but I never figured on doing it forever. It's no use pretending that it doesn't matter to me that I'm not married. My friends tell me to stop worrying about it, that it will happen." She shakes her head, and long dark hair falls loose across her shoulders. "I'm getting older. I want to have children. All of my friends are married, and I'm starting to believe that I'll never find the right person. The guys I meet are jerks."

Poised, intelligent, and strong-minded, Carole believes she has a lot to offer a man. For one thing, she's educated. She's earned both bachelor's and master's degrees. Her bachelor's degree is in art, with a concentration in painting. "I had very little sense of direction when I was younger," she says. "I was a senior in high school, walking around saying, What am I doing here? What does all of this mean? One day I guess I just turned to my parents and said, 'Okay, what should I do with my life?' I wanted desperately for someone to tell me what I was good at, what would make me happy, so I could go and do it.

"My parents encouraged me to do something creative. They weren't practical. To them, a woman gets married and quits working eventually, anyway. Painting was my passion, so I studied it in college and tried to turn it into a career.

"I was good, but never great. I don't think I ever earned more than six thousand a year. My parents were my best customers. Their walls are still covered with my paintings that they bought so that I wouldn't get discouraged.

"It didn't occur to me that I'd go for years on my own without being married, or that I'd have to pay higher rent and electric bills and even think about things like retirement plans. Ten years ago, I wasn't worried about any of that, so six thousand a year seemed okay. I wasn't going to starve. I had a nice apartment. It was a condominium, actually, that my parents bought as an investment."

Carole grins and admits, "Looking back, I realize that my parents were really just subsidizing me. They could have found a lot better investments than a studio apartment in the suburbs. But I wasn't going to argue. They were waiting until the right man came into my life and took over the job of making sure I was taken care of."

Back then, getting married wasn't important to Carole. She was enjoying her freedom. At twenty-two, her lifestyle made her feel very adult and even liberated. "I thought liberation meant earning your own money for a few years, having your own apartment, and sleeping with a variety of men—an adventure you could look back on when you were married and settled. That's as far as it went with me. I wasn't looking to be Miss Independent Career Woman of the Year."

One summer weekend at an outdoor festival where Carole was displaying her paintings, she met Mike. He was an assistant in the promotions department of a radio station that was doing a live remote broadcast from the fairgrounds. He stopped by to look at Carole's paintings during a break, and hung around to talk.

Looking at Mike, Carole's first thought was that he was sexy as hell. Tall. Broad-shouldered. Long, Viking-blond hair that looked almost white in the sun.

They hit it off immediately. Mike, Carole found, was fun and exciting to be around. His impromptu stand-up comedy routines made her scream with laughter and beg him to stop so she could breathe again. He was very romantic and affectionate, often bringing Carole flowers for no reason at all. They took bubble baths together in candlelight with glasses of wine and a toy sailboat drifting in the tub that they christened "the Love Boat." They spent hours together, just talking, content in each other's company. Carole's friends assumed she was in love. After all, what more could Carole want? Two years after they met, however, Carole abruptly broke off the relationship.

The problem for Carole was that Mike wasn't "marriage material." "He was going nowhere fast," she explains. "I didn't see it at first, but Mike was all talk and no action. He moved from radio station to radio station, wanting to be a disc jockey but making a career out of being some big shot's 'gofer.' He figured that if he met enough people, someone would give him a break.

"I wanted to marry somebody who was established, not still searching for his niche in life. I'd always imagined my husband as someone with a solid career, very stable, very successful."

It was an idea Carole had got from her parents. Mike's shortcomings showed up glaringly every time Carole brought him with her to visit them. "They were always nice enough to him, but my mother would say, 'You can't be serious about this guy, can you? You can do so much better.' I lied. I told them we were just good friends. Still, they never missed a chance to put him down.

"It was kind of sad. Mike tried so hard to make my parents like him. He never realized what a nonentity he was as far as they were concerned. It was a good thing he didn't, because it would hurt him terribly."

Over the two years Mike and Carole spent together, Carole's parents kept hinting that she should end her relationship with Mike. If she wasn't serious about him, why did she go on seeing him? "What could I tell them? I keep seeing him because we have great sex together? That was as close to the truth as I could get. They harped on me all the time. I was getting older, my mother reminded me, in the apologetic, I'm-only-telling-you-this-for-your-own-good tone she has. Men would be harder to meet. If everyone knew I was with Mike, other men wouldn't ask me out.

"I tried to tell her that it wasn't high school. Everyone in the world didn't know I was dating this guy, and wouldn't have cared if they did know. Sometimes I just lost my patience and told her to shut up. But then I'd go home and think about what she said. I couldn't help it, and she knew it. I knew she only wanted the best for me, and the fact that she so obviously didn't think much of Mike took the edge off the whole relationship for me.''

Mike and Carole began to fight all the time. Everything about him irritated her. She tried to get Mike to change. She felt that he wasn't trying hard enough to get his career off the ground, and told him so. Mike pointed out that she was making far less than he was selling her paintings at art fairs, but that didn't alter Carole's thinking.

Mike would never change, Carole realized. He was too stubborn to take her advice. In fact, he found her suggestion that he find a ''real job'' ludicrous. What did the money matter when he loved getting up and going to work every day? He worked hard. He'd get his break one day. He was sure of it. She should be patient and have some confidence in him.

Carole just stared at him in disgust. He was a dreamer. It could only get worse. It was time for her to move on. She needed more than a playmate. She'd give up painting and get a master's degree in something—anything—that would make her some money and introduce her to a whole new world of people who really had it all together. She made the decision to ease out of her relationship with Mike and apply to a graduate-school program in journalism on the same day.

Her somewhat confused father agreed to pay the bill when Carole was accepted to a local university's graduate program. Surely his daughter didn't need a second degree, he reasoned, when she'd soon marry, have children, and stay home with them. But if Carole wanted to be a journalist, he was willing to support her.

Carole's mother was also concerned. When Carole was twenty, her goal of having a career for a few years, living in her own apartment, and then getting married pleased her mother, who had done exactly the same thing as a young woman. But why hadn't Carole married already? She was such a beautiful girl. It was time.

Mike was even less supportive when she told him her plans. "Of all things, he asked me to forget about grad school and marry him. I said, 'What would we ever have together, with you at some radio station every other night, working for next to nothing?'

" 'We'd have love,' he said, 'or is that so cheap to you, now?' "

Carole stood her ground. In a battle that lasted all night, Mike shouted that Carole's priorities were hopelessly screwed up. Carole yelled back that at least she had some goals. "It got ugly. He said a lot of horrible things to me. He said that he could hear my parents' words coming out of my mouth and that I'd be sorry one day when I started thinking for myself. Then he started to cry. It turned my stomach. I wanted to shout, 'For chrissakes, be a man.' I couldn't wait for him to leave."

Carole admits that she missed Mike after they broke up. A lot. But graduate school forced her to keep her mind on other things. "My parents were my saviors in those days. I rented out my studio apartment and moved back home. It was my parents' idea. They felt I'd be too busy studying and attending classes to cook or take care of myself. They let me come and go as I pleased. I think they got a real kick out of having me back at home. We were closer than we'd ever been.

"Mike always thought my relationship with my parents was infantile, because I called them every day, confided in them, and didn't make decisions without talking to them. He just didn't understand what it is to have a good relationship with your parents. His father was a very selfish man, in my opinion. He was loaded with money and wouldn't even give his own son some cash to get a better apartment, or buy some clothes. My parents would never do that to me. They always told me, 'No one will ever love you as much as your parents.' I believe this. A family should be close. Why shouldn't I depend on them?"

Fifteen months later, Carole graduated. Her father's partner helped her get a job at a public-relations firm. "I thought it would be interesting, but it was a lot of sitting on the phone, pitching stories to reporters. My paychecks weren't very exciting, either.''

Depressed about her career, Carole concentrated harder than ever on her social life. She joined the health club, took ballroom-dancing classes, volunteered, ran to singles parties. "Over the next five years, I went through a slew of men. It was depressing. Nothing ever clicked for me. There were a few relationships. One lasted about five weeks, and I really thought I was in love. But then I realized that it would never work. He was successful all right, but he was still a little boy, selfish and immature.''

At thirty-one, Carole senses her parents' growing disappointment in her. "You see, they've invested all of this money in me, and they have nothing to show for it. I've got a master's degree and a job, but what they want is pictures of grandchildren in their wallets. That would be something to show.''

Carole would gladly give them those grandchildren. So she spends her time at the health club, at parties, and at charity events, looking. Always looking.

The other day, Carole was at a restaurant with a friend, and she looked up to see her old boyfriend, Mike, standing at the bar. His arm was around his pregnant wife.

She went up to say hello, and both Mike and his wife greeted her warmly. Mike, she learned, was the head of the promotions department at a major radio station and doing very well. They chatted about old times and old friends.

"I'd love to say that his wife was ugly, or bitchy,'' Carole admits, "but actually, she seemed very sweet. She kept looking at Mike like he was the most wonderful man in the world.''

And Mike? "He looked happy,'' Carole says thoughtfully. "In fact, Mike looked really good.''

Everyone looks good in retrospect. That's what Carole told herself when she thought about Mike and his wife, obviously happy together, beginning a family of their own. He was the wrong person for her then, and the fact that he met someone else and married didn't make him the right person now.

Still, something about it hurt. All she ever met, it seemed, were people who were wrong for her. Too fat. Too short. Too arrogant. Too sensitive. Too boring. Too outrageous. Screwed up. A screw loose. Out of their minds. Out for one thing.

Mike, who was exciting, romantic, and affectionate, had come so close to being everything she wanted. But he didn't meet all of her expectations—especially the ones that had to do with the type of career and salary the man she married should have. Even if she loved him, a starving would-be disc jockey didn't fit in.

She was angry at the insinuation that she was too finicky or demanding when it came to finding someone to love, or staying in love with someone she found. Her expectations might be high, but so what? What should she do? Settle for just anybody who came along? It might be frustrating, but she was going to keep searching until she found the right person, even if that search was endless.

In *Perfect Women,* author Colette Dowling writes about such a search, which she calls "shopping for a star." It involves much more than looking for a person who will truly care about us, Dowling believes. Often, it's searching for perfection in another person.

At the root of this search are sharp feelings of personal inadequacy. "The wish for a perfect lover is connected to a deep sense of inferiority and a need to compensate for that feeling," Dowling writes. Although star searchers point to the faults in a lover for why the relationship never got off the ground, it is often the shortcomings they perceive in themselves that cause them to quickly perceive others as "not good enough." What they are looking for in a lover is someone who will complete them.

" 'What can he do for me?' is the hidden preeminent question for a woman who feels inadequate," Dowling writes. "If she thinks he has enough to compensate for what she's missing, 'love' may follow."

Men, too, can be star searchers, always on the look out for the "perfect woman." Such a woman is required to bolster their self-esteem, and "mirror" back a more perfect image of themselves.

Adult children who were overparented become avid star searchers—and for good reason. Little in their history has encouraged a strong sense of self or competence, which makes the need for someone who will complete them potent.

Consider Carole for a moment. Like most adult children who were loved too much, Carole was subtly encouraged to be dependent on her parents. They rewarded her all her life for not being self-reliant, and argued that she should trust their judgment over her own.

Carole's parents had tremendous expectations for her, and especially for the type of lifestyle a husband should be able to provide her with. They encouraged her to find a person who would satisfy them, provide her with a wealth of material possessions, be her caretaker, and more. They said, "You're so special. . . . You have so much to offer. . . . You can find someone better. . . . Don't settle for too little," to the point that almost no one was acceptable. Carole brought Mike into the midst of these expectations. He was judged by a yardstick few mortals could measure up to.

We can argue that everything Carole's parents did and said came out of their love and desire that she have only the best. This was true, but there was another emotion, deeper than love, involved. It was fear.

Underneath her parents' offer of a condominium apartment, their reluctance to see her study for a master's degree, and their constant criticism of Mike was an unconscious fear that Carole couldn't make it on her own. Mike, whose goal was to be a disc jockey and who would have an inconsistent income and erratic hours, quickly became a threat to all of their expectations for Carole's future.

Any threat to a child's happiness becomes an obsession for a parent who loves too much. Carole's parents' pervasive fear was that Carole would be deprived. The thought was intolerable. Families like Carole's are so enmeshed with each other that when a child is perceived to be in pain or at risk, the parent is also in pain or at risk. There is very little emotional separation.

To rescue Carole (and herself), Carole's mother instinctively took control. Through a combination of subtle and direct critical messages, she influenced Carole into reconsidering her relationship.

Carole internalized her parents' fears. She began to believe that she couldn't make it on her own. A future involving independence and separation from her parents was scary. It was essential to find the "right" person, who would be so strong, so wealthy, so stable, that he would fill in the missing places within herself and allay her fears.

Carole seldom thought of love and marriage in terms of an equal partnership, or an opportunity for mutual growth. She didn't question whether she would be able to meet her partner's needs, just whether he'd be able to meet hers. What she wanted more than anything else was a provider: someone she could depend on to take care of her as completely and as lovingly as her parents did.

Given this expectation, it's no wonder that Mike fell short. Years later, Mike reassessed his career goals and found a position with a radio station that was a better fit with his skills. He did what most human beings do as they grow, test themselves, and begin to separate the possible from the unachievable. But by that time, it was too late for Carole. Her expectations of the type of man she should marry left little patience for this type of process, or even belief in it. She had little flexibility when it came to love, and no real confidence that Mike could be trusted to steer his life onto a path that would be both fulfilling and practical. She looked at this man who was struggling, determined to succeed in a career he loved, and wrote him off as a dreamer.

This is not to say that Carole shouldn't have considered the issue of money when she was contemplating marriage to Mike. Money is a very realistic consideration that shouldn't be overlooked when two people think of joining their lives. But, would Carole have married Mike if he had been wealthy?

Carole had little confidence in any of the men she met

after Mike, including several who were quite well-to-do. She found shortcomings in every one of them. Mike might have scared her off with his financial instability, but the truth was, no one was good enough. Not one of these men could calm her fears about the future.

A lifetime of being drenched in expectations and fears that have more to do with our parents' fantasies than our reality is bound to have vast ramifications for our relationships with others. Their expectations become our expectations. Our parents' standards and judgments are internalized in us, and projected onto our friends and our lovers. Whether told to us subtly or directly, their expectations about our future mate form a lot of our assumptions about who would be right for us—assumptions we don't always take time to question.

We meet someone, and make a quick cost analysis of what we see, with a single-minded "what you see is what you get" attitude that gives no quarter to anyone's weaknesses. We want more than potential in a person we marry. We want assurance. We want someone stronger than we are, that we can depend on. That someone cares deeply about us isn't enough. Often only "perfection" gives this sense of assurance.

Given the level of our expectations, it's not hard for us to find something about almost anyone we become involved with that we can use as grounds for rejection. A thirty-six-year-old man told of a "strike-out system" he devised to help him find the "right" woman. "If she smokes, that's strike one. If she's fat, that's strike two. If she expects me to call her every day, that's strike three, and she's out." He had a long list of strikes. The problem was that very few women ever made it around the bases.

Similarly, a thirty-year-old woman explained, "What I always thought I wanted was an older man, who was financially secure and very mature. I've met several men like that, but it wasn't enough. They were dependable and stable, but I didn't feel any chemistry, or spark. I need someone who's creative, too. A self-made entrepreneur who writes romantic songs or poems on the side. Or a serious artist, whose hobby is making wild, lucrative real estate deals. Why can't I ever find a man like this?

Sometimes we search in the classified ads. One woman wrote, "Beautiful, successful, sophisticated yet unsnobbish female, 30's, seeks only very successful, one of a kind gentleman, 26–45, with jet set lifestyle and traditional values. Unselfish, creative, wealthy, warmhearted. Handsome yet modest. Able to balance passionate romance with remarkable top ten percent success."

Two men answered her ad. "Both deadbeats," the woman sighs.

Sometimes we find someone we think might be right for us, but the high expectations remain, and the scenario that follows can be a very sad one. Some children who were overparented find that life has become an exercise in trying to change a partner into what they expect him or her to be, often by scolding, nagging, manipulating, threatening, begging, withholding, and otherwise trying to control. Often the end result is bitter disappointment.

Before we can allow ourselves to love someone, he or she must pass a hundred tests. The conscious goal of a star search is to find someone who will pass these tests and finally fall in love. The unconscious goal, however, is to find a "mirror"—someone to define us and tell us who we are. Why should we need this? It's because we have a very vague sense of our identities. In childhood, we needed our parents to "mirror" us in order to gain a sense of wholeness and separateness. So often, they failed to be adequate "mirrors" because they saw us as extensions of their needs and wishes. As a result, we gained a very shaky sense of separateness. We rarely feel complete within ourselves. Our feeling of wholeness depends on linking ourselves to someone stronger.

The extent to which we went "unmirrored" in childhood determines how great a "star" we'll have to find to make us feel complete enough to love. It may seem that there is never anyone attractive, intelligent, or wealthy enough to mirror back to us a feeling of self-worth, and complete us.

Our self-love determines how much love we have to give

to others. With all our parents gave us, it's possible that they couldn't help us achieve that. If we have a past filled with impossible expectations we couldn't meet, smothering overprotection, and rejection of our true selves, we will shape our expectations of love accordingly. We will face the prospect of love fearfully, with suspicion and hostility. We will feel entitled to love, but not really deserving of it, or open to receive it.

Until we make a decision to work hard on the issue of our own self-esteem and make our first goal learning to love ourselves, we'll be searching endlessly for a sense of completeness no one else can ever supply for us.

CHAPTER 6

THE FEAR OF INTIMACY

*"No one will ever love you
as much as we do."*

"When I knew that my current girlfriend was getting serious, I wanted the first ticket out of town.

"It's happened before. A lot. If I let them get too close and they start depending on me, I feel like I'm choking.

"The second I hear a woman talk about 'relationships' and 'needs,' I cut my losses. I need my freedom."

—Jim, age 37, stockbroker

There's an old story about a woman who longed to sleep with John Lennon. She thought about him all the time. She was positive that he was the only man who could ever make her happy.

One night she met a singer in a bar who looked a little like him. She thought he was terrific, and spent the night with him. The next morning she kissed him good-bye, thinking, He was great, but he was no John Lennon.

She met a lot of other men who reminded her of John. So she went from man to man in a series of romances, always short-lived, always disappointing. She'd break things off, and her friends would say, "What was wrong this time?" She'd sigh and say, "He was great, but he was no John Lennon."

One night in New York, she met a friend of John Lennon's. After a wonderful week together, she told him they were through. After all, he was great, but he was no John Lennon.

The man introduced her to John. She hit it off with him, and it turned out to be the biggest evening of her life. At last, alone with John Lennon.

The next morning, she flew home alone, with no regrets. "He was great," she said, "but he was no John Lennon."

It's happened to us all at least once. The "right" person, with every quality we longed for, came into our lives. Yet after a couple of months, Mr. or Mrs. Right didn't look so good to us anymore. We wanted smart, but now we long for good-looking. We wanted young, but now we want mature. We wanted stable, but now we dream of someone unconventional.

When we're running to parties, handing money over to dating services, writing classified ads, begging our friends to fix us up, the last thing that occurs to us is that we may have fears of intimacy. In fact, a relationship appears to be the only thing we really want in the whole world.

But fears of intimacy are epidemic among adults who were overparented in childhood. It's what accounts for a slew of fits and starts at love, which never end in real intimacy or commitment.

Underneath the high expectations we can't satisfy lie the anxieties of a child who was loved too much, who wants to be safe, above all.

What is it we fear? Engulfment. Abandonment. Exposure. All of these are the risks we take with intimacy. Considering our history, it's no wonder that we fear them so much.

Let's look at each of these fears separately.

Fear of Engulfment

A child who was overparented sometimes grows into an adult who unconsciously fears that if he allows himself to be loved by someone, he'll be engulfed by the other person's needs and lose his freedom, autonomy, and individual identity.

Ron felt that way about his relationship with Chrissie, even though she was pretty and smart and made few demands on him. "We had good times together, but I never felt I was really in love, if you know what I mean. I never wanted her to count on seeing me every Saturday night, or anything like that. I didn't want a situation where I couldn't date someone else if I wanted to."

Chrissie had her own printing company and created signage and other artwork for small businesses. "When business was bad, which was usually the case, she starved. I used to think that if I married her, she'd be moving up in the world, but I'd be moving down. Still, in a lot of ways, she turned me on."

Over the year that they dated, Ron did everything possible to keep Chrissie at a distance. "I knew she was falling in love with me, and I didn't want that. She sent me cards all of the time. If there was anything I liked, she tuned into liking it. She was a chameleon.

"After the first month or so, I never took her anywhere," Ron admits. "We just sat at her apartment, watched TV, and had sex."

Chrissie seemed content to do things his way. Ron admits, "What kept me interested was that she was willing to do anything I wanted in bed. She asked me to tell her all of my sexual fantasies. The darker they were, the more she enjoyed them. Then she'd act them out.

"One night, she asked me to act out one of her fantasies. I said okay, but after about a minute, I told her I didn't want to do it anymore. She was clinging to me, and it was driving me crazy. I got up and turned on the television. Fifteen minutes later, I was dressed and leaving, telling her I was tired."

Sometimes Ron didn't call Chrissie for two weeks or more. "She wouldn't say anything, and when I drifted back into her life out of boredom or whatever, she acted like nothing had happened."

Three or four times, Ron broke off their relationship. "One time I told myself it was for good, and that I wasn't going to get myself enmeshed in the whole thing again. A month later, I was feeling really horny. I went over to her apartment late at night. I guess you could say I seduced her. She tried to push me away at first, but she finally let me.''

Leaving later that night, Ron had to admit that he didn't really feel very guilty. ''To be honest, all I felt was a sense of power from this, like I could get anything I wanted. She'd tell me stories about how her last boyfriend abused her. She said that he was cruel and that all he ever wanted from her was sex, but she stayed with him anyway because it was better than nothing. She confided all of this in me because she thought I'd understand and never treat her the same way. All it did was feed into my feelings that she was nothing special, not good enough for me. Instead of feeling sympathy, I concluded that I really didn't have to give her anything, either. She'd take scraps.

''Do I sound like a real creep? I was. I admit it. It was the worst part of the whole thing. I've always seen myself as a sensitive guy who would never consciously hurt another person. I had this image of myself as someone honest, who really cares about other people's feelings. It's funny how I could reconcile all of that with the way I treated Chrissie, as if everything I did wasn't contradicting everything I thought I was.''

As time passed, Ron became well aware that Chrissie was in love with him, and his keeping her at a distance was hurting her, although she never said anything about it. This was the worst, because the idea of Chrissie hurt and silently suffering made him furious. ''It reminded me of my mother the martyr.''

Ron's mother, a parent who loves too much, still buys her thirty-eight-year-old his socks and underwear. ''I'm over at my parents' house, and I leave the room to go to the bathroom. She yells out, 'Be careful!' What, for creepsake, is going to happen to me on the way to the bathroom?

''She drops by my apartment all of the time, and walks around picking up my things and saying 'Where did you get this? How much did you pay?' Nothing was ever as cheap as she could have gotten it for me, if I'd only asked. Once I caught her snooping in my laundry basket. As far as she's concerned, nothing in my apartment is off-limits.''

Since childhood, Ron has fended off his mother's smothering overprotection. Sometimes he placated her, but mostly he just avoided her. But refusing to tell her anything happening in his life only set her off. ''After all I've done for you, why can't you talk to me once in a while, and give me a little joy?'' she'd demanded. Ron would retreat to his room. He felt that he should try to give his mother what she needed, but he just couldn't do it. He'd look at her anxious face and feel as though he were choking. Nothing was as guilt-provoking as the sight of his long-suffering mother.

Ron's relationship with his mother changed little over the years. ''She still treats me like I'm ten years old,'' Ron complains. ''She calls up and asks me how I am. If I slip and say I have a headache or something, I get a million questions. Am I taking aspirin? What kind? Do I know that aspirin's not good for my stomach? I should see a doctor. I should see her doctor. Maybe it's a brain tumor. She has a friend whose husband had a six-pound brain tumor and the only symptom was a headache. If I'd listen to her and relax more, I wouldn't be having headaches.

''I know she does this because she loves me. No one has to explain that to me. But it never stops.''

Ironically, headaches and constant tension drove Ron into therapy. ''The first time my therapist told me that I had issues with women, I just didn't get it. I was telling her about my relationship with Chrissie, and I thought that because my therapist was a woman, she was just trying to nail me.''

Ron's therapist asked him to list, on a sheet of paper, all of the adjectives he would use to describe women. After some thought, Ron decided to be honest. He listed the following: ''Manipulative and controlling. Fragile and emotional. Smothering. Dependent. Very needy.''

This, Ron assumed, was an accurate picture of what most women were. It was a good indication of why Ron ran for his life every time he found himself in a relationship.

In many ways, Ron's list revealed his perception of his mother, in abbreviated form. Ron's difficulties with his mother stemmed from the fact that she had little respect for his boundaries. By boundaries, we mean the rules that define where others end and we begin, both physically and emotionally.

When we are infants, there are no boundaries between us and our mothers. Our relationship is completely symbiotic, and we believe "Mother is me." One of the tasks of growing up is to separate from our parents, and establish a sense of self and a sense of privacy. The goal is to construct healthy boundaries between ourselves and others, permeable enough to let other people in without fearing that we'll lose ourselves. With healthy boundaries established, we can be needy without fearing engulfment. We can love and give to others without feeling that they'll become so dependent on us that we'll smother.

If our parents have a healthy respect for our privacy and nurture and protect us without overwhelming us with their needs for excessive closeness, we grow up without fears that other people will trap us, engulf us, or invade our space.

In the relationship between Ron and his mother, the boundaries got confused. She had little sense of where she ended and he began. She overprotected, intruded, and invaded to such an extent that Ron felt violated. Ron's mother couldn't back off or allow Ron to separate from her in a healthy way, because of her own needs to hold on to a symbiotic closeness with her child.

As a child, Ron was without resources to stand up and say, "Enough is enough! Give me some room to be me, to do things my way." The only way he knew to fend off his smothering mother was through very indirect means. He trod carefully around her, wearing a mask of studied indifference, fearing to reveal too much of himself. At times he was cold, insensitive, even rude to her. He believed he had to be in order to gain some control. In this way, he attempted to condition his mother to respect his boundaries.

It is very difficult to develop healthy boundaries without our parents' cooperation. They have to be willing to let go, even as they nurture and protect us. Because Ron failed at ever setting a comfortable level of distance with his mother, he projected his experience with her on all women. He developed rigid boundaries as a defense. His feelings of no control in this primary relationship led to defensive overcompensation and a need for excessive distance with all women. His girlfriend Chrissie was not an exceptionally needy woman, but to Ron, all women were too needy, fragile, and dependent, and he projected this belief onto Chrissie. If he got close to her, he was sure she'd devour him with her needs and there would be nothing left of him. So when she appeared too attracted to him, he wouldn't call her for two weeks. When she acted affectionate or loving, he abused her, either by using her body and discarding her or being cold and selfish.

Like Ron, many adult children who were loved too much fear vulnerability in people. A needy person is a threat because, inside, we're very needy. If we were consistently overprotected or given too much by our parents, we enter adulthood expecting always to be taken care of. If we have to take time out to give to another person, will our needs be met? The whole concept of us giving can feel unfamiliar, like a language we never learned.

Sometimes we set up our engulfment. At the point when we sense another person is attracted to us and vulnerable, we begin to distance that person because of our unconscious fears. Our sudden coldness throws the other person off balance, and creates anxiety. He or she attempts to break through our barrier, asking, "What's wrong? Is it something I've done?" We suddenly feel guilty, and because guilt makes us feel uncomfortable, we get irritated and angry. We shrug our shoulders indifferently and say, "Nothing's wrong. Why do you keep asking me that?" The person keeps asking, and we keep evading and distancing him or her even further.

In this way, we incite the engulfers. If we were open and honest, and said, "I'm starting to feel close to you and I'm not sure I'm ready or comfortable with it yet," chances are they'd understand. Instead, because we don't always realize that closeness with others sparks an unconscious fear of engulfment, we use old defenses to fend people off. We become evasive and vague, attempting to distance others by withholding information or emotions. This sets up the engulfment we fear because it causes the people who love us to worry and become more invasive. We run away, searching for someone "stronger."

Relationships demand vulnerability. They also require that we relinquish some of our freedom. This can be terrifying to the adult who was never allowed any boundaries in his primary relationship with his parents when he was a child.

Marriage, it would seem, would re-create the kind of situation the adult may have fought so hard to be free of. One man explains why he never wanted to get married: "I'm so set in my ways. What if she didn't love to ski? What if she hated jazz? What if I never had any time to myself?" He saw marriage in terms of the freedoms he'd lose, the compromises he'd have to make. He saw it as an engulfment of his freedom, rather than an opportunity for mutual growth and fulfillment.

We're most attracted to people who won't activate our fear of engulfment. A woman who endured an intrusive, domineering father throughout her childhood admits that her closest relationships always occur with men who live in other cities or even countries. Her latest love resides in Paris, where she met him on a vacation. She finds this relationship fulfilling, even though she only sees this man once a year. "I hope Peter will eventually move back to the States, but if he doesn't, I don't care. I love him. Plenty of people nowadays have perfectly wonderful relationships, even though they live in different cities."

She's right. They have relationships. But what they don't have is intimacy, and for a good reason: They fear it.

All sorts of involvements with unavailable people assuage a fear of engulfment. Some of us have fantasies about a lover in our past. This person was the real one. No one else can live up to his or her memory. We were too immature, selfish, or brain-dead to realize how we loved him/her at the time, so he/she got away. As life would have it, we hear from this person occasionally, which feeds our dream of getting back together. The problem is, the beloved is married, with three kids. Or lives three thousand miles away. Or lives across the hall and has let us know in a hundred ways that there's no chance we'll ever have a relationship with him/her. We keep digging in the ashes. This is the only person who could ever make us happy, and grounds for rejecting anyone else who comes into our lives. We preserve an empty space in our lives, just in case this person might want to come back and fill it.

A relationship like this is enticing because it involves love without commitment, and therefore no possibility of engulfment. It also prevents us from dealing with the fact that we fear intimacy. After all, we're in love, aren't we?

When we fear engulfment, the people we're most attracted to and allow ourselves to become the most intimate with are very often intimidating, aloof, unavailable, or entirely self-concerned. There's something so attractive about this at first. Believing that vulnerability is a weakness, we mistake indifference and self-absorption for strength. Comfortable enough to risk closeness with people like this, we get hurt when they keep us at a distance. But while these people make us feel safe, the truth is, they have a lot of intimacy issues themselves. The relationship is rarely fulfilling for either of us.

Fear of Abandonment

The fear of abandonment is the fear that we'll lose someone we love. Sometimes there's a superstitious element in this, as in, ''Every time I really love someone, he leaves me." It's as if the very act of loving the person put some negative energy into the universe that caused us to lose him.

To prevent abandonment, some of us "latch on" to other people, give too much too quickly, or try to make ourselves invaluable to others so that they'll never leave us. "I always fell in love on the second date," confides one twenty-three-year-old man. "I couldn't hide it, either. I'd phone her constantly, buy little presents, send cards, show up at her place, put on a real performance in bed. I'd be afraid to leave her alone for more than a day. I thought if I wasn't there, with her, she'd forget all about me.

"Of course, most women backed off," he admits. "I terrified any but the neediest woman. But I couldn't help it. Every time a woman dropped me, my father and mother would take me aside and say, 'She wouldn't have made you happy anyway.' I grew up thinking everybody was going to leave me but my parents. My mother and father would always be there, no matter what."

This man's fears of abandonment became a self-fulfilling prophecy. Unconsciously, he set things up so that he'd realize his fears, over and over again, by clinging too hard. Often, he chose a partner with a strong fear of engulfment, and triggered all of her defenses.

Fears of abandonment destroy our peace of mind. We worry all the time: Can we ever really depend on anyone? Can we ever be sure enough of someone's love? If a fear of being rejected, dumped, or discarded is rooted in our subconscious mind, we don't think so. We're afraid to hope so. A forty-year-old woman confides, "When I have a fight with my boyfriend, I can be furious one moment and then forget all about it the next. But he can't let go of it so quickly. He says he needs time to calm down, to feel loving and affectionate again. Seeing him upset is more than I can take. He says I drive him crazy because I won't relax and give him some space. But I can't just let him go off alone and be mad at me. Until I know everything's okay again, I feel awful, like there's a huge hole in my stomach.''

This woman never learned that people can be angry at each other without abandoning each other. No one was allowed to show angry feelings in her home. The huge hole she feels in her stomach is an outgrowth of the fear of being abandoned. It's a feeling of incompleteness without another person, or another person's approval. The missing place inside only feels filled up when she's in a close relationship.

The feeling that we're not a whole person or complete unless we are "attached" to someone else has to do with the difficulties we had (and still have) cutting restricting ties to our parents. Sometimes our parents hold on to us too tightly, and undermine our efforts to separate and become autonomous human beings, because of their own needs. When we were children, our attempts at separation were met with fear and anxiety: "Don't go near that water—there're bacteria in swimming pools!''; "Don't let go of my hand—you'll get lost!''

As we ventured out, we weren't given the empathic support to become less dependent. We were contained both physically and psychologically, and consequently felt physically safe but rarely emotionally safe. We internalized our parents' anxiety, the nonverbal communication constantly being transmitted.

Even today, shows of independence and self-assertion are met by disapproval or depression, which feels like emotional abandonment. Helplessness, however, is met with attention. Behavior that rigidly conforms to our parents' desires is met with "love.'' Often we take the secure route of unquestioning compliance and dependency. This route appears to be safer.

We end up fearing the responsibility of taking care of ourselves. We grow anxious and fearful at the thought of separation from others. Seeking to fuse with another, we only feel fully alive in a close relationship. Only another person's approval can make us feel strong and secure. Such feelings cause us to cling in relationships and to be overly dependent and demanding, because asserting ourselves triggers fears of abandonment.

Sometimes our parents loved us too much by being too controlling rather than overprotective. This, too, can led to fears of abandonment. Although our parents are not the only source of the picture that we carry inside of us today of who we are, our sense of identity is shaped most by the people closest to us in our early childhood. They "mirror" back to us our earliest conceptions of who we are. If our parents were overly controlling and bent on seeing us only as they wished us to be, they mirrored back to us a faulty picture of ourselves. If they saw us as an appendage of themselves, or a chance to finally fulfill their desires, they may have allowed little room for our individuality or uniqueness.

Parents like this may emotionally abandon their children by becoming cold or depressed when the children can't or won't be what the parents want them to be. They may provide a host of services and material things to their child, but no essential validation or real involvement in his or her life. This can be devastating. Such a child grows up unable to recognize his own strengths, feeling that without someone else to control him—someone to please—he has no direction. The result is a shaky sense of personal identity that needs a close relationship to bolster and sustain it rather than enhance it.

The result is that without a close relationship, we may feel alone and abandoned. We seek other people to replace our parents in giving us a sense of identity. When we love someone, we fear abandonment by them because we fear losing the sense of self we appear to have gained in our relationship with them.

The sad part is that clinging to another person for the shot of self-esteem obtained from his approval puts you in a very precarious position. Basing inner security exclusively on feedback from the outside is a setup for a life of disappointment. The control over our lives is in the hands of other people, and we come to resent it. Security, based as it is on the whims of others—even others who love us—

is never absolute or permanent, because it comes from someone outside ourselves.

While clinging to others is a common way of appeasing fears of abandonment, it's not the only way. A person who fears abandonment may avoid relationships entirely, for fear of getting involved and being left or rejected. As a defense, such a person might act aloof and arrogant, and again unconsciously set up his own abandonment. Or he may set up rigid standards for what he expects in a relationship as a way of protecting himself, and find that no one can meet his requirements.

Consider Janet's story of her relationship with Hal. They met in November and went out just about every weekend. But one Saturday night in December, when Janet assumed they had a date, she phoned Hal to find out what time he was picking her up and he wasn't home. She drove to his house, rang his doorbell, and noticed that the lights were out. Worried, she sat parked in front of his house all night.

Sometime after midnight, Hal pulled up in a car with another woman. Janet drove off, furious. The next day, she dropped in on Hal and accused him of standing her up.

Hal stared at her in frank amazement. "We never had any plans together for the evening," he sputtered, irritated and upset.

"Well, I just assumed—" Janet began, and stopped in midsentence. The look on Hal's face was beginning to make her feel foolish. Worse, he refused to answer any of her questions about whom he had been with, telling her that she was out of line for even asking.

Hal was cool to Janet after that. She tried not to sound hurt the next time they were together, but she couldn't keep the edge out of her voice. The evening was awful, and when Hal dropped Janet off, he said he was too tired when she invited him in.

Janet barely slept that night. The next morning, everything seemed clearer. She wasn't going to be affected by Hal's moods. She was going to have a serious conversation with him about their relationship.

That day, she sent him a bunch of heart-shaped helium balloons, attached to a bottle of wine, sure that he'd invite her over to share it. Hal called to thank her, but something in his voice didn't sound very pleased. He told Janet that he had a million things to do, but if she wanted to come over to his place sometime after eight, he'd be waiting.

That night, Janet confronted Hal. "I asked him where our relationship was going. He acted like he didn't understand what I was asking. He said he was having a good time, and he thought I was having fun, too. That was as far as it went for now. What more did I want? Why couldn't I give it some time and wait and see what happened?"

Janet was angry. "There's something I've learned: I don't have the time, at my age, to wait for a man to make up his mind about whether he wants a relationship or not. You can't spend a couple of years with every guy who comes along, and then find out that the relationship just isn't happening."

All in all, Janet admitted she'd only spent six weeks with Hal—five dates, to be exact. Still she felt, "A month and a half is a long time. I'm not a therapist. I don't want to spend years curing some man of his commitment phobia. I think Hal was just stringing me along. It hurt, but I stopped seeing him."

A need for control in relationships, for people to follow our agenda, often masks a fear of abandonment. Janet was impatient with Hal's wish for more time to allow things to happen between them gradually. The idea of giving Hal even more time than she'd already invested made Janet uneasy.

Janet's need to have a man adhere to her schedule for the relationship was really about self-protection. A month and a half sometimes seems like an eon to people like Janet who were loved too much. Often there's a need to rush relationships with others. Underneath the haste isn't driving passion, but unconscious fears of abandonment. We want another person to be sure, right away, before we invest ourselves in a relationship. We want to make sure we beat them to the door.

Fear of Exposure

The belief that if we let others really know us, as we are, they couldn't possibly love us keeps many of us on our guard. For Denise and Alan, engaged and planning to marry in a month, such a belief nearly meant the end of their relationship.

Denise accidentally discovered the truth about Alan. "I was standing in line in the bank when I spotted a woman two people ahead of me who looked vaguely familiar," she explains. "I couldn't place her at first, but then I remembered. She was the wife of one of Alan's associates whom I'd met briefly at the Christmas party."

Denise caught up with the woman as she was leaving the bank and introduced herself. They chatted for a few minutes about Denise and Alan's wedding plans. As they were parting, the woman turned back to Denise and said, "By the way, has Alan found anything yet?"

Denise stared at her. "I thought I wasn't tracking very well. I said, 'Found what?' "

The woman looked at Denise strangely, and said, "I don't mean to pry, but I just wondered who Alan was working for these days."

Suddenly, Denise felt claustrophobic. Mumbling something that sounded like, "Everything's fine . . . nice seeing you," she took off through the revolving door. What in the world was this woman talking about? she wondered. Feeling anxious and upset, she ran the eight blocks home.

That night, Alan came by to pick her up at seven o'clock as usual, and Denise met him at the door. She told him about the strange conversation she'd had. Alan's face went white. Unable to meet her eyes, he told her the truth. He'd been fired from his job over three weeks ago. He'd been too afraid to tell her. In fact, he'd been too afraid to tell anyone. So each day at seven A.M., he'd left the house, dressed in a suit, carrying his briefcase, as he'd done every day for the last two years.

Looking back, Denise saw things that should have sparked her curiosity if she hadn't been planning their wedding and paying attention to nothing else. Like the fact that Alan told her not to call him at work, which she rarely did anyway, because he was on a project involving a lot of meetings and he'd be hard to reach. Like the afternoons she'd had phone calls from friends who were looking for him that ended strangely and abruptly when she told the callers to reach Alan at his office. Like the evenings he seemed so anxious, and evasive when she asked him questions about his day.

Denise isn't angry that Alan got fired. She feels he's talented and is sure he'll find another position, even better than the one he lost. What stuns her is that Alan could have kept something like this a secret from her. "If he really loved me, how could he not trust me enough to tell me?" she says. "Why would he have held all of that inside, and let me find out from the wife of one of his associates, of all people? I was so embarrassed that I could have died. But that doesn't matter. What matters is that I can't trust Alan anymore. The truth is, he never opens up much about anything, and now I'm suspicious about everything. What else has he told me that's a lie?"

The truth, unfortunately, is a lot. Alan was never the assistant to the president, but one of two assistants to the assistant. The boss he raved to Denise about made it obvious every day that he didn't think much of Alan or his abilities. Looking every inch the successful corporate executive, Alan was never as sure about himself and his future as he led Denise to believe.

Why did Alan lie? He shrugs and explains, "I was getting married. I had future in-laws expecting me to provide for their daughter. Everyone was looking at me to perform. I didn't think I could stand the way they'd start looking at me if I told them the truth. I thought I could find a new job quick, and no one would ever know."

Sometimes the truth seems too terrible to tell. The fear of being found out can cause one small lie to snowball. The lies Alan told Denise aren't a sign of poor character or pathology as much as symptomatic of a deep-seated fear of exposure.

Children who were loved too much are especially susceptible to the compulsion to hide what they perceive as personal failures or weaknesses, or to stretch the truth over shortcomings as Alan did. Underneath is the fear that the real truth—the real self—is so awful, so unacceptable, that others will surely feel sorry for them, or worse, reject them, if it was ever exposed. Deep inside, nothing attained or accomplished is ever good enough. Every "failure" is magnified.

In its extreme, the compulsion to hide the truth can cause a person to turn his or her entire life into a lie. One young woman, for instance, who was rejected from a university that accepted her two best friends, showed up on campus the third week of September saying she had received special acceptance and a full academic scholarship. She moved into a dorm, bought textbooks, and left for classes every day. Suspicious about how this friend could have received such an honor, her two friends called the Registrar's Office. The woman in question was never enrolled, registered, or listed anywhere on the records as a student.

A young man had an older sister who suffered from severe depressions and was living in a halfway house after a series of hospitalizations. This, to him, was a huge skeleton in the family closet. He never told a single person all his life. Instead, he said that his sister was living in Europe. Worse, he broke off relationships before they became too serious, telling himself that he wasn't ready to get married. "All my life I lived in fear that someone would point a finger at me and say that mental illness ran in my family," he explained. "What if it was true? What scared me most was getting a woman pregnant and passing these genes, or whatever it is, on to my child. I was sure the truth would catch up with me. So I never really got involved with anyone, and told myself I didn't need a relationship."

Although these examples are extreme, the adult child who was loved too much often seeks the security of a stronger image. The real self, complete with human fallibilities and weaknesses, doesn't seem good enough.

Sometimes such a person meets someone he or she desires and wants to project an image that is more exciting and therefore more attractive. Overprotected by parents who were too anxious over their child's well-being to allow any risks or adventures, he or she creates an impressive, more adventurous image, very different from reality, by stretching the truth. A woman tells a story about her boyfriend of two years. Seeing a picture of a thoroughbred in his scrapbook, she asked, "Whose horse is this?" He said, "My family's. We've owned racehorses ever since I was a baby." Six months later, she accompanied him to the racetrack, where they ran into his parents, unexpectedly. "Which horse here is yours?" the woman innocently asked her boyfriend's father. "We don't own any horses," he said, staring at her blankly. "It's much too expensive." Her boyfriend didn't miss a beat. "Whatever made you think we owned horses? Did I say that? You must have misunderstood."

While the fear of exposure doesn't necessarily lead to whopping lies about ourselves and others, it often causes us to keep our distance from other people by never sharing our real feelings with them. What if we expose ourselves to someone and he finds out we're insecure? Or depressed? Or not always so smart? Or totally uncoordinated? It feels less risky to play up our strengths and hide our weaknesses.

We guard our perceived shortcomings as if they were horrible secrets. If we take a look at some of these shortcomings or some of the events in our lives that we fear exposing to others, we often see that it's not the event or feeling itself that's so awful, but the meaning that we attach to it. It's this meaning that we learned from our parents.

When parents love too much, they are often absorbed with how good their child looks in comparison to other children. That the child "shows well" to peers, neighbors, teachers, and other relatives is vitally important to them. Heavy agendas exist for what the child should be, whom he should associate with, what his plans for his future should be. Anxious to please his parents and insure their love, the child complies by learning to "package" himself. He may give up hope of ever really being accepted or understood, disavow his real self, and seek attention through his achievements. A hypersensitivity to revealing cracks in his image begins.

Children who were loved too much become adults who believe that they will win other people's love or esteem through "looking good" or hiding perceived shortcomings. This was often true with their parents. The defenses we developed as children to hide our true selves from our parents continue to be used in later life.

The link between the fear of exposure and the fear of abandonment is obvious. The belief is, "If I let you know who I really am, you'll abandon me." Adult children who were overparented are very good at hiding vulnerabilities, but there's always the fear that if people really get close, they'll find out the truth—we're human, and like everyone else, incompetent in some areas. As a defense, we put on our mask, become superficial, guarded, unemotional.

The payoff for hiding our true selves is distance from other people. A fear of exposing ourselves to others that prevents us from sharing our feelings almost guarantees that our relationships will be superficial. People sense that we haven't let them really see us as we are. Or they think that we're invulnerable, and therefore unavailable. We may fabricate or hide the truth because we want to prevent rejection, but inside we may be really terrified of the closeness that might result if we weren't rejected. Again, the fear of exposure is based on a fear of intimacy. Revealing our "secrets" would bring us too close for comfort, but failing to reveal ourselves means that we'll never feel loved completely, for who we really are.

The belief that abandonment, engulfment, or exposure is the natural result of intimacy can cause us to fend off other people without even knowing that we're doing it. The subtle art of distancing other people from our lives includes the following behaviors:

Talking too much. The need to confide our every thought and opinion to others is built on the false belief that this is the way to build intimacy with other people.

We believe that if we aren't talking, the relationship isn't "happening."

Disclosure of our every thought and action was often demanded in our families. Our parents' biggest complaint was that we didn't tell them enough. We talked, and an avid audience listened. Rarely did our parents disclose anything about themselves in return. It was all about us.

Giving up the center stage for others can be difficult, after growing up in the spotlight with an audience who seldom got bored. But intimacy is about sharing. When you talk too much, you don't listen. Intimacy can only develop when two people both share their thoughts and feelings with each other. Talking so much that conversation is a one-way street prevents this from happening. The person on the other end of all the chatter feels insignificant rather than close.

There are other reasons people who were overparented talk too much. Anxiety keeps some of us talking, because silence feels like emptiness or makes us feel exposed.

Sometimes we talk too much to control the relationship, by controlling what is said. Perhaps we're afraid to hear the thoughts and feelings of another person. Holding the monopoly on the conversation means never having to listen to what we don't want to hear.

There are times we talk too much to "puff ourselves up" and make ourselves feel important. It can also be a form of aggression. It frustrates other people, who suffer in silence, waiting hopefully for a chance to get a word in but feeling compelled to be polite and keep listening. Frustration leads to anger, and a desire to get away from the source of that anger.

People are invariably distanced by a person who talks too much. If unconsciously, we need to fend off engulfment by others without being direct about the feelings that give rise to those fears, chattering on and on is bound to work.

Intellectualizing relationships. Reducing emotions to logic and analytically deliberating over your feelings is a way of hiding vulnerability. Too much intellectualization distances other people.

Louise, a twenty-six-year-old systems analyst, tells the story of the first time her fiancé told her he loved her. "Predictably, we were in bed. I was surprised when he held me close and said, 'Louise, I love you.' He'd seemed so aloof most of the time, I wasn't sure I was making the grade with him or not.

"But because I was in love with him, I couldn't help waiting for the next time we were together, when he was kissing me good night, to say, 'Remember the other night? Remember what you said? What did you mean?'

"He thought for a moment and said, 'Well, I've been defining love for myself. I've come to the conclusion that love is extending oneself for another's spiritual growth. That's how I feel about you. I feel you should expand your spiritual growth.'

"I stared at him. 'My spiritual growth? What are you talking about?'

" 'Why are you getting so upset?' he asked, in a calm voice. 'Spirituality is very important. I've lowered my ego boundaries. Don't you see, love is sharing your full essence with someone else, like I'm doing with you.' "

This philosophical analysis of his love would have seemed almost funny to Louise, had she not cared so much.

While it's not wrong to believe that love is about spirituality or to profess an evolved philosophy of romance, Louise's boyfriend articulated his feelings with such a lack of emotion that he might have been giving a speech on economics. The mixed message—I love you, but I feel no emotion—distanced Louise and made her feel foolish and angry. It was months before he confided the truth, and expressed his feelings with all of the emotion he'd been covering with his intellectualizations. For this man, intellectualizing his relationships was a way to express love without risking vulnerability.

Many adult children who were overparented have difficulty saying "I love you." The words seem so loaded. Intellectualization becomes a defensive way of hiding emotions and vulnerability.

But emotions are the cornerstone of intimacy. Without

the expression of feelings, relationships become shallow and unfulfilling, safe but unrewarding. By being intellectual about what we feel and staying in our heads, we avoid experiencing our emotions, often in the same way we avoided exposing our true selves to our parents.

Being sarcastic or arrogant. Sarcasm is indirect anger or hostility, disguised as humor. Little jokes that seem harmless and put other people at a disadvantage can become a habit. But these clever remarks can be used unconsciously to fend other people off.

Arrogance is often a cover-up for shyness; a defense to protect ourselves against insecurity. Rather than expose our vulnerabilities, we act aloof in hopes that we'll fool others and impress them with a superficial show of strength.

Both sarcasm and arrogance are passive forms of aggression. Children who were overparented were rarely allowed to express aggression directly. They developed passive-aggressive strategies for expressing anger, such as being sarcastic, which seems safer. The listener is put off guard and confused, but retaliation is avoided.

Sarcasm and arrogance are roadblocks to intimacy. People view sarcasm as an attack, and arrogance as aggression. They defend against them by pulling away, or attacking back.

Abusing food, alcohol or drugs. Abusing food and becoming overweight can be an unconscious way of appearing less desirable so that the opposite sex will not be attracted. The same can be said for appearing drunk or stoned.

Addictions, whether to food, alcohol, or drugs, create a world of their own. Obsessions take on their own force and diminish real involvement with others as well as contact with them. Our primary attachment is to a substance, rather than other people. The high from sugar, alcohol, and drugs may offer comfort and a superficial sense of self-esteem, but never true intimacy. In fact, it insures an escape from it.

Sulking or "shutting down" so others can't get in. Sulking and looking hurt and sad were some of our best weapons for getting what we wanted from our parents. Ninety percent of the time, such behavior sent our parents flying with solutions to our problems.

We try to use these same weapons as adults, but they are blunt in our hands. "When I sulk and say, 'You don't really love me,' to Craig, he goes crazy," one woman admitted. "We get in the biggest fight, when all I want him to say is that he does love me."

What this woman wants is reassurance. She never learned how to ask for it directly, and feels foolish saying, "Craig, I need to hear you tell me that you love me." Worse, she feels that if she asks for what she wants and gets it, it's not as good as getting it without having to ask.

Is it really better to manipulate people into a position where they give us what we want by whining, shutting down, or sulking? Is that really more fulfilling than asking for it directly and getting it?

Unfortunately, it's often a sure way to distance a lot of people, for a simple reason: Many people have disowned the needy part of themselves—the part that's like a demanding child; that craves love, attention, and affection; that can never get enough. It exists inside all of us, threatens our picture of "adulthood," and causes our defenses to spring into life. Sensing another needy person, the reaction is "Yech! Get me away! This is like the one part of myself that I really hate!"

That is not to say that there aren't people who are attracted to needy, helpless people. There are some who thrive on it. We aren't generally attracted to these people, because we fear that our needs won't get met if we have to take care of them.

Sulking and shutting other people out can be a passive-aggressive way of expressing anger and a way of demanding control in relationships when we feel no control. Such behaviors are an outgrowth of the fear of abandonment. But the truth is, people give us what they want to give us. No amount of manipulation can cause other people to give us love—real love, not grudging acquiescence to our demands—when they don't want to give it, no matter how good our ploys may be. It's our self-esteem that suffers in the end if we have to sulk or play games in order to get what we need.

Acting in an indifferent or hostile manner when others try to get close. Forgetting to return phone calls, being too busy to care, changing the subject when others confide in us, or feeling that people who are affectionate are "weak," "desperate," or "needy" is bound to fend off people who are open to relationships.

If we were pampered too much as children, developing empathy for others can be difficult. Some of us find that when conversations aren't focused on us, we're very bored, although we try to hide it. This isn't so much selfishness as a lack of experience in tuning in to other people's needs. Essentially, we never had to.

Appearing indifferent is an indirect way of expressing aggression, without being overt about it. It's perceived by others as hostility. The message "I'm better than you and I don't really care about you" comes through clearly and breeds anger. It can also feed another person's sense of inadequacy.

True intimacy happens when people enhance each other's strengths and make each other feel good. It is natural to pull away from people who make us feel uncomfortable.

Always needing to be "right." Some of us can't help but say, "Yeah, but . . ." every time someone tells us their opinion. Always needing to be right, to have our say, to put in the last word, to point out the inconsistencies in what some other person thinks, is a way of exerting control in relationships. Too often, it alienates people and makes them feel helpless or attacked.

Sometimes a person who needs to be "right" rationalizes that it's fun and even necessary to always play devil's advocate. I'm just being honest, he or she believes. But there's a difference between being honest when we're asked for our thoughts or opinions, and chiming in whenever we get a chance to point out other people's errors.

For some of us, the more involved we are with a person, the more ready we are to correct them, "help" them, or guide them when we think what they've said is wrong.

Often this stems from our first experience with love—the love our parents gave us, coated as it was with judgments and messages like "If I didn't love you, I wouldn't tell you the truth." The question is, whose truth?

People raised in such an environment grow up thinking that criticizing other people, and pointing out the errors in their thinking or reasoning is synonymous with caring about them. But always needing to correct others—to be *right*—breeds contempt and hostility in the people we've bested. Relationships become a game of verbal volleyball, where people score points off each other, win the battle, and often lose the relationship.

Sharp feelings of inadequacy lurk underneath the stance of the person who is always right. Such a person fears the interplay and flexibility of relationships. Unfortunately, there are many people, ready to love and to share, who are put off by the rigid stance of the person with so little room for the thoughts and ideas of others. But allowing other people to be right seems tantamount to being engulfed, and is actively defended against, even though it shuts out other people and can make intimacy impossible.

Becoming depressed. No one consciously decides to become depressed. Depression can be a serious illness, requiring treatment and a tremendous amount of effort to overcome.

But in addition to the many psychological and physiological causes of depression, the illness can be a defense against intimacy. It can be an unconscious way of eliciting pity and attention indirectly when we have no conception of how to ask for it in a direct way. Depression cuts off open communication from others. It's a lonely shell that breeds helplessness in them. It's this helplessness that eventually leads to anger. For this reason, the depressed person usually finds that the loving support disappears as his depression progresses from days into months. The interaction in relationships with other people that would help most is often impossible to achieve as the depression deepens. Others feel they have failed him, that their love and concern did no good, and inevitably they distance themselves.

* * *

The subtle ways we distance people from our lives are almost never conscious on our part. But if we fear that intimacy will lead to the realization of our fears of exposure, engulfment, or abandonment, we will defend against it.

We may be tempted at this point to blame our parents who loved us so much for our inability to succeed in our relationships with others. But today we are adults. Our relationships are up to us, regardless of our parents' contributions to our outlook. Laying the blame at their door is a cop-out.

"My mother was twenty years old when she had me," one man realized, looking back over his childhood and its influence on his life today. "When I was twenty, I barely knew what I was doing, hanging out in bars, running around and getting into all sorts of trouble. Yet I'm angry that my mother—at twenty years old, with a husband and two children—didn't do a better job and be the perfect mother.

"Now, when I think of my mother, even with all of her faults, I realize she had enormous responsibilities. I'm still angry at the way she smothered me and drove me crazy, but she probably did a lot better than I would have done in the same circumstances. What I forget is that the mother I remember doesn't even exist today. She's grown, too. I might be left with the legacy of her shortcomings, but she just did the best she could at the time. If she had it to do all over again, she might have done it differently. Unfortunately, I'm thirty-five years old, and she doesn't have that chance."

As adults, we are no longer powerless; no longer defined by our parents, whatever they may have thought of us. We can define ourselves. We can grow and change. We will spend far more years out of our parents' home and in homes of our own making. Regardless of the impact of our early childhood, we can be who we need to be. We don't need to rely on our parents' judgments, or use them as an excuse for not correcting things about ourselves that we've realized are causing problems in our lives. If we have fears of intimacy, we can work to overcome them. A heightened awareness of these fears and how they confound our relationships today can be our guide.

CHAPTER 7

THE ROYAL WEDDING

*"We're not losing a daughter;
we're gaining a son."*

"What am I looking for in the woman I marry?
June Cleaver."
—Bob, age 34, designer

At a prenuptial party, the father of the groom toasts the woman who will soon become his daughter-in-law: "You're a lucky girl to be marrying this young man who's given us nothing but joy. He's as precious as gold to us, and tomorrow, we give him to you."

Hearing this, the parents of the bride—parents who love too much—nudge each other under the table. The nerve of these people to imply that their daughter is so lucky as to be getting this gift of "gold." What about what the groom is getting?

Quickly, the bride's father rises to his feet, eyes his future son-in-law, and speaks. "My daughter may be getting gold, but you, young man, are getting something even more precious: My little girl—a true diamond!"

So begins the royal wedding. In spite of fears of intimacy, high expectations, and angst, most adult children who were loved too much marry or become involved in a long-term, committed relationship.

Marriage signals separation from parents, and no one

is more ambivalent about this than family members who have nurtured each other's mutual dependency and enmeshment. It is with much anxiety that parents who love too much let us go and begin our lives with another person, away from their watchful eyes and loving control. Sometimes they don't want to let us go. And sometimes we don't want to let go.

How do children who were overparented loosen the bonds of dependency and enmeshment enough to make a true commitment to marriage? What happens to their relationships with their parents if they force them to let go? What happens to their marriage if they don't? What if they themselves can't let go?

Nancy, an attractive forty-one-year-old woman, grappled with these issues when she married Rob. "We held our wedding ceremony in my parents' living room, and maybe it was an omen," she explains. "My family has always been very close-knit, very involved in each other's lives. Rob became 'the Alien.' "

It·wasn't that Nancy's parents didn't appear to accept Rob completely. On the surface, they did, at least in the beginning. But Nancy didn't kid herself. He was never her best bet in their eyes. "They accepted the inevitable because they had to. So they never forgot things like his birthday, and they always acted nice to him. My mother especially tried to draw him out. But, still, Mom and Dad never really trusted him. They never respected him. Years later, my brother told me that my father never referred to Rob as anything but 'that little twerp' when I was out of earshot, and while it made me angry, I wasn't too surprised."

From the day she was married, Nancy felt as if she constantly had to explain her husband to her parents. Unsuccessfully, she tried to "sell" Rob to them and make them see him in a different light by throwing them together as often as possible.

"I wanted them to like him. It was that simple. But my mistake was confiding in them about Rob's problems at work. Rob's in advertising, and it's a cutthroat profession at times. During the first year we were married, he was passed over twice for a promotion. Although he wasn't concerned about it, to me the writing was on the wall.''

This wasn't something Nancy felt comfortable talking about with her girlfriends. She didn't want them to know Rob was in trouble, and painted a rosy picture of his success for them. But, anxious and worried, she poured the whole story out to her mother and father one night when Rob was out of town.

''I trust my parents' advice more than anyone's, I admit it. They have no reason to steer me in the wrong direction, because they really love me and want to see me happy. I always told them my problems, so telling them about Rob seemed natural. Talking to them was a relief in a lot of ways. But, of course, I didn't want Rob to know that I'd talked to them about him and his job. That would have been terrible.''

Nancy's father was positive that he knew what Rob's problem was: Rob acted like a know-it-all. He shouldn't try to push his ideas down other people's throats. Rob should quit whining about all of the things that were wrong at his agency and be more of a company man. He wanted to sit down and talk to Rob about it, but Nancy absolutely balked and begged him not to.

One night not much later, Nancy and her mother had a heart-to-heart talk, again about Rob. Her mother's opinion was Rob wasn't strong enough. ''Rob is so unstable,'' she maintained. ''Look at how he goes to bars all of the time with his friends. It may not be for me to say, but I don't think it's very mature. Why can't he watch the football game at home with you?''

It was all food for thought, and Nancy, used to listening to her parents, devoured it. It was a mistake.

''Now that my parents knew Rob was in trouble, that's all they talked about. They made these little hints to Rob about what he should be doing, trying not to be too obvious. They were trying to help, but Rob especially resented my father's advice and cut him short the second he started talking. Once, he was so rude to my father that I didn't speak to him for days.''

Nancy fell into a habit of giving surreptitious weekly

reports to her parents about what was happening with Rob, his career, and their marriage. Her parents criticized Rob, and made a host of suggestions for how she should "handle" him.

After a couple of months, Nancy began to resent every word they said. "It seemed like one day, all of this confiding in my parents crossed the line. They were like two amateur psychologists, analyzing Rob's motives for everything he did. They said ridiculous things like, 'Rob should quit watching so much television. He's trying to escape from his problems.' I mean, come on now. The guy was in advertising. He was supposed to watch television.

"The point was, I'd told my parents a little problem, but they blew the whole thing up, and now I had to listen to a constant chorus of, 'Your husband should be doing this, your husband should be doing that.' "

Nancy admits that what followed wouldn't have happened if she didn't keep giving her parents new information. "One day I'd get frustrated and yell, 'We've talked about this whole thing enough, thank you. Can we just drop the whole subject?' The next day I'd be worrying about Rob and start talking to them about him again, wanting at the same time to bite off my tongue. It was a compulsion.

"In the end, I hated myself, I hated the things they said about him, but I couldn't stop. It was like there was some huge pull to pour out my life to them, to never keep anything to myself."

One night Rob told Nancy that the account he worked on was up for review. Nancy exploded, and they ended up in a screaming match. Every criticism her parents ever made of Rob poured out of her mouth. For Nancy, it was support. It was validation. It was ammunition.

Rob was furious. He said, "I expect this crap from your parents, but I never expected it from you. How did they get into this anyway? What makes you think that I'm such a loser that I can't find another job if I have to?"

Embarrassed, Nancy looked away, but she could feel Rob's eyes on her in a look that was long and steady. Finally, he said, "You can tell your parents this: The reason I'm not Mr. Limelight at the agency is because I have a private life. At least I thought I did. Tell them that I didn't want to stay at the office until eight o'clock every night, showing some VP how vitally invested I was in his pizza account, because I was more invested in *you*. I wanted to come home to be with *you*. If I had stayed at the office until all hours, your parents would have said I was neglecting you. I really can't win here, can I?''

Rob and Nancy brooded in silent anger for weeks. Finally, they decided to see a marriage counselor.

In therapy Nancy made an important discovery: she had never really married Rob, in an emotional sense. ''I never trusted him, and I still turned to my parents first. My real loyalty was to them.''

The tension between Nancy and Rob was an outgrowth of Nancy's inability to truly commit herself emotionally to Rob and their marriage. Such a commitment was impossible because Nancy had never separated completely from her parents. By separation, we mean building our own sense of identify, separate from our parents. It means cutting the emotional strings that bind us to beliefs they have that no longer fit our reality.

The fear Nancy had of letting go of dependency on her parents resulted in the construction of a triangle when she married: Nancy, Rob, and her parents. Always, Rob was at the lowest point.

Rob's career problems served as cement for such a triangle. Nancy began to feel shaky about their future, and instead of working with Rob and honestly sharing her fears, she was driven to pull her parents into her marriage as ballast.

The biggest symptom of Nancy's lack of separation was her compulsion to constantly confide in her parents, even when it resulted in little true help or gratification. Her guilty confidences were the cement that held the triangle together. Inside, she was very ambivalent about letting go of her dependency on her parents and placing her trust in Rob. These confidences, hidden from Rob, were evidence of her childlike need for parental approval and control, rather than cries for help.

Why would Nancy have such a problem letting go of her dependency on her parents and their approval? In therapy Nancy looked back on a history of guilt and self-criticism for failing to live up to her parents' expectations. Even her marriage represented a failure to please them or really satisfy them. Nancy's parents had very high expectations of the kind of man their daughter should be married to, and career success was a big part of this. In light of this, Rob's being overlooked for a promotion appeared to be a devastating failure to Nancy, because it was a failure to gain something that might have won her parents' approval.

Nancy didn't bring her fears to Rob because she felt he wouldn't have understood her anxiety. He had his own particular values and goals, and was satisfied with his career as it was. But Nancy felt very uncomfortable if her and Rob's way of operating differed from her parents' way of doing things.

As Nancy and Rob continued in therapy, Nancy began to take a hard look at the relationship between herself and her parents as it existed under the veneer of love and closeness. Nancy admitted that in forty-one years, she could never recall either of her parents criticizing her harshly. Even when she provoked them and made choices that she knew they would disapprove of, such as dropping out of high school at seventeen to work full time, they had appeared understanding, if not supportive. While they lectured her on how much she had to offer and how much more she might accomplish if she were motivated, they generally swallowed their frustrations. When Nancy acted irresponsibly, made mistakes or poor choices, they were always able to find some way of adjusting the circumstances or making excuses for her so that their picture of Nancy as the "perfect" daughter remained intact. They needed this picture, because it validated them. Like many parents who love too much, to accept the shortcomings of their child is to acknowledge their potential failings as parents. Consequently, Nancy's parents repressed any anger or criticism of her.

When Nancy married, they unleashed their frustration

on Rob. In such a family, the spouse, an outsider, can be an ideal scapegoat for anger that the parents cannot express directly to the child. The parents' frustrations with their sons and daughters who never quite lived up to their expectations can be transferred to the son-in-law or daughter-in-law. It's much safer that way, and doesn't risk the "love" that ties the family together. The spotlight is deflected from the problems of their children to the faults of the children's spouses: "If only he (she) were richer, more responsible, more intelligent—more whatever—my daughter (son) would have no problems."

Nancy's parents were quick to ferret out Rob's faults. Although it was more Rob's choice to make his family life a priority than any weaknesses in his skills or motivation that resulted in his being passed over for promotions, Nancy's parents automatically assumed it was Rob's limitations—limitations they had been anxious about from the start. What they saw as shortcomings were really differences between their values and expectations and Rob's. To a parent who loves too much, these differences are threatening. To acknowledge differences between people is to acknowledge their separation from us. Unconsciously, Nancy's parents felt it was vital that their daughter also see Rob's differences as dangerous shortcomings, lest she cleave to Rob and separate emotionally from them.

Nancy also discovered in therapy that there was a part of her that enjoyed her parents' criticism of Rob. It made her feel vindicated. Nancy had certain fantasies of marriage that called for all of her needs to be anticipated and met by her husband. Consciously, she knew that her fantasies were exactly that—dreams of perfection that had little basis in reality. Unconsciously, she was as disappointed as her parents when Rob couldn't fulfill them. When Nancy's parents criticized Rob, they only put her own thoughts into words, without making her feel responsible and disloyal.

Many people who were overparented unconsciously welcome their parents' criticism of their spouses. It feeds the comfortable enmeshment because it places the parents in the role of the adult child's champion, fighting to make sure that he or she has only the best. What could be better evidence of their love, or better reason to continue the mutual dependence? As Nancy later explained, "My parents thought Rob should worship me, do for me, give me everything, and make my happiness his one goal in life. It was the same unrealistic picture of marriage that I secretly had. But I never had to come face-to-face with my own impossible expectations of marriage. Any man would have fallen short. For me to bond with Rob, he would have had to become my parents."

Many of us find that our parents have a large and continual presence in our marriage. It's a signal that we're still attached to our parents in a way that can cripple our relationship.

Sometimes it appears that it's only our parents who have difficulty letting go. They interject unwanted and unasked-for advice, come to our rescue, provide us with money or a home, encourage us to share private details about our spouse, and use a host of other techniques unconsciously to encourage us to depend on them.

Yet we must accept a large share of the responsibility ourselves. Always in such a triangle is an adult child, loved too much and ambivalent about being truly independent of his or her parents. Although we may complain that our parents inject themselves into our lives uninvited, the truth is that we often ask them in, by consulting them on everything we do and seeking their confirmation. Calling our parents five times a day, seeking their advice whenever a decision is to be made, depending on them for extra money, spending far more energy pleasing them than our partner, can all be signals that we're married legally but not emotionally.

Because of our ambivalence about true independence, it's almost too easy for our parents to draw us back in the warm circle of their love and control of our lives. Unconsciously, in order to feel more secure, we may attempt to keep our foot in two doors—our parents', and our own. The keys to our parents' home hang on our key ring, and we use them to move in and out of our parents' door as frequently and easily as if we still lived there.

We'd be wise to return those keys and knock like everyone else. This is not because we are no longer sons and daughters, but because we are separate and independent.

The hardest task all human beings face in a lifetime is that of becoming a separate self. All of us wrestle with the comforts of being a dependent child versus the challenges of being an independent adult. If we have loving parents, with hands outstretched and ready to do for us, buy for us, and solve our problems for us, the hook is even stronger. Depending on our parents is so safe. As strong as the urge is to separate and live our own lives, we will always have the urge to merge with someone stronger, more responsible, more reliable than ourselves. Who can make us feel more secure than our parents who love us so much? Certainly not our spouse, who demands that we give and provide in return for everything we are given.

Incomplete separation and individuation from parents who love too much has devastated many marriages. When families are enmeshed and ambivalent about separation, a spouse may be welcomed, yet unconsciously resented. While in healthy families the separation that occurs when a child marries is welcomed as a sign of healthy growth, for parents who love too much, such separation is met with anxiety. To them, it symbolizes a disintegration of the family structure and a loss of parental control. No wonder our partners are often resented.

If we allow our parents to compete with our spouse for our devotion and allegiance, we will always find ourselves in a triangle rather than a true marriage. The challenge is not to eliminate our parents from our lives when we marry, but to establish an adult relationship with them. To open the path to true intimacy and commitment to another person, we must end the child/parent relationship as it existed when we were truly dependent on our parents. In marriage our primary allegiance must be to our partner. Such a commitment demands loyalty. If we can't muster up devotion or confidence in the person we join our lives with, if our parents can make us doubt that this person is right for us, we're truly not ready for marriage. In fact, it's a perfect setup for failure. When we're angry or upset with our husband or wife and there are two people willing and ready to see things our way, feel our anger, and take away our pain, we'll go where we can find solace rather than real solutions.

Continuing our enmeshment with our parents after we marry has its rewards. Attractive bonuses such as the illusion of emotional security, absolution from responsibility, alleviation of guilt, and financial security draw us in and challenge us to keep our primary allegiance with them.

But there are greater rewards for independence. Feelings of competence. Feelings of being in control. The potential for a full and rewarding marriage, and true intimacy.

Can we do without all of this smothering love and dependency? What will happen to us if we let go, and force our parents to let go?

David is a man who decided to try. The pull of romantic love and the pull of continuing reliance on his parents' approval was responsible for a turning point in his life.

David fell in love with a woman he knew from the start his parents would never approve of. In fact, he never even told them he was seriously involved until after he became engaged. To him, the reason was simple: "You know the movie *Love Story*? The look on the father's face when Ryan O'Neal says he's going to marry Ali MacGraw? It gave me the chills because it reminded me so much of my family. My father's rules were the same: Do it my way, or I'll disown you."

David's parents were against his marriage to Pam from the beginning. "She wasn't Jewish, and they wanted me to marry in the faith. I don't think my father's been in a synagogue since he was a kid, and we never observed any holidays. We used to have Christmas dinner, even. But, still, they wanted me to marry a Jewish girl. I fell in love, and all of a sudden they were devoutly religious.

"When Pam and I got married, neither of my parents came to the wedding. Everyone knew why they weren't there. I accepted their feelings, but still, it hurt.

"In the beginning, I tried to tough it out. I figured I could live without my parents, if that was how they wanted it. But it just didn't feel right not to call them, not to have any contact with them. Pam said to give them time. I got the same advice from everyone. I couldn't. I'd go over and try to talk to them. I'd beg. My father was a brick wall.

"We'd always been so close. I'd done everything else they ever wanted—graduated at the top of my class, went on to law school, made them proud of me. I couldn't believe they were doing this to me. I was their oldest son and I'd listened to everything they ever told me. Until now.

"My mother forgave me enough after the wedding to include me in the family's holiday dinners, so my father had no choice. They couldn't completely exclude their only son from their lives, no matter what horrible thing he'd done. I was naïve. I brought Pam with me, thinking that if they got to know her, they couldn't help but love her, as I did.

"But they never warmed up to Pam. She didn't exist for my parents, even if she was sitting across the table from them. They ignored her completely. It was clear what they thought: This woman was the bad one. She had worked some evil magic on me, to make me go against their wishes. They couldn't accept that all of this was my choice.

"I'll admit, looking back, that there was a part of me that let them go ahead and think I was some kind of victim in all of this. I was only human, and I guess I let Pam take the rap for a while. I thought they couldn't really hurt her—and they were killing me.

"Pam and I made it for about six months, until one day she told me she was leaving me. 'You've got to make a choice. If we're going to have any kind of marriage at all, your parents are going to have to treat me politely, at least. I can't keep going there and standing there while they ignore me, and watch you allow it to happen. I can't live with your guilt anymore, or wait, hoping your parents forgive you. Either I'm your wife, or I'm leaving.' "

David was torn. He tried to convince Pam that she was

being unfair. His parents were really nice people; they'd come around if he gave them time.

Pam didn't buy it. She stood her ground, and David felt helpless. The prospect of taking a stand and demanding that his parents accept Pam triggered tremendous anxiety and fear. It also made David furious at Pam for putting him in the position of having to choose between her and his parents. A true, emotional separation from his parents was something David had never been able to conceive of. Such a separation meant that he would have to say, "I am comfortable with my own choices. Your approval isn't necessary to me. I demand the same respect for my choices as I give you for yours."

David chose Pam. He told his father, "I understand the reasons why you feel as you do about Pam, but she's my wife. I can't allow you or anyone else to be rude to her. I love her. To be happy, I have to be with her. I love you, too, but if you make me choose between you, I'm going to choose Pam. If you can't treat Pam with respect, then we're not coming over here again."

David's story didn't have a storybook ending, where his parents suddenly accept his wife and all of them live happily ever after. But after David's talk with his parents, they were much more polite to Pam. When Pam and David visited, Pam was no longer ignored, and his parents no longer criticized her in his presence.

In truth, it was an uneasy alliance, far from perfect—but good enough. When David thinks about his relationship with his parents today, he admits, "I no longer get the overwhelming emotional support from my parents that I used to get. There's no more constant validation that whatever I do is right. There's a distance between us that's not great enough to be obvious to others, but unmistakable just the same. When Pam and I have problems, like the financial trouble we had a while back when I switched law firms, my parents didn't rush in and rescue us. Before I married Pam, they would have had their hands out in a second. Maybe it's their way of paying me back."

Once in a while David watches his sister and her husband's relationship with his parents when they are thrown together during the holidays. "There's a closeness with them that Pam and I will never have. My sister still talks to my mother five times a day. My brother-in-law, who lets my sister and my parents lead him around by the nose, replaced me as the star of the family, and they can't be sweet enough to him. Sometimes I'm jealous. Sometimes I feel this uncontrollable pull to go to them for advice, to do whatever they want me to do, just so I can feel their approval. I know they still care about me, but it's not the same, and it hurts me.

"I get depressed about it all, then I look at Pam. I hold our son, and I see the future I chose for myself. Maybe I've finally grown up, because I wouldn't trade this for anything. Love is its own reward."

Nothing will bring the issues of dependency and enmeshment to the forefront as will our romantic relationships. We may have gone on for years cozy and secure in the cocoon of our family, perhaps a little resentfully but always comfortable. We fall in love, and suddenly the bough breaks.

Breaking away wasn't easy for David. Nor is it easy for any adult child who was loved too much. But without such an emotional separation, romantic love and a healthy marriage are difficult if not impossible to achieve.

Such a separation will require that we no longer try to change our parents. We give them the same allowance for their thoughts and feelings that we want them to give us. But we allow differences between us, and for those differences to be okay. We learn that we can survive each other's disapproval. We focus on our own lives without needing our parents' approval or guidance, and free our parents to focus on their lives.

It's possible to care deeply about our parents and be cared for in return without enmeshment in each other's lives. A dependent attachment to our parents does not equal love. Neither does allowing them to control us or our spouse, to dictate how we should operate, or to provide us with things we could be providing for ourselves. These are the things we have to give up in order to grow.

Making love work is a challenge. Nothing will test our

maturity as much, but nothing has as much potential for rewards. Beyond the first hurdle of separating from our parents, there will be others. Always, we must be wary of the traps we may set for ourselves in marriage if our early experience was one of pampered deprivation and smothering love.

If you are married or in a committed, romantic relationship, you may notice certain patterns that follow that are causing tension and conflict at times. Awareness will be your guide to changing these patterns.

Searching in Marriage for Mom and Dad

It's only natural to try to re-create situations that are comfortable for us. Often we chose a partner who will re-create the past for us.

Experts in child abuse discovered long ago that abused children unconsciously tend to seek out abusive spouses. The child of an alcoholic finds himself married to an alcoholic. The battered child falls in love with a man who abuses her emotionally and physically. The child of cold, indifferent parents marries someone who is equally unavailable emotionally. None of the above feel free to choose a partner who is capable of love, understanding, and patience. These emotions arouse suspicion and anxiety because they feel so unfamiliar. Abuse is "comfortable" to the child who knows little else.

How much stronger the hook of smothering, controlling, dependent love can be. While we may have resented it at times, much of the time it felt wonderful. Maybe we were under a microscope, but at least someone was paying attention. Someone cared.

People tend to unconsciously arrange a repetition for themselves of both the good and the bad in their childhoods in adult life. Freud called it the repetition compulsion. By this he meant our human compulsion to repeat the past even when we've vowed to ourselves never to repeat it.

Why we seek to repeat the good seems obvious. But

seeking to repeat painful, ungratifying experiences that we resented is also understandable. It can be our way of continuing the battle in our past with a new, stronger, or at least more seasoned arsenal. This time we're determined to win. By restaging the past and rewriting it, we hope to come out victors.

Nowhere do we try so hard to re-create and rewrite the past than in our marriages. Children who were loved too much rarely marry other children who were loved too much. In fact, the person they marry frequently has some form of childhood abuse in his or her background, whether it be alcoholism, physical abuse, abandonment, or just parental indifference. Why? Because childhood abuse, by its nature, creates victims out of everyone close to the abusive person. As a result, many abused children grow up to be helpers and givers, so deeply concerned about the problems of others that they forgot how to care for themselves. In other words, they become people who love too much.

The adult child who experienced too much love is naturally attracted to the adult child who was never loved enough, who makes him feel so comfortable. Such a person who has survived so much appears strong and competent. Better yet, this is a person who will go the "extra mile" for him, take care of him, take control, and show him the way. Often, this sets the stage for a marriage of helper and helpless, admirer and admiree. The bond can be a passionate one, as each person strives unconsciously to complete the unfinished business of childhood.

With a giving, selfless spouse, we search for what felt so good in our childhood: someone to provide for us, take care of us, worry about us, and protect us. Unconsciously, we seek to transfer our dependency on our parents to dependency on our husband or wife.

Yet it's rarely a perfect fit. We ask our partners, "Am I doing this right? What would you do? How's my outfit? How's my hair? What do you think of this? What should I do?" Often the answers are never as satisfactory as the ones we got when we asked our parents. When we can't find or re-create the familiar emotional atmosphere of childhood, we become frustrated and disappointed.

Rhonda, a twenty-five-year-old accountant, married Mark, a man whose childhood experience was full of incidents of parental overinvolvement and overprotection. "Mark wants to be catered to all of the time," she says. "I come home from work and I'm just as tired as he is, but he won't help with anything around the house unless I really get angry. He puts on this helpless act that makes me furious. I can be in the middle of something with my hands full, and he yells that he can't find the aspirin, or his razor, or his car keys. The truth is, he never even looks, because he knows I'll go and look for him. This is a man who has never read the directions to anything. He'll fiddle around with something, break it, and then look up and say, 'I can't figure this thing out,' leaving the pieces on the floor."

These are minor complaints for Rhonda. What bothers her more is the feeling that she's being cheated; that she carries far more than her share of the burden of maintaining their relationship. "Mark can't stand it when he doesn't have my full attention. Yet I can never get his. I've listened to his problems for hours, but he never listens to me. Everything always has to be his way. When I complain, he gets hurt and says that I'm judging him. Somehow those conversations always end up being about all the ways I should change."

In marriage Mark sought to re-create the type of home that he was used to. Mark expected his needs to be met intuitively by Rhonda. Other women in his life, his mother and grandmother, were experts at giving him what he needed, before he even knew what it was. In therapy he explained that he didn't think he was asking so much of Rhonda. He felt there was something lacking in her, because she never made him really feel loved.

When we try to duplicate the pattern of our childhood in marriage, we're bound to feel the tension of constant frustration. We'll feel misunderstood. We'll feel unloved. After a while we'll conclude, "No one will ever love me as much as my parents." If we succeed and find a partner who is as giving as our parents, we will still feel frustrated, because we will also duplicate the same restrictions

and resentments that grew out of a relationship characterized by too much love. We will eventually come to resent
our dependency, passivity, and lack of competence.

The repetition compulsion also means we'll search in
marriage for the other side of our parents: the side that
controlled us too much, expected too much, demanded
too much. One morning we wake up, and in bed with us
are our "parents": a wife who expects us to be a million-
aire before we're thirty; a husband who needs to control
what we wear, what we buy, and where we go; a lover
who withdraws and becomes depressed when we complain
that we're being smothered to death. Here we thought we
picked someone who was the opposite of our parents, and
some inexplicable twist of fate has turned him or her into
our parents.

With this "parent," we re-create age-old battles. Roni,
a thirty-seven-year-old woman, confides, "All my life, I
believed that my mother only loved me when I was thin.
Michael never seemed to care one way or another about
my weight. We were married and I really let things go.
My mother wasn't around anymore to stare at me while I
was eating.

"I couldn't understand why, but I kept telling Michael
about all the things I ate. I'd say, 'This dress really looks
tight doesn't it? I shouldn't have eaten that piece of cake,
right?' He'd look at me blankly and say, 'I don't know,
what do you think? What do you want to do?'

"I backed him into a corner. 'How would you feel if I
never dieted again?' He said, 'What do you want me to
say? I don't want a wife who's a fat pig. You know that.
But you look fine to me. If you think you should lose
weight, then why don't you try?' "

Michael's attitude made Roni incredibly uncomfortable.
Where were her limits? Where was the criticism, the advice, the control? Love had always meant someone else
telling her what she should do and be. Roni actually felt
that Michael didn't love her enough because he wouldn't
be her policeman, a role her mother had played with alac-
rity until Roni got married.

Roni gained sixty pounds the second year that they were

married. Predictably, Michael complained. He tried to be supportive at first, but then, feeling helpless, he got angry and demanding. Roni resented his advice and control, and ate even more. It was a no-win situation that smacked of the past battles Roni had had with her mother.

Roni was compelled to re-create the situation in her past, to turn Michael into her mother. If we relied constantly on our parents' advice and control, even if it infuriated us, we might try to re-create this situation in marriage, sometimes because the conflict is so familiar, but mostly because we want the situation to come out differently this time. A happy ending would ease old hurts and regrets. If Michael proved that he loved her no matter how fat she got, then Roni would have won.

Separation from our parents means separating from the battle of who was right. Such a lifelong battle is as symptomatic of enmeshment as living entirely by our parents' wishes and dreams. If we're bent on restaging past no-win battles with our parents in our marriage—be it over our weight, our accomplishments, our attitudes, or our values—hoping this time to win them once and for all, we're going after an impossible victory, especially if we use the same old, tired arsenal. Rare is the spouse who can't be backed into a corner or made to act the way our parents once did if we act provocatively enough.

While the repetition compulsion can cause us to re-create no-win situations unconsciously, if we become aware of it, we can actually use it in a healthy way, as an opportunity for self-growth. When we bring old issues into our marriage, we can change how we relate.

Lisa was a woman who complained that she thought she'd escaped her father's control by getting married, only to find that her husband's perfectionist standards for her were even more rigid.

She had been attracted to her husband almost from the moment they met. He seemed so sure of himself, so intelligent, so ready to guide and help her. It was enticing. Because he wasn't critical of her as her father had been, she saw little resemblance to the situation she was trying to escape.

Soon Lisa came to resent her husband's "help," which was really control in disguise, not unlike her father's. In the past, she had reacted to her father in a passive-aggressive way, pretending to forget things he had asked her to do, withdrawing and doing the opposite of what he asked whenever she had the opportunity. This was the same arsenal she employed with her husband, with the same dismal results.

One spring, Lisa took an assertiveness-training course at a community college. The teacher was a therapist, and one day after class Lisa poured out her problems to him. He recommend that Lisa join a therapy group of other women who were working on similar issues.

It wasn't long after Lisa first joined the group that the other women confronted Lisa about some of her behavior. They pointed out to her that she became quiet or withdrew when they told her anything that smacked of advice. Lisa paid them back by skipping the next two group sessions. But feeling miserable and depressed, she returned to the third session, ready to work.

Lisa began to express her feelings openly. When she felt pushed or manipulated, she learned to speak up and demand the right to make her own decisions. Instead of becoming overly reactive whenever anyone gave her advice and doing the opposite, she learned to consider it as feedback and accept it or reject it as it fit.

She carried these skills into her marriage. Instead of withdrawing in resentment when her husband attempted to control her, she'd say, "I need to decide for myself what I should do. I know you love me and want to help, but I have to do things my way." She shared her history with her husband, and he developed empathy for her determination to make her own choices. It wasn't that he no longer attempted to control her; she learned to become less reactive to his control, more ready to express her feelings openly and use her own personal power in her life.

When Lisa began to live consciously and confront these issues as they occurred in her marriage, the situation began to change. She learned that she could share her problems without giving up control of her life. Most important, she learned to put words to her feelings of being trapped and confined, and to communicate instead of rebelling in a passive-aggressive way.

The repetition compulsion doesn't have to end in emotional gridlock. If we have the intention to work through old issues of our childhood and not just repeat no-win situations, it can be productive. We can learn that conflict doesn't need to be destructive. It can lead to greater understanding and trust.

Turning to Parents to Fulfill Needs That You're Afraid to Ask For from Your Spouse

We're impatient. We hate to wait. So we go to the people who love us so much that they indulge us. If we let them, our parents may give us things we're afraid to ask for from our husband or wife. It might be affection. It might be understanding. It might be money for a few extra luxuries. In Beth's case, it was her wedding ring.

Beth wanted a big diamond. In fact, it was all she'd ever dreamed of since she was a child and first fantasized about getting married. But there was no way that Gary, her fiancé, could afford a large diamond on his salary as a police officer.

Beth and her mother put their heads together and came up with a way for Beth to get her diamond. Beth's mother offered to take Beth shopping for rings. She took Gary aside and told him she could really understand how overwhelmed he must feel with all of the wedding plans, and that she wanted to do this one thing especially to help him. Gary, who was feeling nauseous at the thought of hundreds of impending decisions and responsibilities, thought it was a fine idea. He told Beth's mother that he could afford five hundred dollars for the ring—six, if it came to that.

Beth came home with a stunning ring, one and a half carats in a beautiful setting. Gary, who knew nothing about carats, points, or prices, thought it was wonderful.

Three years after their wedding, in a brutal argument about money, Beth lost her temper and said, "You couldn't even afford to buy me a decent ring. Do you know how I got this one? My parents paid for more than half of it!"

Nothing cements the triangle more than our taking things from our parents that we are afraid to ask for from our spouse. Beth, who always believed that you never ask a question if you don't want to hear the answer, assumed that Gary could never give her what she really wanted. She never asked. Gary was appalled, not only at his mother-in-law's treachery, but at the fact that he never even knew that a large diamond was so important to Beth. Had he known, he maintained, he might have found a way for her to have it. Or she might have had to wait. Anything was better than this. He neatly skipped over his own complicity in the situation by abdicating an important ritual of marriage to his mother-in-law, and stayed angry at Beth for months.

Nothing will be a bigger roadblock to true intimacy than our failure to truly express our needs and feelings to our spouse while continuing our dependence on our parents. Many of us complain about not getting things we've ached for, for years, from our partners. "He should know I want flowers once in a while." . . . "She should realize that I need her to listen to me more often." . . . "He should know that I need to hear him say, 'I love you.' "

But have we ever even asked?

We don't ask, don't get what we want, and keep wanting. Our needs were often anticipated in childhood, and now we're in a new territory, where no one pays such all-consuming attention to what we need.

Instead of running to our parents with our needs, there are questions we have to ask ourselves: How much do I really want this? If it's something I truly need, do I have to depend on someone else to get it for me? Can I get it for myself? Am I being impatient because I'm too used to having all my desires granted in a way that wasn't always healthy for me? Or am I impatient because this is something I've really earned and deserve and can't get?

We may find ourselves married to people who can't fulfill our real needs. If we find that this is true, we must deal with our partner and make a determination about whether such a relationship can go on. But we must be wary of needs that stem from childish impatience, or a tendency to depend on others to give us things we could be achieving for ourselves.

We can perpetuate the pattern of running to the people who will give us the most—particularly our parents—and consequently maintain our dependency. Or we can choose a healthier route of asking for what we need of our partners. There is a healthy balance between independence and enmeshment, and if we struggle with it enough, we can find it.

Searching in Marriage for Our Parents' Idea of Happiness

Many of our attitudes and beliefs about life are repetitions of our parents' beliefs, formed unconsciously without any independent thought or consideration on our part. This is why our parents' expectations of marriage often sound a lot like our own.

We might commit ourselves to a romantic relationship, but this does not mean that our high expectations about love and marriage have been met, or that they finally vanish, for that matter. Many of us find that once we've married, impossible expectations for a person to mirror us, complete us, give us unconditional love, and end all feelings of emptiness haunt us. At worst, impossible expectations of marriage can cause us to never really be satisfied with our partner. In essence, we spend our married lives still searching, still not satisfied.

This is not to say that we aren't in love with the person we commit ourselves to. We are. Yet at times there's an underlying, puzzling sense of dissatisfaction in our relationship, and we can't always put a finger on what's wrong. For some of us, it's a constant sense of having to compromise, of never feeling that what we get from a partner is enough. For many of us it has to do with the lack of financial security we feel in marriage. Giving up childhood dreams of marrying someone rich, who would take care of us, is difficult. So is giving up dreams of someone who will meet all of our needs.

We leave childhood with a head full of warnings about the kind of person we should marry. Inevitably, we marry someone else. There are moments, frustrated and furious with our spouse, when we conclude, "My parents were right."

Sam tells a story about marrying Karen. "My father warned me about her. He said that if I married her, she'd never be mature enough to make me a good wife. He saw her as selfish and not nearly good enough for me.

"He tried to talk me out of the marriage, telling me that I was too young to really be in love. 'Sleep with her if you want to,' he said, 'but don't believe you have to marry her.'

"I thought this particular pearl of wisdom was pretty gross. I had to laugh. Finally, my father was talking to me about sex, and this is what he had to say."

Sam and Karen married, and after five years Sam concludes, "I'm starting to think my father was right, that she's selfish. She spends all of her money on clothes, when we're supposed to be saving her paycheck for the future. She's always complaining that we should go out more. She can forget it. If I don't save some money around here, who will?

"Karen was the one who wanted us to have children. The moment we had them, she wanted to go back to work. She actually expects me to stay home with the kids when they're sick, so she won't lose her job.

"Sometimes I look at her, and I can't believe she's the same woman I married. It's true that Karen's a warm and sensitive woman, but I want someone who's exciting and stimulating. I have to coax Karen into bed. She says she needs more romance. She complains that I don't support her emotionally. Well, what about me? I want a woman who's supportive of me."

What Sam expected was little more than his mother had

done for his father, and what both of his parents told him to expect. We can become critical and disappointed when our spouses don't meet our expectations, or when they don't relate in a way our parents related to each other.

If we're very close to our parents, we may become furious with our partner when he or she won't join us, mesh with our parents as we do, and create one big, happy family. We're torn if they don't want to go to dinner at our parents' home every weekend. We're angry when we hand them the phone and they have little to say to Mom and Dad.

But have we ever really thought about where these expectations come from? So many times we're disappointed about expectations our partners don't meet when we've never really asked ourselves what it would mean for us if they met them. Would we really be happier? Are the things we ask of our partner the things we really need to have in order for us to be happy? Who made the decisions about what we require? Is this what we really think or feel, or is it what our parents expect of us?

We can feel very uncomfortable in marriage when we don't operate according to our parents' desires. While not everything our parents counseled us to look for in marriage is wrong, not everything is right, either. The choices that made our parents happy may not always work for us, and realizing this is the beginning of true separation/individuation. We have to look at our expectations and values and determine which are our own. Seeking all that makes our parents happy in a partner may gain us a spouse who does just that—makes our parents happy, but leaves us unfulfilled.

Hiding in Our Marriage

Wayne believes he has found the answer to dealing with his overprotective, overinvolved parents who, he felt, would never treat him as anything but a baby. He married at eighteen, left New York City with his wife, and relocated in St. Croix, where he and his wife are elementary-school teachers. His parents can't afford to visit very often. They speak once a month on the phone.

Wayne was careful at first to give his parents as little information about his life as possible, lest he be flooded with letters full of advice. Today, they rarely ask questions, and few letters come.

A happy ending? Not really. Wayne feels tremendous guilt at times, especially now that his parents are well into their senior years. He feels angry and bitter about the past, but the truth is, he misses them. Worse, at times he finds himself fighting silent battles with his father in his mind, especially when he has to make a decision. Most of his life, he realizes, has been lived not according to his own real needs and desires, but to prove something to his parents who smothered him, never accepting his right to have opinions of his own.

There are many loved-too-much adult children who attempt to resolve their issues with their parents by marrying. Marriage seems like their only salvation—the only way to take an independent stand. Some grab their spouse and move three thousand miles away to escape the reality of their relationship with their parents.

Those of us who live in close proximity to our parents may attempt to solve our problems in a different way. Some of us will don the protective armor of a full arsenal of defenses whenever we come in contact with our parents. We'll answer questions in monosyllables. We'll disclose nothing.

"I'm careful never to tell my mother much of anything," one man says. "They complain that I'm secretive, but I have no evidence that whatever I tell them won't be shared with the rest of the family and all of their friends. Everything I did as a child, good and bad, was broadcast to everyone they knew."

This man was recently hospitalized for a hernia operation. He swore his wife to secrecy, and told his parents he was on a business trip. "I didn't want my parents there, wringing their hands over my bed. When you have parents who are ready to call the medics when you have a headache, you have to protect yourself."

We'll lie to our parents if we feel we have to. We'll marry early, move away, resolve to share nothing at all with them about our lives. Such escapes do little to dissolve the enmeshment. This childish cat-and-mouse game with our parents means we're still being reactive, rather than active. We hide in our marriages, but we always bring ourselves with us, and the pain of unresolved issues with our parents remains.

The repercussions of unresolved relationships can come back to haunt us. Bob learned this lesson when he married a woman his parents disliked. Bob felt that by marrying Lynn, he had made a huge step into independence. He cut himself off from his relationship with his parents after a particularly unpleasant argument between Lynn and his mother. But somehow, after that, everything Lynn did aggravated him, and they quarreled constantly.

"The truth is, I couldn't allow myself to be happy with Lynn. I kept picking at everything she did. It was like I was looking for her to make me miserable. You see, I made this big Declaration of Independence from my parents, but the guilt I felt afterward was incredible. It was like it was okay to rebel and marry Lynn, but not okay to be happy with her. It would have been too much of a slap in the face to my parents to be happy—worse, somehow, than marrying her in the first place."

Although Bob loved Lynn, his tactic of hiding in his marriage from his parents backfired. Subconsciously, he sabotaged his marriage.

It isn't that Bob was wrong to feel hurt, disappointed, or angry because his parents couldn't accept Lynn. Such feelings are natural. The problem was that Bob couldn't deal with his parents' disapproval openly, or make a true commitment to Lynn, because his parents' disapproval was like a sword over his head.

The only way out of this kind of trap is through it. If you're in such a trap, getting out will require open communication with your parents, rather than an escape from them. It will mean expressing your opinions, and disagreeing when necessary. It will mean becoming more comfortable with conflict and realizing that the expression of your emotions won't destroy you. It will mean asking for help from your spouse, rather than complicity in various schemes.

To break this pattern, we have to realize that physical distance has nothing to do with our enmeshment with our parents. There are adults whose parents are long dead, and still they feel an incredible urge to satisfy, please, and acquiesce to their parents' desires.

We need to recognize that our style of relating to our parents will transfer to other relationships. Whenever we feel smothered or controlled, we'll want to escape. We can be backed into a corner one day, from which we can't run.

If you truly want to work through certain issues with your parents, you have to speak openly and honestly to them about your needs. You have to get in touch with your resentments, disappointment, and feelings of being out of control. Eventually, you will need to share these feelings. It may be necessary to first share the feelings with an understanding friend or a therapist, someone who isn't emotionally involved.

Understand that when we don't deal with these issues, we're never truly free to be who we are. Our goal is not to change our parents, but to change our beliefs, attitudes, and way of relating. If we change the way we relate, we are changing an important dynamic in our relationships. Although we may not change another person, we will change the rules of the relationship and consequently how people relate to us.

Allowing Grandparents to Love Too Much

For parents who have loved us too much, giving them a grandchild can be the ultimate gift—the big payback.

At best, our new role as a parent can cause us to finally understand our own parents. At worst, the grandchild can become a battleground, a repository of all our old conflicts with our parents. We complain that they stuff our child with food. They spoil him. They make us feel inept. We wonder, Who's got the control here? Whose child is this? Our parents think they are more deserving of control because they have so much more experience. Here's a second chance for our parents, who are getting older, to repractice a craft they've refined all of their lives. After all they've done for us, couldn't we at least allow them this opportunity?

Having children can be a natural breeding ground for resentment on both sides. We want to have our cake and eat it, too. They should baby-sit when we need them, but otherwise make themselves scarce. We may not realize it, but we give out mixed messages: Help me; but do it on my terms.

When we have children, we may really need our parents. Their experience has value. The world is getting scary. Horror stories about atrocities in day-care centers make us toss and turn at night. The safest bet for our child seems to be the safety of being with our parents. We don't want them to be overinvolved in the way we choose to raise our children, but we need them at the same time.

There's no easy solution to this problem. An effort to come to an agreement on boundaries and limits regarding your child that will work for both of you is a beginning. Explain what you believe: If everyone is teaching your child different things, the child will suffer. He may learn to be manipulative. He may become confused if the people who love him fail to present a united front.

Most of all, don't expect your parents to be less than human. If you depend on them constantly, leave your child with them all of the time, and always seek their advice, expect them to try to take control or become overinvolved. If you ask them to be a parent to your child, don't be surprised when they do just that. If you want to be in control, then you have to take control—along with the responsibility that comes with it.

Marriage can be a continuation of the childhood roles we played with our parents. We can turn to our parents, rather than our spouse, and never be truly married. We can continue to play out old family patterns. Or we can realize that now that we are adults, our first priority is our marriage. We have an opportunity to create a new pattern of family relationships that doesn't exclude our parents but allows our own independence.

Truly separating from parents who love us too much is a courageous act. It doesn't have to be an all-or-nothing proposition. The fact is, no one ever gets totally free of his parents, childhood frustrations, or disappointments. Breaking free is a process of becoming a little freer each day, and developing more trust in ourselves gradually. It's a process of becoming aware of issues, repulsing the inclination to hide, and having the courage to confront issues head-on.

CHAPTER 8

THE INNER CRITIC

"We know you'll never let us down."

"When I was in high school, I heard, 'Why can't you get straight "A"s like your cousin Sheldon? You're so much smarter than him.'

"I started applying to colleges and got, 'Why can't you get into Yale? Your cousin Sheldon did, and he doesn't have half as much going for him as you do.'

"Finally, I graduated and got my first job. 'Why did you take such a low salary?' my father asked. 'Your cousin Sheldon's making ten thousand more a year.'

"I learned a great truth from all of this: I really hate my cousin Sheldon."

—Dale, age 30, engineer

"I feel so stupid; if only I were as smart as . . ."
   "I hate my body; if only I looked like . . ."
   "My life's so boring; why can't it be like . . ."
   "I'm never good enough; if only I could be like . . ."
Sound familiar? For many of us, the voices of judgment and self-criticism have become a way of life. An "inner critic" lurks inside of us, sapping our energy with constant thoughts that we're not bright enough, attractive enough, or good enough.
   Why are we such self-doubting adults? With so much

love, praise, and attention in childhood, how did we fall into the trap of constant self-criticism?

The spark that ignites a lifetime of self-criticism for the child who was loved too much is not so much his parents' criticism but their great expectations for him—expectations that breed a sense of failure. Listen as several adults recall some of their early experiences:

Brian: ''My dad is a real hot professional piano player. When I was six, he started giving me lessons. What started out as fun really turned into a nightmare. I'd be practicing in the living room, and every few minutes he would yell out from the bedroom, 'No! It's F sharp not F natural!,' or 'G minor, not major!,' or 'Watch your tempo, you're speeding up!' After a while, I was afraid to touch the keys. Whenever my parents had a party, I'd be sick the whole day, because I knew I'd have to play piano for their friends. All I can say is that Beethoven must have been rolling in his grave, because the *Pathétique* was completely shot to hell. Every time I even get near a piano today, it feels like my dad is lurking in the wings, waiting to correct me.''

Alison: ''I was never spanked, yelled at, or grounded. But any of those would be far better than when Mom turned to me and said, 'I'm very disappointed in you.' I nearly died. It wasn't like she was disappointed with something I *did*, it was that she was disappointed with *me.*''

Andy: ''Every year at Christmas, we had a house full of people, and my brother and I would be 'on display' for the relatives. When the party was over, we got bawled out no matter how good we had been, and for the most ridiculous stuff. 'You were too quiet'; 'You didn't kiss your grandmother'; 'You forgot to show Aunt Judy your swimming medal'; 'Don't you know how to hold a fork?' No matter what we did, it was never enough.''

Billie: "My sister and I got along as well as most and better than some, but my mother expected us to be best friends, to never argue, and to be close all the time. She couldn't accept that we were very different people. There were times we couldn't stand each other. My mother would get depressed because we didn't fit her picture of the perfect family. Maybe if she had just let us be, we would have been closer. But she interfered all the time and tried to force us to be close. Today, just being in the same room with my sister makes me uncomfortable."

Christine: "I was in an advanced math class, and lost from the first day. I said, 'Mom, I've got to drop this class and take something else.' She said, 'No, you can do it. Just study harder.' I failed every test. It was just beyond me. Even the teacher tried to talk to my mother, but it didn't help. She told me she'd rather see me get a 'D' in an advanced class than be in a regular one, and that I just wasn't trying."

Evan: "The message I always got from Dad was to be the best. It was never *do* your best, but *be* the best. Whether it was in sports, school, or even with my friends, I always felt his expectations breathing down my neck. With him, it's not how you play the game, but whether you win or lose."

Expectations. It seems there's nothing we can't do or be if we try hard enough. Or so our parents tell us.

While there's nothing wrong with parents believing in their children or wanting them to succeed, children who are loved too much are often victims of unrealistically high expectations of what they should or shouldn't do. By unrealistic expectations, we mean those that are inflexible, push us past our limits and toward our parent's perfectionistic goals, stress "looking good" and people-pleasing over developing inner qualities, and are motivated out of a need to control and protect us rather than love us.

A simple "You can do better" can be devastating if

"better" is beyond our limits and nothing is ever good enough. Such unrealistically high expectations set the stage for what psychiatrist Karen Horney termed the "tyranny of the shoulds":

> He should be the utmost of honesty, generosity, considerateness, justice, dignity, courage, unselfishness. He should be the perfect lover, husband, teacher. He should be able to endure everything, should like everybody, should love his parents, his wife, his country; or he should not be attached to anything or anybody, nothing should matter to him, he should never feel hurt and he should always be serene and unruffled. He should always enjoy life; or he should be above pleasure and enjoyment. He should be spontaneous; he should always control his feelings. He should know, understand and foresee everything. He should be able to solve every problem of his own or of others, in no time. He should be able to overcome every difficulty of his as soon as he sees it. He should never be tired or fall ill. He should always be able to find a job. He should be able to do things in one hour which can only be done in two or three hours.

Many of us can identify with the tyranny of the shoulds. Because we love our parents too much, when we can't meet their expectations, we feel we have failed. The inner critic is born, and continues to feed on verbal and nonverbal messages from parents and other people important to us. The higher these expectations are, the more devastated and critical of ourselves we become when we can't meet them.

Consider the criticism that Brian, the young man in one of the preceding stories, received from his father. Brian's piano lessons were a fiasco because of his father's high expectations. His conscious intention was to be helpful, yet his perfectionistic standards for his son created a larger problem. Whenever Brian sounded a note on the piano, his father's radar system honed in. Brian's father focused not on what Brian did right, but what he did wrong. The quest for perfection was clearly more important to his father than the enjoyment of playing music.

Brian's father's constant critical evaluations of Brian's playing led to a severe case of performance anxiety. Over time the piano became associated with tension instead of pleasure. Parents who place unrealistically high expectations on their children indirectly teach them to associate pressure with performance. The higher those expectations, the more likely the child is to fall short.

As adults, we excel at embellishing the critical messages we received as children: "You can do better" becomes "I'm not good enough." "You can't do that, let me do it for you" becomes "I'll fail if I do it for myself"; "Don't argue with me" translates to "I'm not supposed to think for myself"; "Always be nice to people" turns into "I should never let anyone know that I am angry"; and "We love you when you're good" becomes "I will only be loved if I become successful. I have to look perfect or be perfect in everything I do or I'm a failure."

While we may not be consciously aware of these early messages, they affect our thoughts and behavior. Jeff, a thirty-four-year-old singer, describes his constant battle with his own inner critic. "When people say I'm a good singer, I always think they're just handing me a line. Maybe I'm neurotic, but I just can't stop comparing myself to all the great singers like Stevie Wonder and Ray Charles. No matter how many lessons I take, no matter how hard I practice, I just never sound good enough.

"In the late 1970's, working my way through college, I started this band with a few of my buddies. We threw together some old Beatles and Stones tunes, and we scored a steady Saturday night gig at this dive called the Hairy Banana. Forty dollars a man and free drinks.

"The people who came to hear us play were totally loose, most of them drunk out of their minds. No one was even listening when I sang, but it didn't matter. In the middle of a song, I'd look out at the audience. I'd see people joking and laughing at the bar and think, They're laughing at me. They think I sound lousy. I'd finish a song sure that everyone was thinking, What a jerk. He can't sing!

"People applauded, and I couldn't understand why. It blew my mind when people came up to me and told me what a great voice I had. It just didn't fit.

"I've been playing music on and off for almost twenty years now. I've come a long way from the Hairy Banana. Still, I've never become less self-conscious. People tell me that I'm too hard on myself. I don't know. I just hate that I don't sound like Stevie Wonder."

A thriving inner critic, nurtured on repetitive negative thoughts, subverts self-esteem. He's thrilled when he catches us in the game of comparing ourselves to other people. He cheers when we become vulnerable to the criticism of people we empower with the right to judge us. Like a movie camera, we begin to project our inner judgments onto others, feeling we're being criticized even when we aren't. Criticism becomes cozy and familiar, hard to resist.

Jeff's story illustrates the deceptive and subtle "tricks" of the inner critic: comparison thinking, projection, invalidating compliments, inflating problems, and black-and-white thinking. If we're as self-critical as Jeff, we may not even notice these distortions in our thinking until they immobilize us.

Let's look at each of the deceptions of our inner critics, one at a time.

Comparison Thinking

There's an enormous emphasis on success in our society. How we look, how much money we make, where we live, and whom we know become reflections of how we feel about ourselves. Caught up in a whirlwind of competition, we rarely feel good enough. Envious of our neighbor's new car, our best friend's money, and our coworker's promotion, we criticize ourselves for not being as "good" as they are. If only we were as successful as these people we envy, we would be happy, we think.

This focus on competing with others is compounded when we grow up in a home where parents love too much. We hear messages like, ''Why can't you be more like your brother?''; ''You know you're a better athlete than Tom, so how come he made the team?''; ''Billy Smith's mother told me he got all 'A's. They're so proud of him''; ''Mary got into Stanford; isn't that wonderful?'' The comparison game never ends.

When parents want so much from us, the stakes of life are high. Our self-esteem becomes tied to our achievements. We judge ourselves on what we do—not on who we are.

It feels like we're loved most when we succeed. Our parents seem to glow when we finish at the top. And while there's nothing wrong with our parents' pride in us and their encouragement, we wonder if we're still loved as much when we fail. We want so much to please them. When we're looking good, they're looking good. But, when we fall short, as we must at times, we feel we've let them down.

The messages we receive as children become the core of our belief system as adults. Life becomes an endless series of competition between ourselves and others, with our inner critic as scorekeeper. We can never relax.

Jerome, a forty-four-year-old car salesman, recalls how comparison thinking ruined his winter vacation that he'd looked forward to for months. ''St. Thomas was beautiful, the weather was perfect, and everything was wonderful, until I decided to sign up for a Ping-Pong tournament. I was matched with this bald guy from New Jersey. After about ten seconds of the match, I could see it was for blood. He was pretty good. We rallied back and forth like it was a matter of life and death. After two deuces at the end of the game, this jerk won by two points.

''Here I am on vacation, trying to relax. I realize I'll never see this guy again, but I'm devastated because I lost the silly tournament. I spend the rest of the day replaying each game, thinking back to every single shot I blew. I'm too antsy to sit on the beach, so I sulk in my room. The day's ruined. My wife, who can't understand what the big deal is all about, tries to cheer me up, but it doesn't help. Even now, I cringe when I think of that Ping-Pong game, and how I lost by two points.''

Jerome's story illustrates some of the costs of a harsh inner critic. It lures us into the games of competition and comparison, yet these games are never fair. Our inner critic is never objective. He is always far more concerned with our failings than our successes. What was this loss of a Ping-Pong game to Jerome? Did it mean his life was a failure, without meaning, without value? Such thoughts seem ridiculous, yet a harsh inner critic is always a master at making us feel miserable when we don't compare well enough to others, even in skills that are relatively unimportant to us.

Projection

Much like a camera projects its images onto a screen, our inner critic projects its negative thoughts onto people in our lives. The following are examples of projections in everyday life:

''When I walk into a room full of people, it seems like everyone is talking about me.''

''Men are all controlling and autocratic, just like my father.''

''My boss is always nice to me, but I know he's waiting, like a vulture, for me to make a big mistake.''

We all tend to project to some extent. This in itself is not a problem. However, when it causes us to feel constantly anxious, to avoid people and opportunities, and to become immobilized by the judgments of others, then the inner critic has gone too far.

To better understand your style of projection, make a list of the messages you give to yourself about yourself. Compare this list with your assumptions of how you think others view you. How are these lists similar? How often have you been surprised by compliments when you thought you were going to be criticized? Begin to check out your assumptions. Identify your projections. In time this process will free you from the distortions of your own thinking.

Invalidating Compliments

Sometimes it's praise rather than criticism that is handed out in excess in our families: "Cindy is the most beautiful girl in her class"; "Marcie is a genius"; "Tommy can do anything if he tries"; "Mary is always a perfect angel." Compliments come flying like confetti at a hometown parade.

It's difficult to believe that praise could have any negative effect on children and cause them to become self-critical. However, sometimes this type of encouragement, if excessive, can be harmful rather than helpful. If from the time we learn to toddle, we continually hear how wonderful, how beautiful, and how smart we are, we may find that we are being set up for a harsh dose of reality when we leave the safety of our homes.

At school we are often stunned as we learn that all of our reviews are not so favorable: "Susie White called me a toad face . . . Mrs. Franklin said I was lazy and spoiled . . . Joey Lee got to be starting first baseman instead of me, and it's just not fair."

We start to feel suspicious and insecure. We wonder, Could my parents have been lying? Where do I really stand? If I can't trust my parents, whom can I trust?

In an attempt to protect ourselves, we stop believing compliments. It's safer. We smile complacently when anyone tells us how wonderful we are, but we don't really buy it anymore.

When praise is overused, children become dependent on others for validation. Conversely, they never learn to recognize their achievements and validate themselves. As a result, self-esteem fluctuates wildly as the individual keeps looking into the eyes of others to find out whether or not he or she is okay. Such a person becomes a people-pleaser, willing to do almost anything to get praise.

Another result of too much praise is that our self-esteem becomes based on achievements. Making the swim team earns much praise from the father who needs his son to achieve in order to feel good about himself. But if this is the only time the child receives any praise, he learns that when he does not meet others' expectations, he has failed. Such a person grows up a victim to a harsh inner critic who demands achievement and assaults self-worth with each passing verdict.

If our self-esteem becomes contingent on praise, our goal becomes to elicit praise from others in whatever way we can. We grow into adults who don't always know that what we learn and accomplish is for our own development—not for someone else's pleasure. As a result, we rarely experience the joy of learning or understanding what would really make us happy or content. We perform for praise, rather than inner fulfillment.

Too much praise also makes us mistrustful of others. When children receive praise for almost everything they do, they tend to become suspicious of the truth. Children who are loved too much are praised excessively for singing off-key, for dancing out of step, for making sounds barely approximating music from an instrument.

There's nothing wrong with praising children for their efforts, if it's clear that the effort is what's being praised. But when we're praised excessively, messages received outside of our homes are rarely as positive as those of our parents. Our music teacher will tell us to keep a steady rhythm. The singing teacher will tell us to keep on pitch. Whom do we believe?

What are our true capabilities? We're not sure. There's no objective way to evaluate our true competency, which was so often inflated by our parents. "You can do anything" translates into "You can do nothing," because we get no firm sense of what we can and cannot do.

A constant overassessment of our strengths can form a basis for our self-criticism. People who loved us very much told us that we were the strongest, the most beautiful, and the best. The world showed us that we were fallible human beings, sometimes accomplishing wonderful things but sometimes failing. We haven't lived up to our birthright. Such feelings can follow us throughout our lives, making us believe that nothing we ever do is good enough.

Inflating Problems

Parents who love too much are never more vital than when they are actively involved in solving their children's problems. Fueled by their own inner critics, parents who love too much have an incredible radar system for problems. They are intuitive. They are perceptive. They are unstoppable when it comes to their kids. They have an insatiable desire to protect their children.

To *protect* one's child is instinctive and healthy. To *overprotect* one's child is destructive. If parents shine a spotlight on every minor mishap their child encounters, they inadvertently create an atmosphere focused on problems.

This is true in Jill's family. She admits, "My parents fawn over me in a way that a lot of people probably find sickening. When I had problems in public school, they took me out and sent me to private school. When I was seventeen and my boyfriend broke up with me, my folks sent me on a skiing weekend in Aspen so that I could take my mind off it. When my parents say, 'How are you?,' I know they're really saying, 'Tell us what's bothering you, tell us how we can make it better.' "

In some families, the only conversation that exists between the parents and the children is focused on problems. As one women put it, "If I didn't talk to my mother about my diet and how much trouble I have trying to lose weight, or if I never mentioned my job and how much I hate it, I can't imagine what we'd talk about."

But our parents don't always see our world accurately or objectively. Problems tend to become magnified. Anxiety distorts perception, and our whole relationship with our parents can be one of "helper" and "helpless."

Sometimes we feel that our parents love us most when we're in trouble. Consequently, many of us learn to manipulate by creating problems to enlist our parents' love. Being melodramatic about our problems can cause our parents to wring their hands over us in a way that is so comforting. Who else in our lives will care this much? We make some of our problems much bigger than they are.

We tend to play out these childhood patterns in our adult relationships. Some of us attempt to manipulate others as we did our parents, by spilling out our problems and magnifying them. Unfortunately, others are not so apt to play our game.

When we shape our lives from the perspective of our inner critic, we develop many self-defeating patterns: We need approval to feel okay. We begin to avoid people and opportunities because we fear rejection. We procrastinate because it takes so much energy to do things perfectly. We have difficulty sharing our feelings with people because we fear our weaknesses will be exposed. Our learning ability lessens as our "inner critic" beats us up every time we make a mistake. Worst of all, a self-critical nature can stand in the way of relationships with others. When we're harsh on ourselves, it's easy to be hard on others. This pushes people we care about away.

There are hefty emotional costs for a self-critical style of thinking: low self-esteem, an inability to make decisions, joylessness, fear of success, guilt and shame, a defensive style of relating, and a lack of creativity. Let's look more closely at each of these costs.

Low Self-Esteem

Self-esteem is a barometer of how we feel about ourselves; a running self-assessment of how well we score against our own expectations of ourselves. Children who were overparented often fare very poorly in such a self-assessment.

Self-concept is developed in early childhood. From a variety of verbal and nonverbal messages, we learn about who we are. As children, we are unable to discriminate truth from fiction. Because we confuse opinion with fact, we listen to the expectations of others and internalize them into expectations for ourselves. No one's expectations are more important to us than our parents'.

As a result of this internalization process, we actually

develop two different senses of who we are. The first is a set of rules as to how we *should* be. The second is a self-observation of how we *are*. If our parents had unrealistically high expectations for us, there is usually a larger difference between these two viewpoints when we become adults.

Marsha sought therapy because her low opinion of herself caused her to be so insecure about her work and ask so many questions of her supervisor that she was overlooked for promotions and excluded from major projects where she might have had a chance to prove herself.

Marsha was asked to compile separate lists of how she saw herself, and how she believed she should be. Marsha's list follows:

I AM	I SHOULD BE
5'2"	5'6"
a little chubby	thin and fit
plain-looking	gorgeous
shy	outgoing and funny
single and lonely	married to a doctor
depressed	always happy

In every category, Marsha "falls short." From these lists, it's not hard to understand why Marsha never felt that she was good enough.

But a further question remains: Whose expectations were these really? In the process of counseling, Marsha saw that she was living out the values and expectations of her parents and society, rather than her own. She recalls her childhood and says, "My parents loved me a lot, but they were always telling me how I could do more. Even their compliments were things like, 'This is really great, and I know if you try harder, you'll do even better next time.' "

Why didn't these compliments about her potential motivate Marsha and make her feel better about herself? After thinking about it, Marsha concluded, "No matter how good I was doing, it was never as good as I could do. I was always hearing that I had great potential. To me, talking about my potential isn't acknowledging. It's like the difference between promises and results. To me, when someone says I have great potential, it's a false acknowledgment; a compliment with shit on it. It's a putdown of where I am today.''

Our parents' grandiose ideas of what we should be able to accomplish can result in unrealistic expectations of ourselves. When Marsha learned to set realistic goals, and accept herself as she was, she stopped wandering through life, looking to others for direction, and became much less critical of herself.

But setting realistic goals isn't all we must do. The development of self-esteem is also directly related to our mastery of tasks and our resulting feelings of competency. Competence is the experience of having sufficient ability to perform a selected task. Parents who love too much, in an attempt to make life easier for their children, inadvertently sabotage their children's opportunities for gaining this sense of competence. As they rescue their children by taking control, they deprive them of the necessary tools and experiences to build a sense of competence and mastery over their world.

Children who were overprotected rarely learn to depend on themselves. They aren't given enough experience in trusting their instincts or their own unique abilities; so they learn to rely on the abilities of others. As a result, they develop a feeling of inadequacy.

Our self-esteem affects everything we do: the quality of our work, the quality of our relationships, the love we express, and the depth with which we allow ourselves to experience life. We respond to people and events from our perception of who we are. If we feel bad about ourselves, we're likely to react to situations with caution and defense. We may avoid opportunities for fear of criticism and exposure. Or we may attack others first if we think they are out to harm us.

Low self-esteem is a multigenerational problem. We cannot give to our children what we do not have. If our parents had a harsh inner critic invalidating their every success, we will tend to repeat this process. To break this cycle, we must cultivate awareness of our needs and concentrate on developing our inner strengths and sense of competence.

Difficulty Making Decisions

Parents who love too much care for us so intensely that they feel compelled to rescue us at the first sign of a struggle. Whether it's help with a homework assignment when we're nine years old or completing our tax forms when we are thirty-nine, our parents are the first to jump in with the answers. Taking control is second nature for them.

When we were young, their advice provided a springboard for our own thoughts and ideas. But as we grow into young adults, too much of it becomes a way of keeping us helpless and dependent. One woman explains, "My mother always brings up my sister, whose life is a mess, whenever she wants to convince me to take her advice or do things her way. 'See, your sister never listened to me, and look what happened.' Well, my sister may have messed up her life, but at least she has a life of her own. I'm still asking my mother to pick out my clothes for me. How old am I? Thirty-three."

Our parents take control because it makes them feel useful, and because they can't stand to see us in pain. Over time we learn to instinctively look into their eyes for the answers. We depend on them because we have never really learned to depend on ourselves. Consequently, making decisions for ourselves becomes nearly impossible.

Mark, a computer consultant, recalls his immobilizing battle-making decisions when he opened his own business. "After putting it off for at least a year, I finally decided to get business cards and stationery for my new office. I guess there are people who go into a store and decide what they want in about five minutes. For me, it was a whole production, I called a graphic artist, who dropped by my office with samples. My worst fears came true when she pulled out three books of logos, eighteen color choices for stationery, dozens of styles for typeface, and at least ten kinds of paper texture. She started flipping through the samples, and my eyes glossed over. I wanted someone else to decide. I sat there trying to appear cool and in control. After all, this was only stationery. Still, I could actually feel myself sweating.''

How did Mark finally make his decision? "Easy. I asked to borrow the books so that I could glance at them at home. I handed them over to my wife, who looked through them and told me what to get in about five minutes.''

Mark's situation is a common one. When we passively give way to our parents' control as children, we never learn to test and trust our own skills. Our inner critic reminds us at every turn that we are not smart enough to make the right choices. So we skillfully manipulate others to take our risks for us. We act cool and indifferent. Yet our lack of competence feeds into our low self-esteem. We may fool others, but we can never fool ourselves.

Joylessness

We complain that life is just not much fun. People sometimes accuse us of being apathetic, bored, and indifferent.

Why do we feel this way? It's because we live in a world of expectations, worry, and frustration. Our inner critic keeps us focused on our shortcomings and inadequacies. He tells us there must always be more. We are unable to fully enjoy our success, because deep down we never feel it is good enough.

When we're so harsh with ourselves, it's easy to be hard on others and to feel unsatisfied with our lives and everyone close to us. This constant dissatisfaction with others causes more joylessness than anything else.

Carole, a recently divorced mother of two, began to realize that this was a problem for her when Jim, her oldest son, told her he preferred to live with his father. "One night he just exploded at me, yelling that as far as I was concerned, he could never do anything right. He was happy with the way he was. Why couldn't I accept him?''

Carole admits, "I'm the kind of person who always sees the glass as half-empty instead of half-full. Jim's shy and quiet. I kept nagging that he should make friends and go out more. I hated to see him miss out on all of the fun things in high school, while he sat in his room playing music. Rather than being happy about all of the things that were right about Jim, like his good grades at school and his musical talent, I could only see all the things that were wrong."

With counseling, Carole began to see that the problem wasn't so much her constant criticism of her son but her own harsh judgments of herself. She became aware that some of the messages she received as a young child were still haunting her today. "My parents weren't the kind of people to give compliments, at least not to us," she confides. "If I brought home a good report card, they never said anything nice about it. They acted like it was expected. And no matter how well I did at school, my father always had plenty of suggestions for how I could improve. He'd make these lists and tack them on the refrigerator. He called them goals, but they were really criticisms."

Carole got a message from her father that nothing she did would ever be good enough. Because she loved him and wanted his approval, she set out on an endless quest for perfection. It was a "perfect" setup for failure. Years later, she was horrified to find herself saying the same critical words to her son that had once made her cringe as a child.

The pain of realizing that her criticism was destroying her relationship with her son taught Carole a lesson. There were parts of herself that she judged bad, such as her own lack of close relationships with friends since her divorce. She had always been uncomfortable making new friends, and lately she'd avoided a lot of social functions and chances to meet new people because she was uncomfortable being newly "single." Since she saw these traits as unacceptable in herself, she reacted negatively when she recognized them in her son.

Once she began to accept such "unacceptable" traits in herself, she became much less critical of her son. Carole took a hard look at the way she tended to focus on the negative instead of the positive, and became more patient with herself.

Many of us are as self-critical as Carole. We know that judgments and criticism are no-win games with heavy costs, yet we let our inner critics hold our happiness hostage. Why? Possibly because we erroneously feel our self-criticism brings big payoffs, too.

If we're taught early in life that the harder we try, the more "perfect" we are, we become hard on ourselves. We may put ourselves down, hoping that it will pay off in affection, friendship, or support.

Sometimes it appears to work. When we adopt the role of "victim," and tell others how awful we are, how depressed we are, and how sad life is, we hook them into playing the complementary role of "rescuer." They try to make us feel better about ourselves by encouraging us. But praise we receive through this kind of maneuver seldom boosts our self-esteem, or does much for our basic feelings of joylessness. In fact, when we continually put ourselves down, those who care for us become frustrated. They begin to tune us out or avoid us.

Fear of Success

Children who were loved too much are often bright and talented people who seem to have an inability to follow through on many of their dreams. Some blame themselves for being lazy. Others make the case that they're really not smart or talented enough. Still others say that they just don't care about success. While all of these factors may play a part, they are essentially defenses that disguise a fear of success.

Max, for example, has bounced from one meaningless job to the next over the last ten years. Although he is a highly creative person, he can never seem to get started on any of his ideas. In therapy Max begins to explore his past.

"It seems to me that the higher you climb, the farther you're bound to fall. I think that's the thing that scares me about success—this incredible burden of responsibility attached to it. Once you succeed, people expect it all the time, and that's a lot of pressure."

When Max was growing up, his father was director of city planning in their community. Active in town politics, photographed and quoted in local newspapers, Max's father was the entire town's picture of success.

In eighth grade, Max ran for student-council president. "I'd been on the student council for three years, and I don't think I really wanted to be president, but my dad had been hinting since sixth grade that I was a 'chip off the old block' and how proud he would be if I turned out to be a class officer.

"The thought of giving a speech to the entire school was terrifying. My dad told me not to be silly, and lectured me on how 'it runs in the family.' As it turned out, he got so involved in the campaign that he ended up writing my whole speech. It didn't sound like me at all. It was something about the youth of America marching on to change the world. Pretty esoteric for a bunch of kids, but he assured me that it was the greatest.

"I'll never forget how scared I was giving that speech, especially since all the other speeches had to do with more school dances and more freedom. I must have stumbled on every other word. It was the most embarrassing day of my life.

"Two days later, the election was held. I got slaughtered. I walked through the streets for at least two hours, because I couldn't stand the thought of going home. When I finally got there, my dad was waiting on the front steps, with a big smile on his face. When I told him I lost, he was ready to go to school and demand a recount, and if my mother hadn't stopped him, he would have. If I can pinpoint one moment in my life where I developed my whole theory of success, that would be it."

Many adult children like Max are immobilized by the

weight of their parents' hopes and dreams. The more they succeed, the more their parents expect of them. It's easier not to get on the ladder to begin with. In the process of avoiding success, however, they sentence themselves to a lifetime of mediocrity.

Another reason adults who were overparented fear success has to do with the fear that if we become independent and competent, we'll lose our emotional safety net. Henry, for example, is twenty-seven and lives in his childhood home with his aging mother. He works part time at a grocery store, a job he dislikes. "But I can't think of anything else I'd really want to do. I don't know, I guess I'm just stuck. I probably should move out, but who would take care of Mom? Since Dad died, she's hated to be alone. So now she takes care of the rent, and I help her out around the house."

Henry has a brother, Frank, a financial vice president, who lost his job months ago, when his company was the target of a takeover. "My mother wouldn't give Frank two cents now. She says Frank can take care of himself. All the years he was a big shot, he only came over once a month, and she still resents it. I feel sorry for the guy now."

To Henry, becoming a success and having a life separate from his parents meant losing an emotional safety net. To him, it was simple. His brother had succeeded, lost the safety of his mother's protection, and then failed. Now, he was out in the cold.

But there were a lot of other underlying reasons for Henry's mother's rejection of Frank that had nothing to do with success. One, Henry admits, was that Frank would never allow his mother to control him. Another was that his mother had wanted him to take over the family business when his father died, and Frank was too involved and happy in his career to leave it. His success didn't cause him to lose the safety net. He lost it because he no longer needed it.

It is possible to succeed and still have a caring, close relationship with our parents. For failing, people like Henry often get protection. This can be a powerful incentive. But Henry also got a life lacking in personal fulfillment. It was no bargain.

Children who remain dependent as Henry did provide meaning and purpose for their parents. They aren't thrilled about their children's failures but take on their responsibilities out of love and a desire to give their children some happiness. A lifetime of caretaking is not easily broken. Both sides are all too familiar with their roles. We may resent these roles but be unable to give up the perks in exchange for our own independence. We don't really want to rock the boat. We may fall over the side and drown. So if we unconsciously choose to remain helpless and dependent, we protect ourselves from our fears of failure and protect our parents from their fears of losing us.

The Guilt Trip

Adult children who were loved too much frequently fall victim to feelings of guilt. What does this emotion really mean? Why does it have such a powerful hold on our lives? Why are overindulged, overprotected children such prime targets for this self-destructive feeling?

Children who were loved too much are constantly tormented by an excessive form of neurotic guilt. Psychoanalyst Selma Fraiberg compared the neurotic conscience to a Gestapo headquarters whose function is "mercilessly tracking down dangerous or potentially dangerous ideas and every remote relative of these ideas, accusing, threatening, tormenting in an interminable inquisition to establish guilt for trivial offenses or crimes committed in dreams."

Guilt is a complex emotion. It's really a smoke screen for two underlying emotions: anger and fear. A case in point is George, a thirty-six-year-old writer, who describes the weekly visits to his parents' home:

"Every Sunday night, Marcia and I pack up the kids and go over to see my mom and dad. Driving the forty miles out to the suburbs, with Marcia complaining the whole way and the kids fighting in the backseat, I wonder, Why am I doing this?

"We get there and Mom's depressed. Tonight, she's griping about my sister, who hasn't been over to see her in two weeks. When my sister's there, she complains about me. She keeps a scorecard of how many times a month each of us visits her.

"My kids ask if we can go home so many times that I finally bribe them with five bucks to get them to shut up. Now, Marcia's really angry at me.

"We drive back to the city in silence. Now, I've got guilt up to here. I've got mother guilt. I've got father guilt. I've got wife guilt.

"Forty years old. Ten years of dragging my family out to see my parents. That's five hundred and twenty Sunday nights, and an equal number of Rolaids. And for what? Just so I don't have to face my fear that I'll tell Mom we're not coming anymore and she'll kill herself."

George's words reflect his acute sensitivity to his own feelings of guilt. Yet underneath, he is less aware of his "unacceptable" feelings of fear and anger.

George suppresses his anger at his mother for fear that she will be devastated if he openly expresses it. In an attempt to protect both of them, he turns it back on himself in the form of self-punishment.

He also chokes back his anger and frustration toward his wife for fear of her disapproval, abandonment, and possible retribution. Again, he turns it back on himself and feels like a failure.

He swallows his anger at his kids' behavior because they're only saying out loud what he feels and can't express. He internalizes his rage at being trapped, and reaches for another antacid tablet.

Trapped between his sense of obligation and his own frustration over family relations, he is left immobilized and guilt-ridden.

George grew up in a family that gave with strings attached. In return he was required to "be a good son." To many parents who love too much, being a good child is to love, honor, and obey one's parents at any cost. To challenge their rules is to be bad. If we had experiences similar to George's, any step in the direction of disobeying our parents' rules is a trigger point for our guilt reflex. As a defense, we victimize ourselves, and as a result we feel unlovable, unworthy, and self-blaming.

This sensitivity to guilt is exacerbated when we grow up with a martyr parent. Martyr parents manipulate their children's behavior by intentionally inflicting guilt. Consider this common scenario:

Mom: Are you coming to brunch on Sunday?
James: Sorry, Mom, I can't, I have too much work to do.
Mom: Oh, I understand. I guess all of my children are too busy for me these days.
James: It's not that at all! I would be glad to come Wednesday night, when I'll have more time.
Mom: I remember when you were a baby. I was so busy then with all three of you, but never too busy to be there when you needed me.

Martyr parents are masters of manipulation. With their arsenal of verbal and nonverbal guilt-inflicting messages, they maneuver their children into the position of compliance. Children who were loved too much have few resources to deflect this guilt and to maintain any sense of objectivity. So they suppress their emotions and walk on eggshells around their martyr parent.

However, when we are not honest with our feelings, we are like a time bomb waiting to explode. For we can only hold in feelings so long. This "explosion" may take the shape of an inappropriate blowup, an emotional or physical breakdown, or even a suicide attempt. Coupled with an array of psychosomatic symptoms such as headaches, ulcers, or high blood pressure, we are like a boiling pressure cooker with the lid held on tightly.

Guilt can be used as a way of punishing ourselves. We wallow in self-deprecating thoughts in an attempt to do penance for our "sins." Irrationally, we feel that the more we suffer, the more we will be forgiven. Unfortunately, it just doesn't work that way. Playing the victim and suffering just keep us from getting to any solution.

We also use guilt as a way of manipulating others. Children who were loved too much know that their parents can't stand to see them in pain. Some take advantage of this leverage to manipulate their parents by playing up their inner pain. The worse they appear, the more likely they are to enlist the rescuing parent. In this way, we don't have to take responsibility and action in our lives. We don't have to own our anger or fear. We remain children.

Guilt is immobilizing and prevents us from taking positive action. It focuses us on the past, which we can't change, instead of the present, which we can do something about. Underneath our feelings of guilt often lies a more insidious and self-destructive emotion: shame.

While both of these emotions are generically associated with feelings of self-blame, remorse, or worthlessness, there is a clear and important distinction between these two emotions. Guilt is recognizing, I have done something wrong. Shame is feeling, There is something wrong with me.

Thoughts such as the following are evidence of feelings of shame:

If you knew me, you wouldn't like me.
I always feel like I'm letting everybody down.
I know I finished second in the class, but inside I feel like a failure.
Why try? I just can't seem to do anything right.

In many ways, shame is a more self-destructive feeling than guilt. It runs deeper. The fault does not lie in our behavior, but in our opinion of ourselves. Shame forms the core of self-doubt and self-criticism.

Ironically, too much love can lead to shame. As pampered children, we know our parents will do almost anything for us. The problem is that if we spend most of our lives allowing them to rescue, guide, and indulge us, we accumulate an enormous sense of debt. Over time we become uneasy with the imbalance. We manage a token gift here and there, perhaps on birthdays or at holiday time, but it does little to assuage our sense of obligation. Our efforts feel so skimpy. It's like trying to pay back the national deficit from our checking account.

But it's not money or gifts our parents want from us. It's compliance with what they wish us to do and be. So to protect ourselves from an onslaught by our inner critics, we distance friends our parents disapprove of; we hide our hurt and anger so that their positions will not be challenged; we choose careers that will make them proud of us. In other words, we often sell out in terms of our true selves.

If you find that persistent feelings of guilt and shame are a problem for you, first ask, "Whose expectations am I trying to live up to? Have I done something that I really feel is wrong? Or is it someone else that is making this decision for me?" Realize that if you are spending your life trying to be the apple of your parents' eye, you may be selling out the person who you really are.

Compile a list of "shoulds" in your life: "I should never spend money on myself. I should never get angry at my children. I should call my parents twice a week. I should never say no when someone asks me for a favor."

How many of these do you really want to keep? Living up to someone else's shoulds is a perfect setup for guilt and shame. Who told you you should do these things? Consider the source. Develop your own style. Accent your own uniqueness. Find out who you are.

A Defensive Style of Relating

When we develop a self-critical style of thinking, we assume that others are judging us just as harshly as we judge ourselves. Feedback from others feels like criticism, and criticism means we've failed. To protect ourselves from attack, we hide our true selves behind a fortress of defense:

Teacher: Jimmy, you need to work a little harder on your spelling.
Jimmy: It's not my fault! My brother took my workbook, and it was a really hard week, and I've been feeling sick.

Wife: Honey, could you please put your tools back in the toolbox?
Husband: Stop nagging me! You're always leaving dishes in the sink and clothes on the floor!

Firing a round of defenses and excuses for our behavior at others when a simple "Okay," "I'm sorry," or "You might be right" would do becomes a habit. Defense is a learned pattern of thought and action intended to protect us from real or imaginary pain. In childhood, it was an adapted response to a threatening situation. In adulthood, it is often a replaying of childhood fears and expectations.

Styles of defense are as individual as one's set of fingerprints, but can nonetheless be grouped into predictable categories. Children who were loved too much most often use the defenses of avoidance, rationalizing, and looking good.

Avoiding people or experiences that we fear will demand too much of us is a primitive form of self-protection. It prevents us from experiencing our fears of rejection and criticism. We figure if we hide out, we can't be hurt. No risk, no pain. Unfortunately, such a defense also insures that we'll live in a world of missed opportunities and isolation.

"There's this really cute girl in my history class," one young man told his friend. "Blue eyes, long hair, and a great smile. I'd give anything for a date with her. But even the thought of talking to her scares the hell out of me, so I don't." By avoiding the girl he's attracted to, this man avoids rejection, but he also avoids acceptance.

Other clues that we are defending ourselves through avoidance are failing to send out résumés, filling out applications messily or incompletely, oversleeping, drifting off into space while others are talking, not returning phone calls, and never making eye contact.

Closely related to avoidance is rationalization. Rationalizing is building a case, no matter how flimsy, that justifies our position and makes us believe that we are right. We justify our position and blame others, finding an excuse for being mad at people who are mad at us. Consider the following example:

Laura: Do you know who put that dent in my car?
Mike: I guess I did, but I was going to get it fixed.
Laura: I can't believe that you didn't even tell me!
Mike: Who are you to talk? Remember when you lost my overnight bag? You're not so perfect. And why are you making such a big deal out of a silly car? Who do you care more about, me or the car?

Again, a simple, "I'm sorry" would do, but people who rationalize are compelled to find ways of justifying their position. To them, admitting fault means "I'm bad," so they protect themselves.

"Looking good" is another defense that masks our true feelings. It involves putting up a "front" that will impress others, rather than sharing who we really are. Such a person becomes achievement-focused and emotionally suppressed, while always fearing that he or she will be accused of being an imposter.

Defenses are used by everyone to some extent. In early life, they helped ensure our survival. Much like the warrior needs armor to protect himself from physical attack, a small child enlists defenses to protect himself from psychological attack.

The major problem with defenses is that they do not provide any real solutions to problems. In fact, they set up more difficult problems than the one they were intended to fix. If we rationalize every problem, take no responsibility, and seem invulnerable, we tend to alienate those around us, create polarized work relations, and feel victimized and unhappy.

Overparented children have a higher tendency toward defensiveness due to the following personality traits:

Entitlement. If we're rarely encouraged to take responsibility for anything we do wrong, and are consistently rescued and overindulged, we begin to believe that we're always right. It seems natural to expect others to cater to us in the same way that our parents did, and we can feel outraged when they don't. We sharpen our defenses to validate our position.

Underlying shame. Underneath our well-groomed package, many of us feel vulnerable. A person who was never able to fully meet his parents' expectations feels a pervasive sense of not being good enough. A defensive style of relating gives the illusion of protection from these feelings.

Fears of engulfment, abandonment, and exposure. A combination of overinvolvement, conditional love, manipulation, and high expectations lead to the development of these primary fears. The overparented child is forced to use defensive strategies to avoid emotional pain he or she assumes is the result of intimate relationships with others. Paradoxically, the more defensive we are with others, the more likely it is that we'll be abandoned, engulfed, or exposed by them.

It is important to remember that defenses are blind spots in our vision. We don't realize when we're being defensive, which is why breaking through our defenses is a difficult job. It requires taking responsibility for our own part in creating problems, and realizing it's okay to be imperfect. Where do we start? By noticing our own styles of defense and making a conscious choice about whether we want to continue the pattern. Friends can help us identify our defensive style, as can a good therapist. Once the pattern is identified, the next task is to take a risk a day. Say, "I'm sorry," or "You could be right," when you feel the urge to defend yourself, and watch what happens and how you feel about it. The more comfortable you are with who you really are, the less urge you will have to be defensive.

Lack of Creativity

Creativity is a process of exploration and discovery. At best, it opens up new pathways of expression. At its more basic, it's in a child constructing his first sand castle. It is not the level of complexity that defines creativity, but the act of creation.

Creativity is born in each of us. While it has been proven through research that genetics plays a role in the development of our personalities, it is primarily our early environmental conditions that encourage or discourage our creative attitude.

A parent who loves too much may stifle the creativity in his children while attempting to do the opposite. Although the parent may provide an endless array of opportunities for outlets, such as tennis lessons, music instruction, or private tutors, sometimes there is such anxious monitoring of the child's progress that the child represses himself in an effort to please the parent.

"When I was a kid, my favorite class used to be art," one woman recalled. "My teacher let us play with water colors, papier-mâché, and clay. I remember making a total mess and having a ball.

"I brought a lot of my 'creations' home to show my mom. 'What is this supposed to be?' she'd ask. I'd say, 'An octopus eating a pizza.'

"She'd get all pissed off and tell me that I wasn't taking my art classes seriously. She told me I should draw things that were real. This is a woman who couldn't tell a Van Gogh from a Picasso but thought she was an art critic.

"My mother had confidence in me, though. I have to admit that. If I had an interest in art, she was going to see that I had everything I needed to develop it. I got an easel and watercolors and brushes. But it stopped being fun. I couldn't draw the way my mother wanted me to and still enjoy it. The message was, 'Go be an artist, but do it my way.' So I quit."

Creativity is suppressed when someone forces us to comply with his or her standards. Inherent in the creative process is the ability to take risks. Adult children who were loved too much were rarely allowed to risk. They were encouraged to create and achieve, but through the safest, most proven routes.

Children's creative explorations often provoke anxiety in the parent who loves too much. The child who is creating can't be controlled. Creativity encourages us to break the rules. Find new pathways of expression. Be willing to fail. Parents who love too much are so self-conscious about their children that they are unable to allow the freedom that creativity requires. And creativity is nearly impossible with someone breathing down your neck, anxious to see you succeed and rescuing you from your mistakes.

Taking a creative stance is getting in touch with your own unique self. Looking good is the antithesis of creativity. A need to conform, to please others, to be what they want us to be, stands solidly in the way of creativity. No two people are alike. Each person has a different way of perceiving and interpreting life. It is this unique perspective that allows each and every one of us to be creative.

Why hang on to an attitude that carries such a high personal cost? If you're dancing to a familiar song that goes, "I'm not good enough . . . I look awful . . . I need your approval to feel okay," consider this: The inner critic can be disarmed. You can crawl out of the trap of self-criticism and free yourself. Fortunately, there are several ways to combat your inner critic and end his control over your life.

- Awareness is the first step. Compile a list of critical messages you received from each of your parents. The following is a sample:

MOM	DAD
You're too fat	Don't be so shy
I'm disappointed in you	Make me proud of you
You're lazy	Lose weight
You should get better grades	I'm disappointed in you
You should never be angry	You could do so much better
Crying is for babies	Don't ever embarrass me

From early messages, we can come to many negative conclusions about ourselves. Some of these are: "I'm unlovable"; "I'm not good enough"; "I shouldn't share my feelings"; "I'm lazy"; "I'm disappointing my parents"; "I'm a failure."

While many of these statements may be overreactions to our environment, they are honest feelings about ourselves nevertheless, which need to be acknowledged before we can combat them.

Study your own list. How does this compare with the list of critical messages that you give yourself? Do you wish to keep rehashing these messages? Are they really accurate? What do you really believe?

• Get to know your inner critic. Try to visualize him or her. What does your critic look like? A drill sergeant? A perfectionistic schoolteacher? A parent? Have a conversation with this critical part of you. Why does it put you down? What does it need from you? How can you work as a team, rather than as opponents?

• Monitor the behaviors that grow out of your self-criticism. During the next few days, notice how you empower certain people in your life. Do you feel intimidated and "shut down" in certain relationships? Much of this stems from unresolved issues with our parents and significant others that we "transfer" onto similar people in our lives, often authority figures. If this is a problem for you, remember that no one can shut you down unless you give them that power. In the final analysis, we are responsible for our bad feelings.

Once we realize that we're reacting to our boss or coworker in the same manner we once reacted to a father or mother who loved us too much, we're able to change our expectations and reduce other people's power over our feelings.

• Practice accepting yourself more fully. What parts of yourself have you judged as bad? Do you fear anger, jealousy, or vulnerability? If you feel that such traits are unacceptable in yourself, two things will happen: You will be afraid that these traits will be "exposed" by someone else and will be very cautious and defensive in your relationship as a result; or you will react negatively when you see these qualities in others. Once you become aware of these feelings, you can become less critical of yourself and others and begin to accept these "unacceptable" traits. Learning to accept, trust, and appreciate yourself as you are is essential.

- Start looking at criticism from others as feedback. You don't have to accept other people's judgments as facts. There are no strings tying what other people say or think to your own self-worth. Criticism from others only hurts because we translate it into an all-encompassing "I'm bad" rather than taking it for what it is: someone else's opinion of our actions. Have sympathy for your critic. Remember that many people who find fault with others often do so because they themselves feel insecure.

- Remember that it takes courage to kick the criticism habit. You may come up against everything you were once taught as a child. One key is to give yourself credit for your accomplishments. Even small successes should be acknowledged on a daily basis. Lower your expectations of yourself. Make goals attainable.

- When your inner critic becomes a long-winded bore, drown him out. Replace negative, repetitive thoughts with positive statements. Repeat several times each day: "I accept myself, regardless of my imperfections."

Create your own positive messages. Write them down. Tack them up somewhere where they can remind you each day that you have the strength to challenge the messages of the past and to fully accept the person that you are today.

CHAPTER 9

HUNGRY FOR LOVE

"There're people starving in China!"

> "My mother's answer to everything—black eyes,
> bad grades, fights with friends, broken engage-
> ments—is always the same: 'Don't worry about
> it, honey. Have a cookie.' "
>
> —Marci, age 22, manager

Some of us find ourselves in an intimate relationship that
allows us to be comforted without being vulnerable, to
take without giving, and to feel intimate without the risk
of being abandoned. This relationship is with food.

What is the connection between growing up in a home
brimming with excessive love, attention, protection, and
high parental expectations, and the initial development of
an obsession with food, weight, and dieting? It's widely
accepted that abnormal patterns of food consumption are
expressions of underlying problems. Once physical causes
have been ruled out, it's a sign that our psychological needs
aren't being met. Food is being used to meet our emotional needs and to accomplish what we can't accomplish
in healthier, more direct ways.

Food can seem like an elixir to the child who was loved
too much, whose childhood experience resulted in a host
of inner conflicts he has yet to solve. Such a child can use
food in an attempt to accomplish the following:

- to avoid feelings
- to avoid conflict
- to relieve anxiety caused by the high expectations of parents
- to wrest control away from controlling parents, when active resistance is too threatening
- to get into the family spotlight
- to nurture oneself
- to fend off intimacy
- to punish oneself in response to guilt
- to quiet restless dissatisfaction
- to rebel against "looking good"
- to avoid maturity

But, why do we turn to food? Why not alcohol or drugs or some other obsession equally "useful" for this purpose? There's a very good reason for this. Food, and to a certain extent obsessions with food, are socially acceptable. Our entire culture appears obsessed with dieting and weight at times.

Children who were overparented and schooled in "looking good" are keen observers of what's acceptable to others. They find a lot of company in other people equally obsessed with their bodies, their diets, and their weight, and feel safety in numbers.

Unfortunately, a predisposition to using food to fulfill emotional needs can lead to the development of full-blown eating disorders such as bulimia and anorexia nervosa.

Bulimia is an eating disorder characterized by rapid consumption of large amounts of food, or "binges." During a binge, the person often has fears of not being able to stop eating voluntarily. Self-critical thoughts and depression generally follow. Because this type of compulsive eating results in weight gains, the person suffering from the disorder sometimes attempts to prevent gaining weight by vomiting afterward or by abusing laxatives and diuretics.

Anorexia nervosa is a less common eating disorder characterized by self-starvation. It is estimated that between 90 and 95 percent of anorexics are female. The person suffering from this disorder controls her weight through rigidly limiting caloric intake and sometimes also through excessive exercise. Symptoms of the disorder sometimes overlap with the symptoms of bulimia, as the victim may also attempt to prevent weight gain through self-induced vomiting or the abuse of laxatives and diuretics. Terrified of becoming obese, the anorexic sees herself as fat no matter how much she weighs.

Compulsive overeating, while not technically classified by medical experts as an eating disorder, nonetheless plagues many children who were loved too much. The compulsive overeater is obsessed with thoughts about food, dieting, and weight. Eating may be continuous, and food is so rapidly consumed—almost inhaled—that the result is often obesity. Life is a roller coaster of overeating, vowing to diet, feeling anxious, moody, and deprived, and "blowing the diet." The cycle is repeated, making the compulsive overeater feel guilty and hopelessly out of control.

Eating disorders are family illnesses. Our family is the setting in which we became a separate self. When a family member develops an eating disorder, it's a cue that something is wrong within the family, not just within the individual. The family rules, traditions, lifestyle, and practices are not meeting the needs of the individuals, although the person who develops the disorder may be the only one showing the stress outwardly.

In families characterized by obsessive love, closeness, and protection, this is especially hard to see. It's important to parents who love too much that the family present a united, harmonious appearance to the rest of the world. Conflict, distance between family members, and other problems are jammed under layers of denial. On the surface, everything looks fine, except for the fact that a child has developed an obsession with food that is controlling his life.

Not everyone who uses food to fill unmet needs becomes "addicted" or develops bulimia or anorexia. However, if we need comfort, love, or respite from anxiety and we repeatedly turn to food for relief, we set the stage for an unhealthy dependence that can turn into a full-scale

eating disorder. Food works. It will comfort us—but only
for a short time. But until we can find healthier ways of
meeting our needs, we will be hard put to give it up and
recover.

Let's look at each of the ways food may be used to meet
emotional needs separately.

Using Food to Avoid Feelings

Obsessions with food, dieting, and our weight are convenient ways to keep our minds engaged and unavailable for
dealing with our feelings. Jamie, for example, a twenty-
five-year-old administrative assistant, became completely
absorbed with food and dieting when the emptiness of her
marriage became intolerable.

Jamie grew up in a family where everyone eavesdropped
on each other's private conversations, jumped in to answer
questions directed at other family members, and barged
boldly through closed doors without knocking. "You
couldn't even count on any privacy in the bathroom," she
admits. "People strolled in when you were in the shower
or even on the toilet. My feelings were never my own,
either. I was the youngest, and if I had an opinion, four
people stood there dissecting and analyzing it, telling me
why I should feel differently. It was better to say nothing
at all."

Feeling smothered by constant doses of attention and
advice throughout her adolescence, Jamie escaped her parents' control when she married Bill at age nineteen. "All
my life I'd had someone standing over my shoulder, telling
me what to do and how to act. It was the fact that Bill
didn't hang on my words or try to orchestrate my life all
of the time that attracted me so much at first. He was ten
years older than I, which was also a real turn-on. He made
my other boyfriends seem like infants."

Bill was a successful real estate accountant. Although
Jamie knew that he worked long hours and traveled frequently before she married him, she was still surprised at
how often the responsibilities of his career took him away

from her after the wedding. Bill was almost never home. When he was, he'd fall into bed, exhausted, early in the evening, and Jamie would be left alone.

"I didn't know what to do. I wasn't used to being ignored by someone who supposedly loved me. I had no idea how to go about asking someone to give me more attention, or at least to show a little interest in what I was doing. I'd spent most of my life fending off people who were too interested, too intrusive. So I sulked around looking hurt and rejected, hoping Bill would get the message. He never even noticed."

Jamie spent many evenings puzzled and alone in front of the television set with a bowl of buttered popcorn or a pint of Häagen-Dazs for company. "I had always been slightly overweight, but after the wedding I really started to gain. I'd heard that a lot of women gain ten pounds in the first year of marriage, so I laughed it off, telling my friends that it was a sign of contentment."

Jamie recalls her first full-fledged binge vividly. She was at her office one morning, thinking about Bill, and decided to call him at his office. It took his secretary ten minutes to find him, and when he finally came to the phone, he sounded harried and upset. Jamie quickly babbled something about reservations she was thinking of making for the weekend, apologized for interrupting him, and hung up.

"For a long time afterward, I sat at my desk, fantasizing about surprising him at lunchtime by taking a cab over to his office," Jamie remembers. "I imagined walking in and asking his secretary to call him out of some important meeting. He'd come out smiling and put his arms around me. I imagined him proudly introducing me to everyone there, then taking me to some romantic place where we'd talk and laugh together over lunch. I started to cry thinking about this, right at my desk. You see, I knew Bill would never do any of that. He'd probably be furious if I ever stopped by his office in the middle of the day."

Jamie pulled herself together and worked through the day. Feeling childish for crying, she lectured herself that she had a good husband and a great lifestyle. What more could a person expect?

That night, home alone in an apartment that seemed too empty, Jamie stood in the kitchen, suddenly feeling ravenous. "I ate an entire cake that I'd bought to bring over to my mother's house the next day. I just put my fork in at one end and ate through to the other. Then I washed it down with a pint of ice cream. I couldn't stop eating. My stomach was full, but my mouth felt like it could never get enough.

"Looking back, I realize that it was what was happening with Bill that was making me act so crazy. But at the time, I didn't see any connection. All I knew was that after I was done, I felt better than I had all day."

Jamie never spoke to Bill about what she sensed was happening to their marriage. It hurt too much, and Jamie had learned to deny her pain. She continued to overeat compulsively, and consequently gained weight quickly. "All I thought about was food. I was obsessed with it. I tried to control what I ate, but I couldn't. I'd start a diet every Monday and give it up by Wednesday."

Jamie hit rock bottom months later, when Bill told her he was no longer in love with her and that their marriage had been a mistake. "He said he couldn't love someone who didn't love herself enough to take better care of herself. By that time I weighed over a hundred and eighty pounds. I didn't fight him over the divorce. In fact, that night I sat on the phone, crying to my mother, and shoveling in this huge spread of corned beef and potato salad that I'd put in front of me. I swear there was a part of me that said, 'Well, he's gone, and now I don't have to bother trying to diet.' It was years later before I learned to deal with my feelings directly, instead of bingeing over them."

When we're constantly absorbed with food, our weight, our diets, our sudden loss of control, we don't ask, Am I happy with my life? Is this what I really want? Am I still in love with my husband? Does he love me? Is what I feel still important to him? If I share what I'm feeling, will he listen?

We prefer not to think about these things, because

thinking about them would bring feelings we don't want to have. Instead, we eat. In comparison, our problems with food, dieting, and our weight are much easier to deal with than our feelings about our marriages, our careers, our friendships, and other aspects of our lives.

When we're taught in childhood, as Jamie was, that our feelings are not as legitimate as others', we search for ways to stuff what we feel, numb it, or shut it off. Jamie's feelings were always held up to the scrutiny of other family members. Her opinions were minimized, and sometimes even laughed it. It became important to keep a tight lid on what she really felt.

There's no better way to frustrate yourself than to set limits on what emotions you will allow yourself to feel. Compulsive eating is a way to avoid our feelings. So is compulsive dieting. Both are absorptions with food, and passive ways to express hurt, anger, guilt, anxiety, and other feelings that we might not even be aware of.

As children, we were strongly influenced by the unconscious needs of our parents. Today, we still have a tendency to lean toward what they unconsciously wanted us to be, and how they wanted us to act.

So often our parents told us what we should feel as we were growing up, with statements like:

"What do you mean you're not hungry? You must be hungry. Eat!"

"Calm down! Don't get so excited!"

"You're silly to feel guilty when it's not your fault."

"How can you say you're not tired? Go lie down—you're exhausted."

"Don't look so hurt; it's really not such a big deal."

"Don't scream at me. Well-bred children don't lose their temper."

It may have been perfectly fine to express hurt, frustration, and depression, but if we vented anger, the entire family system got upset. Or perhaps our parents kept their composure when we screamed our heads off, but lost it completely when we cried or showed other evidence of our vulnerability. While they didn't hold a sign in front of us that read, THESE FEELINGS ARE OKAY, THESE FEELINGS

ARE NOT, we got the message just the same. We loved our parents, and lived in continuous fear of not being loved and acknowledged by them. We became very vulnerable to their criticism and learned to hide our feelings to protect ourselves.

No longer children, we're still affected by our childhood experiences. We can't turn off the voices of our parents. Somehow, our true feelings seem suspect, open to debate, or clearly unacceptable.

Feelings can't be wishes away, or forced out of our minds. The only option we have is to express them or hold them inside. Obsessions with food, dieting, and weight are indirect ways to express hurt, anger, guilt, anxiety, and other feelings in a way that seems more acceptable to us.

Dealing with feelings directly can be painful. It's much easier to avoid it. We grow up in homes where avoidance is the model. We're encouraged to package ourselves in a way that will be socially acceptable and a source of pride to our parents. We live our lives uncomfortable with the idea of offending anyone with our anger or neediness. Our one emotional outlet is our appetite. Eating makes us feel better for the moment, but never for long. The only thing we can do to feel better in the long run is to deal with what's going on inside of us directly.

Using Food to Avoid Conflict

One man recalls that his mother would grab her chest and accuse him of trying to give her a heart attack whenever they had an argument. "She'd turn beet red and run out of the house to her car, and my father would say, 'Go get your mother! She's liable to drive off a cliff or something.' I'd run out to the garage, swallowing my rage and apologizing like crazy. I knew it was probably an act. But what if it wasn't? I never knew how far she'd go to make a point."

This man's story is an extreme example of how some families react to conflict. However, many of us can remember our parents becoming unglued whenever any of the family members got into an argument.

If you've every wondered why they reacted so strongly, consider this: The child who is loved too much is responsible for holding up his end of the WE ARE THE PERFECT FAMILY banner that is so important to his parents' self-esteem. When there was conflict in your home, your mother or father may have believed it meant they weren't good parents, that they hadn't raised you correctly. They may have believed that conflict shouldn't exist among people who really love each other. Angry outbursts and arguments threatened the facade of "perfect parents" raising "perfect children."

Thinking back about how our parents handled their own conflicts can further explain why they so often tried to prevent us from having ours. Often, we can't remember our father ever expressing his true feelings. We may have grown up watching our mother hold in her anger and frustration, purchasing peace in the family at all costs. We adopted a style of coping with conflict and differences of opinion that was modeled by our parents.

Parents who love too much set few boundaries between their feelings and their children's. Your conflict was their conflict. For this reason, when we were angry or upset, they seemed bent on distracting us from our feelings with offers like, "Let's go out for a ride, dear, and you'll forget all about it." Often they sent us to our rooms to calm down, or otherwise excluded us. In this way, they taught us something they believed—that no good could come from working through these feelings, that dealing with issues between people is fruitless and should be avoided.

If this was our experience, today when we sense we're about to get into a conflict with someone, we look for something to distract us. Often, we choose food.

Elaine, a twenty-seven-year-old mother of three, tells a story about a night when her husband promised to take all the children out bowling so that she could have a much-needed evening to herself. "At the last minute, he said he didn't want to take the baby. So much for my evening to myself."

Elaine kept the baby home with her rather than fight over such a little thing, but found herself in front of the television set with a large bag of cookies, crunching and munching on her anger, while the baby cried in her lap. "I got so disgusted with myself for going off my diet that I really lost it and had something like a fit." She ran to the kitchen, tossed the leftover cookies into the sink, mashed them down the drain and watched them go down the disposal with glee.

It's interesting how so many of us who grapple constantly with dieting and our weight will express all sorts of angry feelings and conflicts in relation to food, and how we're denied it, yet not about anything else going on in our lives. We'll say, "I'm so mad, because I'm on this diet and I can't have any sweets," or "I could shoot myself for going off my diet," or "It really galls me that I look at food and gain weight while everyone else eats like a horse and never gains a pound." Elaine wouldn't argue with her husband about staying home with the baby, but had a fit, instead, with a bag of cookies.

We're very passionate in our fits over food, but will we look at a loved one and say, "I'm so hurt because you don't keep your promises to me," or "You're drifting away from me, and I don't feel like you really understand me or care about what I need"? Will we say, "I'm furious at you for never doing what you say you'll do and for expecting me to give you more than you'll give me"? Elaine felt all of these things, but would never express them because she was afraid of the conflict that would result.

Many of us aren't even in touch with these feelings of rage when we have them, let alone feel comfortable talking about them. We choke back our feelings by choking down food. Then, the next morning, we finally allow ourselves to feel our rage, but over the food we ate the night before rather than what's really going on in our lives. Self-hate, anger, hurt, and disgust erupt in a flood of conflict over what we ate the night before.

Using Food to Relieve Anxiety Caused by the High Expectations of Parents

Parents who love too much often have such high expectations of their children that their children live in a constant state of anxiety trying to live up to them. The stress can become unbearable. The result? The children try to fend off the anxiety through any acceptable means available. Obsessing about food and dieting can be an attempt to relieve stress caused by the high expectations of parents who love too much.

Sharon's story is an example. "When I was seventeen and a senior in high school, I weighed eighty-nine pounds," she begins haltingly. "I'll never forget the exact number, because it had to do with a goal I had set for myself, which was to weigh less than ninety pounds. I believed that was my natural weight."

Sharon was hospitalized the summer before she started college. "I don't remember much about the hospital, except that I kept trying to convince my doctor that I wasn't eating more because I felt full, and that if I ate as much as he wanted me to eat, I was going to blow up and look like a cow."

Looking back ten years later, Sharon can admit that she was literally starving herself in those days. "You have no idea how painful it is, how much it actually hurts to starve. I feel something like horror today when I think that I ever did that to myself. But you don't feel that way when you're doing it. What I felt was a kind of sick sense of pride in myself, that I was strong enough to do it."

The youngest child of a wealthy family, Sharon received excellent medical care and psychiatric counseling after the onset of what was diagnosed as anorexia nervosa. But when Sharon's psychiatrist insisted that her mother and father also receive counseling prior to Sharon's release, her parents balked. Both took the idea that there may have been underlying family problems that contributed to the development of Sharon's illness as a personal affront.

Intelligent, talented, and attractive, Sharon had always

seemed to be the ideal child. She lived with her family in a large ranch house on about an acre of land in a suburb of Atlanta. The family was well-to-do by most standards, and Sharon's childhood included private schools, horseback-riding lessons, and expensive summer camps.

On the surface, Sharon appeared to have the perfect childhood. It was this picture of perfection that caused her parents' defensiveness in their approach to Sharon's illness. They had always been close to their children and given them everything, they maintained to the doctor who treated Sharon. Everything was fine, they believed, up to the point where Sharon refused to eat.

Sharon saw it differently. She remembers feeling anxious all her life, as if she wasn't quite making the mark with her parents. "In our town, my parents were local celebrities. My father was a politician. My mother's background was generations of old money. She's a beautiful woman, and I always wanted to look like her. But she's also a little eccentric, even flamboyant. People are always talking about her clothes, and the things she's doing, and I think she enjoys that, as much as she enjoys having her own way."

Given plenty of privileges, Sharon felt pressured and undeserving. "I felt like we were this special family, and because of it, I had to be special. I was given the perfect childhood, and I felt like I hadn't done one thing to deserve it."

Although Sharon got a lot of attention for the excellent grades she received in school, her parents' expectations seemed frustrating and devouring at times. "So much was expected of me, and the more I did, the more my parents demanded of me. My mother always needed to know what I was doing, thinking, or feeling."

A good athlete, Sharon made the Girls' Varsity Volleyball team during her junior year, shortly before she developed anorexia. "One night both of my parents came to watch me play before going off to a dinner party. After the game, my father kept talking about Lori, the star of our team. He said she played aggressively, just like a man, and for him, this was the highest compliment. I felt so jealous listening to him talk about her. Then he smiled at me and said, 'Why'd you let that ball go over your head, shrimp?' ''

Sharon became determined to improve her performance on the court. Constant volleyball practice made her already healthy teenage appetite enormous. One day her father, watching her wolf down her dinner, said, ''You'd better watch that, or you're going to get fat.'' He was smiling and teasing her, but Sharon took him literally.

That night, Sharon thought hard about herself, and decided that her body was at fault for what she saw as her poor athletic performance. It wasn't lean and strong enough for competition. She became obsessed with trimming and honing her body.

Sharon's attempt at trimming her body slowly slipped into a starvation regiment. Her rapid weight loss horrified her parents. Her father came home early each night and sat stolidly at the table, forcing her to eat under his gaze, while Sharon insisted that she was ''stuffed'' and that he was trying to make her fat. It did no good; he made her eat. Afterward, she'd run outside to the back of the yard, squeeze between the bushes that separated her house from the neighbors, and vomit on the grass. ''I thought it was a pretty clever solution. I was fooling everyone.''

Each morning her mother would stand over the scale and watch as Sharon weighed herself. Sharon sewed quarters into the hem and cuffs of her robe to pass her mother's inspection. One morning Sharon's sister borrowed the robe and discovered the quarters. She immediately told her mother.

''They confronted me that night at the dinner table, after I had eaten an enormous meal. My mother calmly brought the robe into the dining room and asked me what it meant. That was just like her, always in control. I felt like an animal in a trap. I looked at my father, and something held so long inside of me broke.''

Sharon stood up, ran to the kitchen sink, and vomited. She did it over and over again, unable to stop, while her terrified parents looked on. Finally, she fell on the floor, raging hysterically at herself, her mother, and her father. "I screamed about everything that had ever happened to me in my whole picture-perfect life."

The next day, Sharon entered the hospital, where she stayed for four weeks.

Sharon experienced a childhood where her needs appeared to be met but in fact were not. Everything a child can need for physical and intellectual development had been provided. However, under the well-polished surface, Sharon's youth was full of anxiety and stress. She constantly worried that she would be found lacking, not good enough, or not up to what she sensed were her parents' expectations. She had little confidence in her own value, and was preoccupied with trying to be somebody she thought her parents wanted her to be.

Children who grow up as Sharon did, with too many expectations, become very dependent on other people's opinions to determine how they feel about themselves. When we're obsessed with the need to outguess people so that we can do what we think they expect of us and win their approval, our lives are no longer in our control but in the hands of others. Refusing to eat gave Sharon a much-needed feeling of being in control of herself.

If our childhood was like Sharon's, all that we are given may arouse an obligation in us to prove that we're truly worthy of everything we receive. We may feel hungry for approval, starved for validation, thirsty for acknowledgment. A preoccupation with food and dieting serves as an emotional elixir to the stress of trying to live up to incredibly high expectations. "I'm not good enough" becomes "I'm not thin enough." Sharon's eating disorder calmed her anxiety by providing an escape from the real issues in her life. Planning meals, counting calories, reading diet books, obsessing about her weight while secretly purging, nurtured her. These activities distracted her from her failure to meet her parents' high expectations, and her weight loss gave her an illusion of "success."

Using Food to Rebel
Against Our Parents' Control

When we're grappling with an eating disorder, control usually means one thing: "I had a small salad with lemon juice; I'm in control. I had a chocolate sundae; I'm out of control."

A more vital issue, however, is not so much our control over food, but our control over our own lives. Measuring our food only gives us an illusion of control.

We need most to be in control when we feel strongly controlled by others. When a child is loved too much, his or her parents' control is always an issue.

Compulsive eating or dieting can be a way of rebelling against our parents' control, either consciously or unconsciously. We use our bodies to send a message to our parents that we would never say aloud: "You can't control me. I'm not going to fit your image of the thin and beautiful perfect child."

Jane's story is a case in point. In her home, her father's wishes came first. What the other family members wanted was acceptable only if it didn't infringe on his demands. "We all catered to him. Especially my mother. Everything he believed, my mother said she believed, too, even though I never thought she was being honest.

"Dad liked to golf, so we were out on the course by seven o'clock every Saturday morning. Because he thought it was important to be a cultured person, I was forced to take piano lessons and art lessons even though I hated them. He went to parochial school, so I was stuck in a Catholic school that was horrible."

Jane learned to conform to her father's wishes or be abandoned. "Golf outings, the country club, traveling, the symphony—these were the things my parents loved. I learned to behave so that I could be around them. If I didn't behave, I was left home, or sent home to stay with a baby-sitter. And although I would have been cared for, I wouldn't have been included." To Jane, nothing was as important as being included.

As Jane got older, the weight of her father's control became a burden. Everything had to correspond to his tastes, interests, and preferences. "He couldn't understand why I wanted to be out with my best friend instead of with the family. My mother tried to reason with him, but she gave up. 'He loves you very much,' was what she always told me as an excuse. No one could reason with him. Worst of all, how could you get mad at someone who loves you so much?"

One thing Jane's father couldn't control was Jane's appetite. "What was he going to do? Lock me in a closet so I couldn't eat? I started to gain weight when I was about thirteen years old, and I just kept gaining. I was an incredibly mature, well-behaved teenager, and perfect except for one thing—I was terribly fat. My eating was totally out of control."

Conform or be abandoned. It's an important message that children who are loved too much grow up with. Abandonment can be emotional or physical. In Jane's family, to openly rebel was to be physically abandoned, left home with a baby-sitter. Jane was raised in a way that fulfilled her parents' needs and wishes more than her own, and her father's control extended to all areas of her life except her diet. Food was used to fend off her parents' control, to sabotage their picture of the perfect daughter; thin, beautiful, accomplished, and a credit to them.

It is no accident that the onset of most eating disorders occurs at some point in adolescence. At this point, children become aware of the need to be their own person, separate from their parents. They start looking around for ways to establish firmer boundaries between themselves and others. Food preferences are one of the first and foremost things adolescents use to "define" themselves. Potato chips, hot dogs, pizza, soda, and other foods are eaten constantly, and such a diet results in a battle with parents over nutrition. Such a battle is important. It's a cue that the teenager is asserting himself as separate and in charge of his own body.

Parents who become overly rigid about their teenagers' diets, who forbid certain foods and force them to eat others, set the stage for a more rigid response in return.

Strange, ritualistic eating patterns can develop as a way of saying, "This diet is my idea, and the first thing in my life that I've ever taken a stand on."

A sense that we have some power over our own lives is critical. A vital issue for children who are overprotected by their parents is the lack of control they feel. In families where parents love too much, rules don't shift readily to adapt to changes in the needs caused by our increasing maturity. As teenagers, and later as adults, we no longer need our parents to keep shielding us from harm or guide and mold us, but they can't stop. In families where overprotection is severe and rules are rigid, refusing to eat or bingeing secretly can be resorted to when such smothering becomes overwhelming. Either device gives an illusion of being in control: "I'm powerful enough to resist my feelings of hunger; I can starve myself," or "I'm powerful enough to resist gaining weight; I can eat all night and purge myself, never gaining a pound."

An obsession with food that develops into a full-blown eating disorder can help us wrest control away from controlling parents in an even greater way. An eating disorder, once it's discovered, creates a family crisis. It becomes a family problem that gives the victim increasing control over other family members. Maybe no one will be able to eat dessert in front of him/ her because it would be tempting. Maybe someone will have to stand over him/her to make sure that the food is eaten. Maybe the family will have to give up their free time to go for counseling.

Although we may have physically left our parents' home long ago, an obsession with food can still serve a similar function in our lives today. We get an illusion of being independent or in control of our own lives through our secret food habits, as outrageous as they may be.

Using Food to Fend Off Intimacy

Julie, a twenty-four-year-old computer programmer, has been trying unsuccessfully to have a long-term relationship with a man for the past five years. She blames her weight for her inability to attract the kind of man she wants. While it's true that Julie's excessive weight has the effect of keeping men at a distance, her unconscious desire to keep relationships superficial is a hidden agenda underlying her obsession with food.

Julie grew up in a home where she was constantly dragged into her parents' battles with each other, as the mediator or peacemaker. Finally, her parents divorced. Julie's mother clung to Julie afterward, talking to her at length about her loneliness, how Julie's father had let her down, and even about her need for sex now that she no longer had an intimate relationship. "She wanted me to be with her all of the time. If I had a date or plans with my friends, I'd feel guilty telling her."

Because Julie couldn't set any limits, her mother became increasingly enmeshed in her life. Julie felt suffocated by all of her mother's attention, and helpless to fend it off.

It was at this point that Julie became obsessed with food. Food provided solace from her mother's increasing demands, and Julie gained forty pounds in the years following her parents' divorce. Her fat said, "I'm separate, I need space—keep away!"

Although Julie's mother's neediness was extreme, many of us grew up in homes where our parents became enmeshed in our lives to one extent or another. We got love, attention, and material things for which we were grateful, but at times we couldn't breathe. It seems to us that along with the love people give us comes an expectation for too much in return. This has been a burden all of our lives. The people closest to us, whom we relied and depended on, also expected the most from us.

Food may be used to "solve" a wide range of issues we have with intimacy. Intimacy is scary. If we let someone know us and love us, will he or she become enmeshed in our lives as our parents did? Will that person demand more from us than we're comfortable giving? At two hundred pounds, or eighty pounds, we don't have to worry too much about intimacy. We stay absorbed in our food-related issues that seem safer than tackling the issues of intimate relationships, or for that matter, the entire issue of our sexuality.

If we're in a relationship that's full of emotional distance and discord, we can focus on our problems with food instead. Food is much easier to deal with than dissatisfaction with a husband, wife, or lover. We blame our weight and tell ourselves that things will get better once we lost those extra pounds.

If we can't find the "right" person, we can say it's because of our weight. We never have to deal with the terrifying question of what would happen if we lost weight and still were unable to find the perfect love.

In any case, we never have much energy for relationships anyway. Our relationship with food is too engrossing.

Using Food to Nurture Ourselves

"Food was in a constant state of being prepared in my house," Karen recalls. "I can't remember the kitchen ever being closed. Some kind of activity was always going on in there. The minute the meal was done and the dishes put away, the baking began. It was never one pan of brownies, but two or three.

"My parents always said, 'You must be hungry. Eat! You've got to eat! There're people starving.' If any of us didn't want to come to the dinner table, it sent the whole house into an uproar.

"If I didn't eat what was set in front of me, my mother would say, 'I've been cooking all day, but I guess no one likes it.' Cooking was the way she showed her love. The way to show her that you loved and appreciated her was to eat. The way you showed her you were angry was to refuse to eat. Eating had nothing to do with hunger. It was the way we communicated back and forth."

Food is especially symbolic in many of our families. Certain behaviors around the dinner table are telltale signs of enmeshment: Someone is in someone else's soup, everyone is grabbing for a taste of someone else's dinner, and no one's meal is his own.

Parents who love too much long to provide for their children and comfort them. They worry that they aren't giving enough. Many of these parents stuff their children with food from the moment they are born, as a way of showing their love.

The consequences of our parents' stuffing us with food in response to any of our needs—nutritional or not—can be devastating. When parents mistake a variety of their children's physical and emotional needs for hunger and provide food as a response, a pattern is set that can lead to eating disorders later in life.

An infant has one signal for announcing every need he has—crying. A parent has to be empathic enough to "decode" this signal and respond appropriately to it. Sometimes a parent will consistently make the wrong response. Perhaps the baby is crying because he's lonely, tired, or cold. The parent feeds the child, misreading the "cue." Or perhaps the parent is adhering to a rigid feeding schedule. The baby cries, and the parent doesn't realize that the child is hungry, or believes the baby will be harmed if taken off his schedule. Both of these types of unempathic responses to the baby's needs result in confusion. The baby doesn't learn to distinguish hunger as different from other needs or discomforts. "I'm tired" becomes "I'm hungry," just as "I'm scared" or a host of other emotions translate to "I'm hungry." A foundation is set for a lifetime of using food to solve a host of complex emotional problems.

Compulsive eating may be the only way we know to nurture ourselves today. We don't know what we really need, or what we're truly feeling inside. It becomes habitual to reach for food when we feel lonely or unloved. Food becomes affection, rather than fuel for the body. As one woman put it, "Ice cream is an inner hug."

Using Food to Rebel
Against "Looking Good"

Mark, a thirty-year-old accountant, remembers an incident that occurred when he was a high school senior. He was applying for a student loan for college, and the plan was to meet his father downtown in front of the bank. That morning, getting dressed, he realized, "Everything in my closet was either blue jeans or workshirts. I went to high school dressed like a slob, like everyone else."

Knowing he couldn't meet his father dressed in jeans, he ran down the block and borrowed his cousin's shirt, tie, and dress pants. "I thought I looked pretty good. My father didn't say much until we were walking into the bank and he happened to look down at my feet. 'Look at those shoes!' he said, swelling up like a toad.

"I looked. They were pretty bad. I was wearing the same beat-up loafers I wore every day.

"Right there, outside the bank, my father yelled at me, his face all red like he was having a stroke: 'You look like a ragamuffin! I'm ashamed of you!'

" 'I didn't know you had to look rich to go and borrow money!' I yelled back."

Today, Mark still looks anxiously for his father's judgments on his wardrobe every time he visits, even though he says he has contempt for his father's hang-ups over appearances. "At thirty, I should be able to wear what I want when I go to see my parents. But, somehow, I still find myself dressing up for them, getting a haircut, and thinking, Will Dad think this tie's too loud?"

Many of us have had similar experiences with one or both of our parents. Even innocuous comments like, "Aren't those pants a little tight?" or "I think it's time for a new jacket," drive us crazy today. Chained emotionally to our parents' approval, we can be just as devastated by their failure to say anything at all about how we look. We imagine, then, that their judgment is so negative that they can't bring themselves to say it.

It's true that most parents care a great deal about how

their children look and behave. But with parents who love too much, it can become an obsession. They feel that the responsibility for how their child looks and behaves is theirs, rather than the child's. And they expect perfection. They demand that we "look good."

Some of us can shrug off our parents' obsession over "looking good." But others are very vulnerable to it and resent the rigidity of their parents' views about what qualifies as correct behavior and what does not.

But confronting our parents directly on these issues has never been easy. This is why we turn to indirect methods. Food can be used to rebel against "looking good" in a very powerful yet indirect way. What could be a more negative reflection of parenting than a fat child, or one so thin that he or she looks emaciated?

With our obsession with food, we speak up. We say that everything is not all right. We rebel against "looking good" in a way that seems safe, but is often so powerful that the entire family system is knocked for a loop.

Using Food to Punish Ourselves in Response to Guilt

Some parents are skillful guilt-inflicters. They maintain control over their children by making them feel responsible for their own suffering, frustrated hopes, or unfulfilled lives, repeating, "I gave up a lot for you, I tried to give you all the things I never had, and just look at how you act in return."

What inspires so much guilt is the implication that if we loved our parents, we'd do what they say. We'd be who they want us to be. We'd pay them back for all they've given us by fulfilling their expectations of us.

Guilt is one of the primary emotions children who were loved too much tend to eat over. Guilt is immobilizing, and eating gives us the illusion of doing something—of taking action. Food is also comforting and distracting, helping us numb helpless feelings of remorse.

The guilt-inflicting messages our parents laid on us are internalized so well that they tend to pressure and control us with far more intensity than our parents ever attempted to. Guilt carries over to other relationships. If someone else is unhappy, we feel responsible. If someone is angry at us, we automatically assume we're at fault. What a surprise to our parents, who never felt we were as responsible as we could be, to find that we feel responsible for the feelings of the entire world.

Guilt becomes a habit. One woman tells a story about being awakened at midnight when her three-year-old came down with a high fever. Soon the older child woke up complaining of a headache. For the rest of the night, she ran back and forth between children, trying not to worry about work the next day, how she might not be able to go in, and how she'd missed so many days already she'd probably never get the promotion she wanted. By four o'clock in the morning, she was ready to throw both children and her husband, who slept peacefully through it all, out the window.

This woman felt terribly guilty about these feelings, especially about being angry at sick children. Her own mother, after all, wouldn't have felt this way. By 6:00 A.M. she was in the kitchen, gorging herself on a breakfast of Cheetos, banana cake, ice cream, and stacks of Oreos.

Food can be used to alleviate the guilt we feel when we can't meet our own internalized expectations. This woman felt that she had to be the perfect mother, as she felt her own mother had been. Her guilt over feeling angry at a sick child was unendurable. She drowned out the inner critic with food. Realistic thoughts about the fact that it was late, that she was exhausted, that she was only human, were wiped out by the specter of her mother, a parent who loved too much, who seemed to thrive on self-sacrifice when it came to her children.

The problem with using food to cope with guilt is that the more (or less) you eat, the guiltier you feel. Now added to your wrong doing is the sin of going off your diet, of losing control, of bingeing or purging. It becomes a vicious cycle: The more you use food to cope, the more guilt you feel. The more guilt you feel, the more you need to use food to cope.

Using Food to Quiet Restlessness and Dissatisfaction

One man confided that when he was a child, his parents felt so guilty about going out and leaving him behind that they hired clowns and other performers to entertain him until they returned. "No wonder I go crazy when I'm home alone. I guess I expect to be entertained."

Boredom is an uncomfortable feeling for us. When we're bored and have nothing to do, we tend to look at ourselves. For some of us, this is alarming. The high expectations that we've internalized creep up on us: "I should be exercising. . . . I should read more. . . . I should write a résumé and try to get a better job. . . . I should do something about my social life. . . . I should practice the piano. . . . I should get organized. . . ." It all crowds in at once, and because we can't do it all, we end up immobilized, doing nothing at all. Thinking about food, planning meals, trying new diets, are a solution; something to do and plan. These activities distract us effectively from looking at ourselves.

Using Food to Get into the Spotlight

There are several reasons why the child of parents who love too much would want to be the one in the family spotlight. Consider Ann's story.

A twenty-one-year-old student, Ann wakes up each morning thinking, Can I eat like a normal person today?

Since her early teens, Ann has gone on secret eating binges for no apparent reason. At these times, the urge to eat seems uncontrollable. "I don't feel like I have a choice. Once I start eating, I can't stop."

As Ann explored her childhood, some of the circumstances that contributed to her developing such a pattern emerged. Ann had an older sister, Julie, who had Hodgkin's disease. "She was in and out of the hospital all of the time, and my parents were always very worried."

Ann's mother felt helpless about her older daughter's illness. "She couldn't control it, and it broke her heart."

Up to the age of twelve, Ann had been quite skinny. "When I started gaining weight in high school, my mother took me to one diet doctor after another. My problems with my weight were something she felt she could do something about. She forced me to diet, threw food away so I wouldn't find it, and sent me off to exercise classes and special camps. When it worked, she felt happy. But I'd always go back to my old ways."

In Ann's home, the spotlight of her parents' attention was focused on her sister who was ill. So much worry and concern was focused on her sister's unsolvable problems that Ann felt she had to take control.

Ann attempted to move the spotlight to herself by developing a pattern of compulsive overeating. With the spotlight redirected on her weight, Ann "solved" her family problems. Her parents' concern and helplessness over her sister's illness made Ann feel vulnerable and frightened. Children are often very protective of their parents, especially if the family is enmeshed. Ann's solution was to focus her mother's attention on a different, more "solvable" problem, her compulsive overeating. Her mother appeared less concerned and depressed about the other more painful and distinctly unsolvable family problems when she was involved in controlling Ann's eating.

Many of us can identify with Ann's protectiveness of her family. We may be determined to remedy the problems that we can sense are very painful to our parents. We're so dependent on them that their pain creates great insecurity. There are few boundaries between us. Some of us can barely separate our feelings, thoughts, and biases from what our parents would have felt, thought, and decided. We open our mouths to speak and wonder if what comes out is really what we think, or what our mother or father would have said. This is the consequence of a lifetime of having our parents speak for us, define our needs, and tell us what we should feel.

Eating disorders become significant family problems that scream for attention. Unconsciously, we may hope to shift the focus of the family from our father's alcoholism, our mother's depression, our sister's or brother's troubles, to our eating disorder. If our parents have a troubled marriage, their sudden collusion over our eating disorder can appear to be new closeness and intimacy. We deflect the spotlight off of these problems, shine it on ourselves, and avoid a showdown over all that our parents feel helpless about.

Using Food to Avoid Maturity

Food can be used as a means of hanging on to our childhood. Children who were loved too much are often ambivalent about true independence from their parents. This fear stands in the way of ending an unfulfilling infatuation with food and dieting.

When we're consumed with thoughts about whether we can stick to a new diet, whether it will work fast enough for us to stay on it, or whether our secret purges will be discovered, we displace what we really fear: having to take charge of our own lives.

We've become accustomed to being taken care of by our parents. Parents who love too much often hamper maturity by sabotaging our separation from them and doing for us what we could be doing ourselves. Their hidden agenda is often to keep us children, dependent on them. Our obsession with food and the resulting problems create a focus for their lives, while increasing our dependence on them. They are often the ones we turn to most to reveal our daily struggles with our weight and our triumphs and disasters in dieting.

Some parents who love too much unconsciously sabotage their children's attempts to free themselves from their obsession with food and dieting. Carrie, a compulsive eater, joined Overeaters Anonymous and became embroiled in a battle with her mother. "The crazy thing was that my mother had been after me to join Weight Watchers for years. She'd always told me that I should do something about my weight. But since OA isn't about dieting as much as dealing with your feelings, my mother was against it from the start.

"I'd go out with my mother, and she'd ask me a million questions about the program: 'What do you talk about in those meetings? Do you talk about us? Are you sure you're eating enough? You know, it's not good to lose the weight real fast, you'll just gain it back.'

"My mother and I have always been close, and I usually didn't mind her constant questions, but I didn't want to keep talking about my diet and thinking about it. I told her flat out to stop asking me about it. She said, 'You're so irritable lately. I think it's that group you go to. Maybe you should try something else. I don't want you to get sick.' "

Carrie was still going to her parents' house every Friday night for dinner. After Carrie started attending OA, her mother would phone every Friday morning and say, "You know, it's too hard for me to make special meals for everyone who comes to dinner. We're having the same thing we always have, so I hope you can find something to eat."

"She'd serve lasagne or pork chops, and I'd be forced to bring my own meal. Some lavish dessert would be served, and she'd say, 'I know you're on a diet, but surely you can have a little sliver?' "

Carrie eventually stopped going to her parents' home for dinner. Her parents were hurt and accused her of neglecting them.

Carrie found a solution, however. "A girl in my OA group had similar problems with her parents, and talking things out with her helped. She talked about how the entire focus of her relationship with her parents had been her eating problem, and how hard this connection was to break.

"I realized that since I'd left home, I'd spent most of my time with my mother complaining about how fat I was, how lonely I was, all of this while we were cooking together or going to restaurants and eating. I fumed with her over my 'bad days,' and she made me feel better. My mother had felt needed and included. My new resolve to lose weight was threatening to her, and she felt left out because I wouldn't talk to her about it.'' Carrie's task was to begin to establish other foundations for closeness with her mother beyond her need for a parent to monitor her weight and despair with her over her losses of control.

We make our parents feel needed by going on and on about our problems controlling our weight. If we're bulimic or anorexic, they come to the rescue. They pay hospital bills, psychiatrist bills, food bills—anything that will help. We remain childishly dependent.

This is not to say that our parents consciously or even unconsciously enjoy our eating disorders, or would want us to be ill to make them feel needed. There is no simple cause-and-effect relationship. However, our perception that our parents need to be needed and have a void that only we can fill can be one of many unconscious motivators for us to stay involved with food, dieting, bingeing, purging, and emotional overeating. The progression of these symptoms into an eating disorder will inevitably mean that we will develop health and emotional problems that will send a clear message of our needs. It will say, "I still need you to parent me, whether I'm thirteen or thirty-five." The message will be poignant and compelling, and they'll take care of us again because they love us so much.

Using Food for What It Is: Fuel for the Body

If you recognize that you've been using food to meet needs you've been unable to meet in other ways and want to change your ultimately unfulfilling relationship with food, you're going to have to work hard on your relationship with yourself. The following steps can help:

Acknowledge that you have a problem that you are unable to solve alone. Give up your hope that the next diet will be the one that works or that you'll stop vomiting tomorrow. An eating disorder is an addiction. It can destroy your life by robbing you of the joy of self-esteem and inner peace.

Go for help. If you have an eating disorder, real help is not in a diet book. It's not in this book or in any other book. All of these are guides that can provide insight, but insight alone isn't curative. You may have a better idea of how your past has influenced your behavior today, but such knowledge is not the same as taking action. An eating disorder requires specialized treatment. Don't make the mistake of thinking that if you only cure your depression, stop criticizing yourself, absolve yourself of guilt, or come to terms with your unrealistic expectations, you will magically stop eating or dieting. All of this will be helpful. But true action will mean acknowledging that you have a problem and making a commitment to halting behaviors that have become habitual. This will be difficult and frustrating. You will need support from others who are on the same road. Overeaters Anonymous will give you the support you need as you try to change. Try them, or find another support group in your community.

When you get that sudden urge to eat compulsively, or find yourself obsessing about food, ask yourself what you really need. Eating disorders serve a purpose in our lives. Increase your awareness of what that purpose is for you.

Are you angry? What do you need to do with that feeling, other than eat over it? Are you bored and restless? What can you do to add some excitement and adventure in your life, other than eat?

Are you still rebelling against your parents' high expectations? How can you detach, and set your own course for your life?

Is your weight a shell in which you hide from intimate relationships? Intimacy is scary, but a lot more exciting than dealing with food and weight.

Becoming aware of your feelings and needs will give you a better sense of control over your life, and provide you with options. You will be able to choose ways to meet your needs other than obsessing about food, once you realize what's behind that obsession.

Be on the look out for codependents in your life. Codependents are the people who actually become so involved in our eating problems that they unconsciously prevent us from achieving the independence that is necessary to our recovery. They take on our responsibilities and try to ease the consequences of our behavior. They are very often our parents.

We need to be the ones making the decisions about what we will or will not eat. The more control we allow others to have, the less we will have to acknowledge that the problem is ours alone.

If your parents or anyone else in your life is codependent, they need help as much as you do. There are support groups available to them. You can suggest that they join one, but, again, it is their responsibility to follow through. You must disentangle yourselves from each other's responsibilities. Both of you will have to detach.

CHAPTER 10

HOOKED FOR LIFE

"You can always count on your parents."

> "My parents send me presents with the price tags still on them. They don't admit it, but it's because they want me to know how much they've spent on me.
>
> "I'm getting too old for these games. I asked my mother, 'What's with these price tags? Why do you do it? What are you trying to tell me?'
>
> "She apologized. After that, when she sent me presents, the price tags were still on. But she drew a single blue line across the numbers."
>
> —Randy, age 44, mechanic

When we stop to consider our past, we begin to see our parents as human beings with needs of their own that they were driven to meet. We see why our accomplishments were so important to them. We gain a better understanding of their motivations for giving us too much.

At the same time, we may discover that we've spent much of our lives trying to be whatever would make our parents happy. We do this because we love our parents too much in return.

Strong defenses have always been in the way of our seeing the full extent of the trap we've set for ourselves, or of realizing how great our dependency on our parents can be at times. We don't think about these things when we can help it. Although it frustrates us, and we sometimes hate ourselves for it, we keep returning to our parents for "help." We're broke, or we want a better job, or our spouse expects too much of us. We know we shouldn't need our parents' help, but somehow we're at their door.

Usually, our parents are more than willing. They may criticize, lecture, and humble us when we come knocking at their door, but our parents always take us in.

We may dislike our dependency and realize that we might be better off if we started to give to ourselves. But the hook is too strong.

Our parents' generosity seldom stops when we become adults. It doesn't stop when we have children of our own. But when so much is given to us now, it's even more problematic for us. At a stage when we know we should be standing on our own feet and taking less, our parents offer us a host of "goodies" that are so seductive and enticing that we can't refuse.

Many of us don't refuse. We embrace the danger of being hooked for life.

What keeps adults hooked into mutually dependent relationships with their parents—relationships that are both restricting and demanding? More than guilt and responsibility anchor us to our parents. What ties us to them is the security they can often provide us with. Sometimes it's the promise of a lifetime allowance. Or an inheritance. A down payment. An important connection. These are the perks of being loved too much. Each is a blessing and a trap.

The Lifetime Allowance

Every month when the check arrives in the mail, we're relieved. It may be paying our rent, or providing us with vacations, clothes, and evenings out we couldn't afford otherwise.

But the lifetime allowance insures a continuation of childhood. Most of us feel guilty about this money. We hide where we got it from our friends. Sometimes we marry and attempt to hide from our husband or wife the fact that we're still taking money from our parents.

But it seems ridiculous to say no. We tell ourselves that other people are just jealous when they make rude remarks about grown adults who take money from their parents. If our parents are particularly well off, we tell ourselves they couldn't possibly spend all of their money on themselves anyway.

Whatever rationalizations we use, we never quite get to the point of returning the money. It's difficult to say, "Hey, thanks a lot, but I can make it on my own," when we're not so sure we can, or we'd be less comfortable if we did. We're reluctant to pull up the safety net under us. We'd have to change our lifestyle to do it.

We really could make it alone, but perhaps not as comfortably. There would be risks involved in returning this money. So we cash the checks, and that does little to bolster our self-esteem. It does even less for our feeling that we're truly mature and independent of our parents.

The Family Business

"Vice president" is the most common title parents who give too much bestow on us shortly after our induction into the family business. There is no bigger blessing and curse for us than the one we get when we decide to follow our parents' footsteps into the company they own.

First of all, we may be surprisingly good at our work once we get there. We may work harder than anyone else, just because we have such a tremendous stake in the company. Yet great or lousy at what we do, we will always be suspect in the eyes of our coworkers.

We feel very sensitive when anyone even hints that we might have had an advantage—that we didn't earn our title. Our whole lives, it's a source of insecurity. Are we really as good as we think we are? Would we have made it in a different career, had we chosen one? We'll never really know.

When we've been forced into the family business, all of our insecurities are compounded with resentment. We rebel, and test the limits of our parents' patience.

One man's father had to hire two assistants to "help" his son in his new role as vice president. The son arrived late and left early. He always left the lights on in his office, hoping to delude everyone that he was still there. Or he left at noon and signed out to miscellaneous clients, assured that his staff would never have the gall to call and check. His attempts at subterfuge were the office joke. All day long the people he supervised heard him on the phone with his friends, discussing his plans for the weekend. They watched his mistakes. He had one of the largest departments in the company, with the least work. His father didn't want him to be understaffed and overworked. And anyone who complained about his management was promptly fired.

The worst thing was, the man knew exactly what the situation was. Every day he sat at his desk feeling as if he were an imposter, but he was too frightened to really take command or use his natural abilities.

Regardless of whether we chose to enter the family business or if we fell back on it when we failed elsewhere, or got dragged into it kicking and screaming, we're in a situation that encourages our parents' lifetime control over us. They set our salary, and define our standard of living. Indirectly, they determine when we can buy a new car, take a vacation, or even afford children of our own. We're under the greatest obligation of all, because they're providing us with a living. We've got an uneasy bargain in exchange.

The Inheritance

"One day I'll finally kick the bucket," the parent who gives too much sighs, "and you kids will split half a million dollars."

Now what are we supposed to say to this? What if we said, "That's great. If it's soon, maybe I can get a terrific deal on a Porsche."

We don't know what to say, so we stand there with a simple-minded look on our face, feeling like the child who hears what he's going to get for Christmas.

This should be a sober topic. It's important to our parents to tell us about their insurance, their savings account, and all the money they've saved throughout their lives that will form our inheritance. They see it as the final evidence of their love. And it's true, of course, that our parents have to discuss their eventual demise with us so that we may carry out their wishes.

But why must they dwell on it? It seems to come up at every holiday dinner, along with morbid monologues about the many relatives who have passed on and are no longer sitting at the table.

When our inheritance comes up for the hundredth time, we repeat, "Come on, don't talk like that. You aren't going to die." Another favorite reply is some variation of, "Why don't you and Mom spend the money on yourselves?"

We really mean this. But, deep down inside, we hope that if they decide to spend some money, they'll be frugal about it, so that there will still be a lot left for us. After all, we're only human.

It sounds horrible. It's also true of many children who were loved too much. The guilt we feel over thoughts like this is formidable. Thank goodness there's safety in the fact that no one, especially our parents, will ever know what we're thinking.

We shouldn't feel so guilty. Our thoughts are an obvious response, given such unrelenting provocation.

The promise of an inheritance can make us alter our behavior. As beneficiaries, we may suddenly have good reason to fear arguing with our parents or telling them anything we truly feel about our relationship with them. We might lose our inheritance. Some of us have excellent reasons for depending on it, having always counted on it as an eternal safety net underneath us.

What a dilemma. If the inheritance that awaits us in the future is large (and parents who give too much often insure this by depriving themselves so that they can give more to us), never in our lives do we really have to give 100 percent of ourselves. It's like money in the bank. We're frustrated over the raise we didn't get at work, our best friend's promotion, our neighbors taking off on an expensive vacation, until we realize, So what? When my parents die, I'm going to be rich.

We hate ourselves for these thoughts, but almost every person who was ever told of an eventual inheritance thinks them at one time. If you look at it closely, you'll realize that your parents unconsciously encouraged this type of thinking by bringing it up so much of the time.

An interesting thing happens to some of us when we finally receive our inheritance. Do we go out and spend it, travel around the country and vow never to work another day in our lives? Rarely. We put it in the bank, at a good interest rate, and only use the income. The money has come to represent the security and love of our parents. The subtle meanings they attached to it make it difficult for us to really use the capital and enjoy it.

The Down Payment

Parents who give too much often offer us the down payment on things like houses or cars. We're happy to have it. But sometimes we'll receive it only if it's for a house in a neighborhood they approve of, or a car they think we should own.

In exchange for the down payment, or any other large sums of money they offer us, we make some bargains, often unspoken but binding just the same. We may unwittingly sign a silent contract with our parents that reads:

- never challenge us
- never express anger at us
- never disappoint us or embarrass us
- come visit us once or twice a week
- never move out of town
- never talk about family problems to outsiders
- never cause problems
- take care of us in our old age

The implication is always the same: You have a good deal, but in exchange you're under your parents' control.

The Referral

Our father knows the best lawyer in town. With one phone call, he can get us out of the lease we signed.

Our mother knows a woman who's the cousin of the man whose wife sits on the college admissions boards. One word and we're in.

A man who just happens to be the majority stockholder at a company we're dying to work at plays golf every Saturday with our father's best friend.

So it goes. Our parents' connections smooth our way more than we'd like to admit.

So what's wrong with getting a little help? Everyone does it. Lots of people are proud of it. They call it "networking," and trade connections like baseball cards. Why shouldn't we take advantage of the people our parents know?

On the surface, all of this is our good fortune. But, again, what happens to our confidence in ourselves and our ability to make it on our own? We never really learn to take initiative or develop our own contacts when we can rely on our parents'. We find ourselves depending on them in areas of our lives where our own independence would foster our self-esteem. We may also blindly take on their values and preferences. The path we end up on isn't really our own, because when we came to a fork in the road, our parents' friends and connections determined our course.

Overindulgence was a pattern that was foisted on us as children by our parents. We weren't responsible for it then, and our parents were only doing the best they could with the resources they had.

But we are responsible today. If we don't give up the passive expectancy that other people will provide for us, we can't begin to provide for ourselves.

It isn't that parents give with an expectation of receiving something in return because they have some special character flaw or deficiency. The majority of people in the world, ourselves included, expect something in return for what they give, and our parents are really no different. We have to learn to look at reality. The idea that we can ever get something for nothing is disproved so often that we ought to vow to give it up once and forever. There is always a debt, no matter how subtle.

But because these are our parents, we somehow kid ourselves that we don't really owe. We think, My parents bought me a seat on the stock exchange because it was an investment for them. It had nothing to do with the fact that I desperately needed a career. I really don't owe them anything.

We fool ourselves in thinking, My parents sent me this check because they like to give money to their children. They don't expect anything of me in exchange.

Yes, they give to make us happy and because our happiness is important to them. Yes, they are benevolent and loving and may not want anything tangible in return. But there's a debt just the same, even if it's only that we'll appreciate what we've been given, or finally be able to stand on our own two feet. Often, the debt involves giving over our independence to their loving control. Whatever is expected in exchange, we should determine whether we can comfortably give it before we make the bargain.

The question for our lives then, is how much debt we want to take on. How much independence can we manage? How many risks can we comfortably take? What do we accept from our parents, and what do we refuse because it fosters childish dependency, or even self-contempt?

The more we take from parents who give too much, the more we become hooked for life into a pattern of mutual dependency. This pattern is responsible for our self-criticism, lack of direction, difficulties in intimate relationships, and our feeling of unrequited entitlement. For many of us, it's a way of getting our needs met that will never work—a pattern of loving that hurts.

Learning to love and be loved in healthier ways means finding a balance between living our own lives and loving our parents. It requires risk. It requires giving up some of the comforts inherent in dependency. We must give up impossible expectations of our parents, and they must give up impossible expectations of us.

II

The Parents Who Love Too Much

CHAPTER 11

THE PARENTS

"Maybe we loved you too much, but we couldn't have done it any other way."

What is it like to be a parent who loves and gives too much?

Typically, a parent who loves too much senses that he or she is overly devoted when such all-consuming involvement brings pain rather than fulfillment. The mothers and fathers who speak out in this chapter are perceptive and insightful about the patterns of their relationships with their children. Although the details differ from story to story, several features stand out:

- an overinvolvement in the events of their children's lives, even when these children become adults
- the obsessive desire to be a "good parent" and to raise "good" children
- great anxiety over their children's successes and failures; the feeling that their children were capable of much more
- an awareness that the constant anxiety they feel over their children is robbing them of much of the joy inherent in being a parent.

Karen S.: Parents Who Would Give Anything

"I grew up in a single-parent home. My parents divorced when I was so young I can barely even remember it. My father never paid any alimony or child support, so my mother had to work full time. Every day she would come home exhausted and say, 'If I didn't go to work, you wouldn't be eating or have a roof over your heads.' She complained that no one would ever marry a woman with four children and said, 'I should give you all up for adoption!' It was constant verbal abuse, and I never felt secure for a moment, despite the fact that I knocked myself out trying to please her.

"My mother turned me into an adult when I was nine years old. I was expected to go home straight from school every day. I wasn't allowed to play with my friends, or have them over. I had to wait for my brothers and sister to come home, make sure they did their homework, set the table, make dinner, and play the mother role.

"I wanted my own children to have childhoods. I decided that I would never, ever, allow my children to worry about money. I wanted them to have security, so they wouldn't feel what I grew up feeling. They were going to have wonderful, carefree existences.

"Looking back, that's where I see the motivation for everything I did. It came out of my own deprivation. I went the opposite way with my children, and gave them everything—not only what they needed, but everything that they wanted.

"When Scott was a little kid, we bought him a train set that took up the whole basement. It cost five hundred dollars, and he was only four years old. He had little Italian suits when he was no more than a baby. His birthdays were catered affairs—extravaganzas with clowns and musicians and entertainment. When I look at pictures of those parties now, I think, My God, what was all this nonsense?

"Scott had trouble in school from day one. Well, that's not exactly true. He loved nursery school, where they were wonderful and kind and nurturing to him. But when he went to regular school, where there was one teacher to thirty kids instead of one teacher to nine kids, he didn't get much time or attention. He had trouble with that. I was busy getting him a therapist when he was five years old.

"I had Scott tested immediately when the problems started. I was constantly testing him, making sure he was okay, which was a mistake. All I was doing was pointing out what I thought was wrong with him, but I didn't know that then.

"I hired reading specialists, math specialists, therapists, or whatever else all the experts thought he needed. I didn't feel I could help him in these areas, but I always felt that I could buy somebody else's talent, and this would somehow translate into my helping Scott.

"You'd think I wasn't doing much myself, with all of these specialists running around my house helping Scott, but I was spending enormous amounts of time and energy organizing all of these things for him. It took all of my time to drive him to lessons, to therapists, to tutors, and to constantly be at his beck and call.

"I thought it was important that this child, who was my first child and the first grandchild, get everything. I suppose, like most mothers, I wanted him to be a star, and if he was getting everything, there was no reason for him not to be. I was saying, 'You have all of these things—swimming, horseback riding, wonderful vacations, tutors, baby-sitters. The least you can do is be an outstanding human being.'

"Well, he wasn't doing that. Things never improved for Scott at school. More often than not, I'd tell his teachers that they didn't understand him and that it was their problem. Then I'd hire another tutor.

"I realize now that my expectations really had more to do with me than Scott. I had unrealistic expectations of myself—of being the perfect parent. The perfect parent was going to raise the perfect child. If you give and give, then you're going to end up with a perfect child, I thought.

"As Scott was growing up, I felt we were very supportive as parents, and that we were doing a very good job.

After all, Scott was never alone. He just had to snap his fingers and there was somebody there. He never even had to pick up his own toys. My husband couldn't stand to come home to a house with toys all over the floor, so I picked them up when Scott was a baby, and when he got older, the maid picked them up. My husband didn't like the kids being noisy at the dinner table, so I made sure they were finished eating and playing quietly when he got home. I was always trying to make things better for everyone else.

"My husband and I never talked about being parents, or what we wanted for our children. Our marriage wasn't the greatest. I'm not even sure he wanted children. He never got as involved as I did, and we had a lot of problems communicating. We never discussed our own values and what we wanted to instill in our children. We didn't go anywhere to find out how to be parents, or talk to anyone about it. We just thought, Well, we're having a good time, and the kids seem to be having a good time, so it must be okay.

"My days were full. I was a den mother. I sat in the rain at Little League. I went to watch Scott's bowling league. My whole goal was to make his life happy, solve his problems, and work through his frustrations. But despite all of this, Scott never found out who he was. He never got a strong sense of self. He just learned how to do all of these things.

"He got more and more spoiled and obnoxious and lazy. Underneath it all, he was very unsure of himself, something I never could understand.

"After a while, the only gratification I got from being his mother was that I looked like a terrific parent. I'm sure that's how it looked to the outside world. Today, I see the cost. Last month he dropped out of the fourth college he's enrolled in. He was planning to lie on our couch for the rest of the semester—he's done it before—when I demanded that he leave.

"There's been nothing but time, effort, and money spent on Scott, and it's never been appreciated. He's twenty-three now, and somebody had to stop playing the game.

Maybe it sounds hard, but I had to throw him out of the house finally, because of what all of this is doing to me. I feel like I've given and given and given, and there's no more left. I'm tired. I'm worn out.

"I don't like my son, and I don't like what he's become. I don't like what he's allowing himself to be. He's a person I wouldn't choose to spend time with if he wasn't my son. This is a young man who wants a quick fix for everything. He smokes, overeats, has no goals, thinks that his father and I will always take care of him. Most of the time, he's obnoxious. He has very unrealistic expectations of everyone—not just us, but his own friends. Scott lives in a fantasy land, as far as I'm concerned. It's a tough world for him, because no one's going to treat him the way we did.

"It wasn't easy to ask Scott to leave. I sound stronger than I am about this. I was the type of mother who cried the first time I saw my son walk next door to play when he was just a little boy. I was crying because he didn't need me anymore. It was so important that he need me. But I've been getting help recently. Finding out who I am in therapy is changing all that. Now, I realize that I have needs, too. I want to sleep through the night without worrying about Scott. I don't want to spend the rest of my life making things easier for him while he treats me like a servant. For any parent on the verge of taking the same path, I'll be the first to warn you: It just doesn't work.

"I can't go back and redo what I've done. But still I wish there was some way to turn some of the negatives into positives at this point. Now, I have this son—this adult—who's obnoxious and rude, and I don't know what to do. Essentially, Scott and I have no relationship today. It hurts, even though I'm trying to be strong about it, and handle it. I'd like to be able to be friends with my own son. I know one thing for sure, though: It has to be on very different terms than the ones Scott offers me today."

What stands out so vividly in Karen's story is a lifetime spent giving to others with too little coming back in return. When we give and give, yet nothing helps and there's so little gratification in it, we have to look more closely at our giving and what it really means for us.

Karen was a woman who had never experienced a childhood. Belittled and hurt deeply by her own mother's indifference, she entered adulthood with an empty and longing heart.

Karen overcompensated for her earlier deprivation by giving too much to her son. Being a perfect parent was supposed to heal her of her perceived shortcomings and faults and take away the pain of her abusive childhood.

Unfortunately, Karen's needs continued to go unmet in the family life she helped create as a parent. This was not a coincidence. Karen was driven to set up a situation in her adult life that repeated the familiar situation of her childhood.

Our family history contributes to how our lives develop and the kind of parents we become. Unconsciously, many of us re-create our past so that we might have another chance to fight old battles. The setting and characters change, but the script remains the same. Karen merely continued the childhood role of being an unselfish giver and caring for others who took her for granted. Putting her own needs last was comfortable to her, even if it resulted in a kind of comfortable misery. Karen's sense of self-esteem, shaky as a result of years of giving and never receiving much in return, didn't command much respect from others. She accepted her husband's underinvolvement in the family's life, and repressed her anger at a man who didn't want to be bothered with toys on the floor—or anything messy or imperfect, for that matter. She accepted Scott's growing irresponsibility and obnoxious behavior and gave even more, hoping to change it, just as she had once hoped to change her mother into a loving, supportive parent.

Karen wanted more than anything to be a perfect parent in order to bolster her self-esteem. Yet she felt very insecure in her role as Scott's mother. Because she never learned to trust herself, she was constantly hiring experts and helpers to raise her son and fix the problems she felt incapable of solving. She based her self-worth on her ability to procure the right kind of help for Scott, and ran herself ragged obtaining it. When nothing she gave succeeded in really helping him, her self-esteem plummeted. But this was an old story for her, one that she had almost come to expect. Nothing she gave in her childhood seemed to solve her family situation, either.

We tend to think that we can't possibly fail as parents if we give everything we have. Why is it that all of this giving so often results in children who never appreciate it—who thank us by becoming sullen, irresponsible, and obnoxious human beings? It's more complex than the simple explanation that we've spoiled them: When Karen took control of every aspect of her son's life, he felt out of control. He had no experience in solving his own problems, and no emotional resources for dealing with frustration. The more emotional support he got, the needier he became. He leaned on his parents to the point that he lived his adult life as a dependent baby, a pampered/deprived adult child. This is almost always the result of too much giving. The child who receives an avalanche of goods, services, and attention wonders, Don't my parents think I can do it on my own?, and it's the beginning of deep feelings of insecurity.

Often our children resent our sacrifices in a way that hurts us deeply. This isn't because they're insensitive. They are, in fact, very sensitive. They sense that there are motives behind our generosity—motives that are so unconscious that we don't immediately recognize them ourselves. When we give and give until we're exhausted, as Karen did, usually it's because we feel that this is the only way others will accept us or maintain a relationship with us. If we stop giving, our children will stop loving us. They could never accept us for who we are, rather than for what we can give them. We believe this because we have so little real trust in our own value—in our own selves. On the deepest level, we fear we're lacking in things that are essential to being a good parent. Without our grandiose gestures of self-sacrifice, our children, our spouse, our neighbors, our own parents, will see through us to our lack. We aren't giving what our children need, so much as what we think will shield them from seeing whatever it is in us that we think we lack. So we center our lives around our children, tolerate abuse, and keep giving.

Because we give and give to the point of exhausting ourselves and our resources, we give the appearance of being overinvolved. In fact, we're underinvolved. We haven't risked being ourselves with our children, and letting them see who we are apart from what we can provide. We can't believe that they'll love us for ourselves alone. We keep giving, devastated that our children are so ungrateful, yet we never realize that they sense our unconscious motivation—to be needed; to have our weaknesses overlooked; to produce a sense of obligation. Our children end up resenting all that they're being given because they feel it isn't genuine, that it's manipulative.

Our tendency to love and give too much is understandable given our expectations of parenthood and all we want from it. If our needs weren't so compelling, we'd stop giving when we see the effect of all of it in our grown child who has no resources to give back in kind.

It's vital that we begin to see that there is a difference between giving out of love and out of the desire to provide for a child's needs and overcompensating because of our own needs. No one's needs are truly met in the latter situation. Our children can never be the answer to a lifetime of pain, problems, and grief. No one relationship can provide this kind of solution. It must come from within ourselves. Too much giving, too much absorption in our grown children's lives and problems, creates a distraction that keeps the focus off ourselves. We keep looking at our children's achievements and accomplishments, hoping to fill our own deep needs. Often, out of our love and need, we do our children a big disservice. When we take over our children's responsibilities; when we conscientiously try to "fix" all that's wrong in their lives; when we provide what they could provide for themselves, we help create people who never see the necessity to take responsibility for themselves. Our children fail to develop a sense of self-sufficiency. They learn to have great expectations of others, to make excuses for their inability to give back in kind. They drift and flounder as adults, dissatisfied with their lives and resentful because they feel entitled to start at the top.

When we give too much, we create the antithesis of our aim. We stop giving too much only when we determine, as Karen eventually did, that enough is enough, that our own welfare is as important as our children's, and they control their own lives rather than us. Our children will do well to release the bonds of their dependency on us, and we will do well to focus for once on ourselves and our own needs. We can choose to pause before we give in, once again, and ask ourselves the following questions:

Could I be allowing my children's problems to provide a distraction from my own pain and guilt?

Am I giving my children what they really need, or what I've determined they should have?

Am I afraid to ask for anything in return? Do I question whether I'm worth it?

Am I pampering my children because I get vicarious satisfaction out of indentifying with my child? In other words, am I really indulging myself?

Am I comfortable teaching my children to take from others, rather than create satisfactions for themselves?

Dan M.: Making Up the Difference

"Linda was in kindergarten when we first realized there was a problem. She didn't know the alphabet, and all of the other children did. She came home from school one day crying because of it.

"We didn't know what to make of it. Our pediatrician told us that children mature at different rates and warned us that we could actually make things worse by getting too anxious. His attitude was, 'Wait and see.' Still, we worried.

"We spent hours trying to teach her the ABC's. She finally got it, and then we read volumes of stories to her, asking her questions about them. She'd barely listen and interrupt, asking about things that had nothing at all to do with the story. But, we thought, what can you expect from a five-year-old?

"We got called into school for a conference in June. They wanted Linda to repeat kindergarten. My wife said, 'What are you saying? She flunked? How can you fail a kid in kindergarten?' Neither of us could believe they would do such a thing to a child that young. We couldn't allow it.

"That summer, we moved to a different suburb, where we knew the schools were better. We didn't tell Linda's first-grade teacher anything about her past problems in kindergarten, because we were afraid she'd be treated differently and never get a clean slate.

"Parent-conference nights were something we dreaded. For the next two years though, the only complaint was that she daydreamed in class.

"One of us did her homework with her every night, making sure she got it done. Already it was a big fight trying to get her to pay attention. Teachers warned my wife that Linda was getting too much help at home and not learning to do things independently. But as long as she was keeping up with the other kids, neither of us cared.

"When Linda's third-grade teacher said to us, 'Can you stay a few extra minutes?' on conference night, I thought, Okay. This is it.

"She said that Linda was having problems with phonics and had been sent to the school counselor for something they called a screening. The counselor thought that Linda might have auditory-perception problems. They wanted permission to do psychological tests.

"I was furious that they had done any screening at all without telling us. My wife and I marched into the principal's office and I gave him hell, but he told us it was standard school procedure. My wife was trying to calm me down, but I was furious. You can't imagine what it's like to hear someone tell you that your child isn't normal. I felt like my guts were being ripped in two.

"To the psychological testing, I said no. No way. By this time, I had read plenty about children with learning problems. I knew all about psychological tests. Nothing was definitive about them, and too much was left up to interpretation. With the wrong interpretation, Linda could be labeled for life. I wasn't going to trust Linda's future to some school psychologist.

"We had Linda tested that summer, but by someone we trusted, recommended by our pediatrician. She told us that Linda's problems weren't severe, but that the test indicated a slight learning disability. Because she felt Linda might benefit from extra help in school, she broached the subject of placing Linda in special education, but said it wasn't absolutely necessary. When she saw how dead set against it we were, she assured us that the school couldn't force us to put her in special classes, and that made me feel better.

"We worked with Linda every night. We hired tutors. I really believed at this point that we could 'fix' whatever was wrong, if we just kept at it long enough. But then she started having other problems. She couldn't pay attention in class. She'd talk to other kids, goof off, I don't know. We'd punish her. It didn't matter.

"When she was in junior high, other things started to bother us. My wife pointed out that Linda wasn't invited to parties. At first I thought, This is the least of our problems. Still, I wanted her to grow up like other children.

"My wife would make suggestions to her, like 'Why don't you invite some friends over? Join the Girl Scouts? Take ballet lessons?' The more she talked, the less Linda listened. All Linda wanted to do was watch TV.

"Do you know what it's like to know that your child isn't liked by other kids? My wife would leave work to drive by the school-yard and watch Linda at recess. Linda was always alone, or playing with kids who were much younger than she was. My wife would call me at work, sounding depressed, and the rest of the afternoon would be a waste because I couldn't think about anything else. It made me furious to think of other kids treating Linda like this. I wanted to kill all of the children in the neighborhood for being so cruel.

"One day we got a notice, registered mail, of an 'interdisciplinary staffing' on Linda. Can you believe they can do this to parents? My wife was throwing out all the mail that came from school at that point. I know this was pretty childish, but we felt we had the situation under control. We didn't want to hear what Linda's teachers had to say because it was too frustrating. Registered mail was the only way they could get to us.

"We couldn't keep the meeting a secret from Linda. My wife was hysterical, we were screaming at each other, and still we tried to tell Linda that it was just a normal meeting, and not to worry. Who were we kidding? Linda looked terrified. I wanted her to know that I'd protect her, and nothing bad would ever happen to her with me there, supporting her.

"I'll tell you what one of these staffings is like. You walk into a room and there's about ten strangers staring at you—psychologists, administrators, teachers, counselors. Even the school nurse was there, and I thought, What the hell is she doing here? Are they going to tell me that Linda has some disease on top of everything else? I resented every one of them. They were responsible for putting my child in large classes where she got no individual attention at all.

"This time they insisted that Linda belonged in special-education classes because she required more attention than the regular class teacher could give her. 'She can get the help she needs,' the school psychologist said. I said, 'You haven't helped yet!', and they all looked at each other. My wife kicked me under the table to try to get me to stop, best I didn't care. Who were these people to tell me what was best for my kid? Who were they kidding, telling me that it was better for her to be in special education, where she'd be stigmatized for life? I got up and left the room, and my wife had no choice but to follow me.

"We kept Linda out of special-education classes, and looking back, the strain was showing on us all. We were exhausted from forcing Linda to do her homework and get organized for school each day. Her organizational skills were so bad that there were moments I just wanted to shake her. There were times I thought, We're wearing ourselves out. Maybe she really belongs in special education.

"Linda entered high school, and I thought, here's another chance for a clean slate. But, again, a notice came for a staffing. Each of Linda's teachers reported on the problems she was having—attention span, English, math. Always problems.

"We walked out of that meeting, too. But Linda's homeroom teacher ran after us, down the hall. She looked like a child herself, so small and skinny, with long hair and huge eyes. I tried to walk past her, but looking like she was ready to cry, she grabbed my arm and said, 'I have a younger sister like Linda. My father would rather have seen her dead than see her in a special-education class. But she's so much happier now. She's so much more confident. Did you ever ask Linda what it's like to compete with other kids, and fail over and over again, in front of them? To have kids laugh at your mistakes? Did you ever talk to her about what she wants? Ask her! I care about her, too, I can see that she's changing. She's getting quieter, more depressed and anxious. She's so scared to fail, she won't even try anymore. She's giving up.'

"The truth is, I'd noticed it too. But I said, 'I'm sure this is none of your concern. She's our child, after all.'

"Still, all the way home in the car, I thought, I haven't asked Linda. I've always figured, What could she possibly know? She's just a baby.

"That night, I talked to Linda. 'They want you to be in a special class, a couple of periods each day. They said you'd get extra help. What do you think?'

"She looked at me and said, 'Daddy, I think I need all the help I can get.' It just about broke my heart.

"Linda went into special-education classes, and I went to observe. To me, the other kids looked like a bunch of delinquents. I lost ten pounds that year, all of it because my stomach was constantly churning. My wife and I dropped most of our friends. We couldn't stand the comparison game of how well their children were doing, when ours was having so much trouble.

"I felt helpless. It was ironic. My whole career as a

marketing consultant was built on my ability to solve problems. Why couldn't I solve the problem at home?

"Linda adjusted better than we did. She'd come home with an 'A' on an assignment, and say, 'Daddy, look!' I'd look and think, This is some silly crossword puzzle. When is she going to really learn anything? My biggest hope was that Linda would spend a few months in special classes and then return to regular ones. When they told me she'd need this kind of help always, it was the lowest point of my life.

"My wife and I finally went into therapy, but it was a year or so later, when we could barely stand each other and what was happening to our family. We had almost no marriage, no sex life, no anything. All we did was try to help Linda and worry about her.

"The therapist looked at us that first session, after hearing us out, and said, 'You feel responsible for everything your daughter has suffered, don't you?' I looked at him like he was crazy.

" 'Of course we're responsible,' I answered. 'We're her parents.'

"I've always felt that I was responsible, as the man of the family, to solve any problems. When I was a boy and anything bad happened, my mother would say, 'Wait until your father gets home, and everything will be all right.' Dad was the last resort, and somehow he always knew what to do. Everybody loved him, and I admired his strength. The only picture I have of what a father is supposed to be I got from him.

"I couldn't solve Linda's problems, no matter how much I tried, and it completely frustrated me. The therapist warned me that I had to begin to accept Linda's learning disability, and that nothing I could do would take it away from her. I thought, This man has no idea what it means to be a parent; I'll bet all of his children are screwed up.

"It was hard on my pride, but my wife and I became involved with the Council for Exceptional Children, and were referred to a support group of other parents with similar problems. I went to the group meetings basically because I thought I was going to learn how to help Linda succeed in school from these other parents who had gone through the same experience. Instead, the parents in the group lectured me to detach from Linda and her problems at school. They said we should step back and allow Linda more independence.

"Facing up to my need to control Linda's life, and the fact that my need could be harmful to her, was something I fought against for a long time. One thing that I've learned is that as parents, we don't realize how much we need our children to validate us and make our dreams come true. Now, I see that I kept Linda away from the help she needed because, above all else, I needed her to be normal. If she wasn't a normal child, then how could I be a good father? I poured all of my energy into doing what I thought was helping her, but I was actually desperately trying to help myself.

"Now, I look forward to these group meetings. I find a lot of support and understanding. Not everyone in the group has a special child, but they've all been caught in the trap of expecting more from their children than is possible. For the first time, I've learned to look at my own feelings and Linda's feelings as separate. Because I'd feel stigmatized if I was in special-education classes, I assumed Linda felt the same way. I couldn't have been more wrong. Linda just wanted to get through school, no matter what it took. It was the beginning of the realization that my daughter was an individual, who didn't feel the same way I did about everything.

"I sit back and listen to the other parents talk, and I realize we all do this. We all want so much for our children that sometimes we don't really see them clearly. Linda's learning disability isn't what made us react the way we did. We would have reacted the same way to any problem she might have had. We couldn't stand the fact that things weren't perfect for our daughter. All of the parents in the group see it in each other—this driving need to protect our children, not so much because they'll be safe and comfortable, but so that we can sleep at night.

"What I've learned, and what's made such a difference, is to let go of some of my control over Linda's life. Al-

though I can support her, and encourage her, I can't change
the cards she was dealt in life. I really can't solve her
problems, and even if I could, it might not be the health-
iest thing for her. That's the hardest lesson for any parents
to learn. Once you learn it, though, your whole role as a
parent begins to make much more sense.''

Linda's parents faced one of the hardest experiences a
parent ever has to face: learning that for inexplicable and
unexplainable reasons, their child will never learn the way
other children learn. Any parent who has ever been told
that his child will never function physically, emotionally,
or intellectually the way "normal" children function can
identify with their pain and anger.

Much has been written about underinvolved fathers and
protective mothers, resulting in a false assumption that
only mothers become obsessed with helping their children
and solving their problems. Dan's story demonstrates that
the driving need to "help," guide, control, and change a
child that forms the basis for overparenting can be as much
the province of fathers as mothers.

Dan's need to help his daughter—to cure her—became
an obsession. Parents like Dan, who have handicapped
children, can carry an enormous burden of guilt. "I've
created a damaged child," was a notion that was so intolerable to Dan that he spent years rigorously defending
himself against it. If he allowed Linda to enter a special-
education class, it would make her learning disability an
undeniable fact, so he avoided it at all costs.

Dan's denial blinded him to a crucial fact: Linda needed
special help. No amount of love or parental involvement
was going to change that. All of his help—doing her homework, fighting with her teachers, moving to a new neighborhood—actually produced more serious problems. While
there are kinds of help that will make a child stronger and
more competent, Dan's kind of help fostered dependency
and insecurity in his daughter. Linda sensed that both of
her parents wanted—and even needed—her to achieve in
school to a point that was beyond her capabilities. She
internalized her parents' anxiety to such an extent that she

gave up, rather than attempt a task and fail. Avoidance was her way of "looking good," because if she never tried, she couldn't fail.

Why was it so difficult for Dan to accept his daughter's limitations? An achievement-oriented performer, Dan saw his daughter as an extension of himself. Linda's problems made him feel inadequate and inept. The specter of his own father, the consummate family problem-solver, haunted him and was responsible for the erroneous belief that all of life's problems are solvable. His self-esteem plummeted as Linda's difficulties continued and he over-parented her to bolster it. Unconsciously, his heroic attempts to keep her in the regular classroom were aimed at meeting his own needs and unfulfilled hopes, rather than at providing what Linda truly needed.

Dan learned that what he really needed was help managing his own feelings, rather than advice on how to control his daughter's life or improve it. Linda didn't need his constant help and overinvolvement as much as she needed encouragement in finding ways to help herself and her father's acceptance of her limitations.

Those of us who are lucky enough never to see our children faced with problems as extreme as Dan's daughter's can still identify with the need to have our child achieve and excel. All parents grapple with this compulsion to get overly involved in their children's lives in order to "help" when the going gets tough. But when "helping" becomes an obsession, we take on a burden of anxiety and frustration. We hear that our child has fallen short, failed, disappointed, or dissatisfied, and we feel sick with anxiety. He or she receives a "B" instead of an "A," fails to make the team, or doesn't get into the college of our choice, and we're terrified. What does this mean? Have we failed as parents? What are we doing wrong? What more can we do? We feel we must charge in and wrestle the problem from their hands, no matter how insignificant.

It's not that we're naïve. Many of us are "authorities" on child psychology, having read scores of it to "help" our children. But it's difficult to apply what we know intellectually to what we feel so intensely emotionally. We wrestle with the knowledge that it would be healthier for all if we stopped solving our children's problems and let them fend for themselves at times. But when our children are unhappy, such a stance seems too cruel, too cold. I'll help, we think, just this once.

Some parents' behavior when their children are troubled makes Linda's father's attitude seem like indifference. There are thousands of parents who cannot eat, sleep, or think of anything else when their child has a problem. They worry, react, and obsessively take up the reins of control. They give and keep giving until they are emptied and aching inside, but they can't rest until the problem is solved.

This type of parent defines "problem" loosely. It may be major school failure, illness, chemical dependency, or depression. But it may also be five extra pounds, a bad headache, or a less than desirable steady boyfriend. The degree of the problem is insignificant, the reaction to it extreme.

The problem that consumes such parents is often no more than that the children have failed to live up to their expectations. They believe that they know better than their children what they really need, even if these "children" are well into middle age themselves. At worst, they can become nagging, scolding doormats to their children, resentful that their advice is taken so lightly. And because they feel such intense responsibility for their children's lives and problems, their children feel almost none.

In the 1970's, the term "codependent" began to be used by researchers in the field of drug and alcohol dependency to describe people whose lives were troubled as a result of being closely involved with family members whose problems centered around the abuse of drugs or alcohol. In her book *Codependent No More*, Melody Beattie broadened this definition to include anyone who "has let another person's behavior affect him or her and who is obsessed with controlling that person's behavior."

It seems obvious that most of us are affected by other people's behavior, especially the behavior of those we love. Codependents, however, feel much more than loving concern or a warm desire to help. They allow another person's behavior and problems to become their obsession. The need to solve these problems controls their lives.

Consider for a moment the characteristics that Beattie and others have found symptomatic of codependency. Codependents:

- anticipate other people's needs
- feel safest when giving to someone else
- feel responsible for the thoughts, actions, needs, and destiny of other people
- feel guilty and anxious when someone they love has a problem
- feel compelled to come up with the solution to a loved one's problems
- seldom develop their own interests, yet become consumed in their loved one's
- put their own needs last
- drop whatever they are doing to come to the rescue of someone in need
- feel angry and upset if their help and suggestions don't "cure" the problem
- do for others what they are capable of doing for themselves
- feel other people's pain more deeply than they do
- do little to maintain a social life of their own, so that more time is available for their loved ones
- deny painful realities about their loved one, even when these realities stare them in the face

Experts in the field of mental health are beginning to discover that relationships that wrestle with the problem of alcohol or drug dependency are not the only ones that create codependency. The parent who loves too much shares many of the characteristics of the codependent. Notice the similarities. Parents who love too much:

- anticipate their children's needs
- feel safest when giving to their children

- feel responsible for the thoughts, actions, needs, and destiny of their children
- feel guilty and anxious when their children have a problem
- feel compelled to solve their children's problems
- seldom develop their own interests, yet become consumed in their children's
- put their own needs last
- drop whatever they are doing to come to their children's rescue
- feel angry and upset if their help and suggestions don't cure their children of their "problems"
- do for their children what they are capable of doing for themselves
- feel their children's pain more deeply than they do
- do little to maintain a social life of their own, yet become enmeshed in their children's social lives, love lives, and married lives
- deny painful realities about their children, even when these realities stare them in the face

It is clear that parents who love too much are very much codependent people. Their energies are focused on their children's lives and concerns to the exclusion of almost everything else. Their enmeshment in their children's problems is intense and painful. They may actually become depressed, isolated, withdrawn, or ill because of them.

An important part of being a parent is fostering our children's ability to develop independence and self-reliance. Codependency too often results in helpless children who never seem to gather the resources they need to solve their own problems.

We need to become better at distinguishing minor problems from major ones that really require our involvement. We need to understand that many problems resolve themselves over time. We need to believe that our children will solve their problems if we stand back and allow it to happen naturally, and that our standing in the way actually exacerbates the problem. Our children might not solve the problem quickly, or in the way that we would have, but the only way they will ever become self-reliant is if we allow them responsibility. Most of all, we need to accept that some of our children's problems may be due to things that we cannot possibly change. Accepting our children's limitations without our stomach churning, our heart pounding, and our obsession to try to change what can't be changed is as vital to their well-being as to our own.

Sheila K.: Working Mom

"When Karl and I decided to have our first child, I didn't think about changing my life as much as rearranging it. I knew I would keep working. I'd just started a new position in special-events marketing when I found out that I was pregnant. The thought of walking away from my career—of losing the momentum it had taken me years to build—was unthinkable. It wasn't a question of money. On Karl's salary, we would have managed very well.

"Was I selfish? Maybe so. My job has never been ideal for balancing career and family life. There's a lot of stress, and I'm exhausted all the time these days. I look at the younger men and women who work for me who are single and have no real responsibilities at all, and I envy them. Still, I think Karl and I have done a pretty good job with Barb and Todd. Or at least I did until recently.

"It's strange, but when I'm at work, I look at the pictures I have of Todd and Barb on my desk and I think about them, and there's something that's almost romantic about the feeling I get. I can't wait to get home to be with them.

"What ends up happening? The second I walk in the door, we all start fighting. Their homework isn't done, the stereo is blasting, Barb's been on the phone for over two hours, and I lose my patience with both of them.

"The littlest things set us off. I'll ask Todd what he got on his math quiz, or how his computer class went, and he'll say, 'Here we go again!,' because he thinks I ask too many questions. A simple question is an interrogation to him.

"Barb and I have been arguing with each other for a month because I want her to take a review course to prepare for her SATs this spring. She doesn't want to spend two nights a week taking the course, although last year, when she took driver's education, two nights a week for private lessons was no problem.

"I can't make her do anything she doesn't want to do. Still, I can't understand why she won't take advantage of an opportunity to prepare for tests that can mean all of the difference in the world for her future.

"I can't get my kids to see that these years, while they're in high school, are so important to them. I don't expect them to be perfect. I don't want to put too much pressure on them. All I want is for them to be prepared to go after everything they can get in life.

"My mother says, 'You can't just direct the kids the way you direct the people who work for you.' It's hard. I wonder, When do you hold on? When do you let go and trust your children to make the right choices for themselves? How do you stop the constant worry? At times I want to shake them and say, 'Listen to me! You think you know the answer to everything, but I've already been there. I *know*.'

"I love Barb and Todd more than I can tell them. It hurts me that all we do is yell at each other these days. I expected these years to be difficult, but never like this. Barb and Todd get along so much better with their father, and at times I'm almost jealous. They run to confide in him, but tell me I'm prying if I ask a question. Karl just shrugs and says, 'You worry too much. Leave them alone; they're good kids.'

"Sometimes I wonder if I've given them enough. I think every woman who works and cares about her career wonders about what she may be doing to her children in the long run. You take every step you can to see that they have everything they need, but you still worry about the choice you made.

"My own mother lectured me about all the hours Barb

and Todd spent with baby-sitters and in after-school programs when they were young. She used to say, 'Children raised by baby-sitters develop the IQ of the baby-sitter.' That really got to me, because nothing is more important to me than my children's education. I've been very involved with their schools and teachers over the years, and I know that I have nothing to worry about in terms of Todd and Barb's intelligence. Both of them are very bright. What concerns me is that they take the easiest way out of everything. It's an attitude that didn't come from me. I would have loved to have the opportunity to take advanced courses in high school, while my children want the easiest classes and the least demanding teachers. I would have gone to summer school if it would have meant I could have taken the courses I needed to get into a better college. Barb and Todd think, Why bother? They don't understand how important it is to have an edge in the world today. They've been given everything, and they'll never understand how much it took to get them all these things they take for granted.

"I wake up at five in the morning, arguing with them in my mind, and I think, Why is this so damn important? I should be satisfied that my kids do well in school, aren't on drugs, or having any of a hundred problems kids have today. Why do I want more? I should just give up and let them be who they want to be.

"But, the truth is, I don't really believe this. What kind of parent just gives up?"

Perhaps there is no greater element than stress that induces well-intentioned parents to become parents who love too much. Add guilt and high expectations, and you have all the ingredients for overparenting.

Sheila, who had never truly dealt with her guilt over the hours and energy she devoted to her career, transposed her growing anxiety over her choice into unreasonable anxiety about her children. She tried to cram all of her parenting into the three hours she spent with her children in the evening. Todd and Barbara reacted strongly to what they felt was an anxious, nightly cross-examination by a mother so stressed out that she easily lost her patience and perspective.

It is difficult to be empathic and to tune in to a child's needs when we're under tremendous pressure. Stress makes us feel out of control. Sometimes we overcompensate by trying to control others. Sheila bickered and argued with Barb and Todd partly to alleviate her own anxiety. Without meaning to, she set up a power struggle that began to feed on itself. Control invites resistance. The more Barb and Todd resisted, the more helpless Sheila felt and the greater her need to exert control over their choices grew.

Many parents who are heavily invested in their careers find it difficult to make the transition between work and family life at the end of the day. This can be especially difficult if we maintain a position of power at work and have grown used to directing others. As one company president jokes, "After a half hour at home with my kids, I want to run back to my office, where nobody says no to me and everybody does as I ask."

A parent who desires the same control over his children that he experiences at work runs the risk of discouraging the child's independence or creating passive or active resistance. Perfectionistic demands for higher and higher achievement can be overwhelming to a child, leading him to conclude, "I'll never be good enough to satisfy my parents, so why bother?"

This is not to say that there is something inherently wrong in attempting to motivate and encourage children toward achievement. The problem comes when we're never satisfied. Sheila, for example, admitted that she was rarely satisfied with her children's accomplishments, even when she had reason to be, because she felt they were capable of so much more. Never feeling satisfied and forever attempting to effect a change in another person's life is the cornerstone of loving too much.

When we're very achievement-oriented ourselves, as Sheila was, and frustrated because our children don't appear to be imbued with the same drive, we have to consider a number of things. First, is it possible that from somewhere in our own background we hear the voice of a screaming and overly demanding parent who was never satisfied with us? (Take a closer look at Sheila's comments about her mother, and you'll hear this screaming voice.) Are we still reacting to this voice and feeling inadequate? Are we unconsciously repeating the same stance with our children because we're overly concerned with their reflection on us?

What do our children's achievements mean to us? Do we simply want them to gain fulfillment through a sense of accomplishment? Or do we need them to succeed in extraordinary ways so that we can scream back to that voice in the past, "See, I was good enough after all. Look at the incredible children I've raised!"?

Sometimes we overestimate our children because of our own needs to have them reflect well on us. When they fail, it's because the world has misjudged and mistreated them, we feel. When our children's weaknesses become clearer and we can no longer blame the world, we redouble our efforts and try to change them so that they might come closer to what we see as their potential.

How much of what we take on is true parental responsibility? At what point does all of our helping become a means of meeting our own need for a perfect child who will reflect back glory on us, bolster our self-esteem, and prove that we're good parents?

There's an enormous price we pay for all of this. When we see our children as extensions of ourselves, we believe we can exert control over everything that happens to them. We can't, and as a result, we end up feeling constantly out of control. Worrying and obsessing don't leave us grounded enough to really help when it's truly needed. Caught in the web of anxiety, we sometimes make small problems large and large problems worse.

Our perfectionistic demands, our anxiety, our entanglement in their problems, create children who find security only in their accomplishments. When we see our children as extensions of ourselves and try to mold them into the image of our highest expectations, they are seduced into a kind of self-aggrandizement that results in painful feelings of worthlessness every time they fall short.

Sheila was on the right path when she began to ask herself, "Why is this so important to me?" It's a critical question. When we're bent on changing our children, and "helping" them to become more of what we believe is best for them, we have to take a hard look at whether our expectations of them are realistic. We should be wary, because unrealistic expectations breed a sense of failure.

How do we know if our expectations are unrealistic? While this question is difficult to answer, there are some essential guidelines for determining if expectations of children are healthy or unhealthy:

- Healthy expectations focus on developing the inner qualities of the child, the true self. Unhealthy expectations stress "looking good" and people-pleasing.
- Healthy expectations are flexible. They take into account how the child is feeling at that time. Unhealthy expectations are rigid. They attempt to fit a child into a preexisting picture of how he or she should be.
- Healthy expectations are realistic. They make success attainable by taking into account the child's limitations. Unhealthy expectations push the child past his limits and toward perfectionist goals.
- Healthy expectations are motivated out of love. Unhealthy expectations are motivated out of the need to control.
- Healthy expectations encourage the child's sense of self-esteem and competence. Unhealthy expectations are really motivated toward enhancing the parent's self-esteem.

What if, after we take an assessment of our expectations, we conclude that we're realistic and our children are acting out destructively? Then we need to ask, "Why are my children resisting? What do they need so badly that they'll sabotage their own futures to obtain it?" These needs seldom are material. More often they are needs for understanding within limits, acceptance without harsh judgments, and the opportunity to assume a level of personal responsibility.

When our children fail to meet our expectations, it's critical to think less of our "failure" as parents and more about our children's perspective. If we can begin to separate our children's needs from our own and try to truly understand them as people separate from ourselves, we start on the right track to giving real help and guidance.

Kathy M.: Supermom

"There are worse things I could be accused of in life than loving my children too much. We all get a little crazy when our child is hurting. We all get superinvolved. Intellectually, I know that if I let my children be independent and make good decisions, bad decisions, and their own mistakes along the way, it should be okay. But I'm being honest. It's really not okay. I know what the 'right' thing to do is. I'm telling you how it really is, not what the right answer is.

"When I was a child, if something had happened to me like what happened to my daughter, Nanci, the other day, my mother would have ignored the whole thing and not said a word to me. But, when Nanci's hurting, I want to help her.

"She came home that night acting a little funny. I didn't think anything of it at first, until dinner, when she seemed depressed and didn't eat.

"She went to her room to do her homework, and I couldn't stop myself. I had to call the mother who'd driven Nanci and her friends home from school, to see if anything had happened.

"The woman picked up the phone and said, immediately, 'Is your daughter upset? It was just awful!'

"It turns out that in the car on the way home, Nanci's friends talked about a party planned for that Saturday night. Nanci wasn't invited to it, and the girls knew it, but they talked about it—and all the fun they were going to have—right in front of her. Nanci just sat there, pretending not to care.

"I was devastated. I was sick that she had been hurt.

" 'Couldn't you do something?' I asked this woman. Still, I know how it is. What could she do?

"I should have just let the whole thing drop, or waited to see if Nanci came to me to tell me about it. Why was it my business, anyway? I realize that Nanci has to learn to solve her own problems with her friends. But at the same time, this is the kind of thing I've never been able to ignore.

"It's strange, but you'll swallow your own pride so easily for your children. If someone doesn't invite me to something, I say, 'To hell with them.' But when it's my child, locked in her bedroom and feeling miserable because of the spoiled brats in this neighborhood, I can't stand it. I'm ready to go into battle. I knew it was probably a mistake, but I was on the phone that same night with the mother of the child who didn't invite Nanci to her party.

"This woman was lovely. She understood. She had a talk with her daughter, and at about ten o'clock her daughter called Nanci, just to chat, and was really nice to her. Nanci went to bed feeling better.

"After the kids were asleep, the phone rang, and it was this mother again. She repeated everything her daughter had told her: 'Nanci always has to have her own way. She acts like she knows everything, which starts all the trouble.' I couldn't sleep well after hearing that.

"My daughter has this self-righteousness about her that I've noticed myself many times. Over breakfast the next morning, I had a talk with her. I told her that I don't want her to change who she is, but that she doesn't always have to have the last word. I could see I hurt her feelings, and that she couldn't really understand what I was talking about. She'd forgotten all about last night. To her, the whole thing was no big deal.

"But what else could I do? I don't want Nanci to be excluded from things. My getting involved in stuff like this has been very detrimental at times. For all I know, this little girl might have gone to school that day and told the whole fifth grade that I called her mother. I might have caused a disaster.''

It's interesting how much support we can find from other parents for being totally preoccupied with our children's concerns. Here was a whole cadre of mothers who love too much burning up the telephone lines to orchestrate their children's social lives. Why? Because they love their children, want the world for them, and would go to any extreme to help and protect them.

Kathy hurt when her children hurt. She empathized, understood, sympathized, and felt her daughter's pain. There was little separation between what her daughter was feeling (or what she surmised she was feeling) and what Kathy herself felt. A lack of separation from what our children are feeling and what we are feeling is so much a part of our loving too much that we rarely see anything wrong in it until we're in so much pain over our children's lives that we can't stand it.

Kathy worried that her overinvolvement in her children's lives was detrimental. Perhaps no real harm would come from her phone call to another parent or from the subtle manipulation she used to ''buy'' her daughter friendship. But her need to act, to control, to solve this small problem, is evidence of how frantic she becomes whenever her children are threatened. It's this frantic, often chaotic reaction to our children's problems that so often becomes detrimental. Helping becomes an obsession. With our minds and stomachs churning in pain over our children and their problems, we lose our ability to think clearly, or to act in our children's best interests. The anxiety is so intense that in our state of emotional turmoil we must do something—anything—fast.

In such a state, we rarely solve anything. We need some distance and separation in order to stand back and think, rather than to react quickly, doing anything and everything willy-nilly in hopes that it will help our children.

Had Kathy been able to stand back and consider Nanci's unhappy experience with her friends, she might have seen that constantly rescuing Nanci was fostering the "self-righteous" attitude that was the root of the problem. Her daughter's "self-righteousness" was, in fact, the beginning of a feeling of entitlement—a belief that she was entitled to special attention, deference, privileges, and consideration by others. It's the prime result of a childhood experience of being continually pampered by parents who are obsessed with helping their children manage their lives.

Overinvolvement is about control. When our children do it our way, we feel successful and powerful. We become addicted to the "fix" our children give us when they let us solve their problems and control the events in their lives because we feel all-powerful and all-necessary. The problem is, we become completely dependent on our children to continue this wonderful feeling of control and importance. We become "addicted" to the thrill we get when they need us, and can't let go because we've grown dependent on them to continue to validate us in this way.

If you're concerned that you may be overinvolved in your children's lives, ask yourself the following questions:

Am I relying on my child too much for companionship? Am I afraid to let go and separate because I fear facing an empty nest, an empty marriage, an empty life?

Can I embrace the idea that all people—even my children—are ultimately responsible for themselves once they're grown, and that I really can't solve problems that aren't my own?

William T.: Parents Who Love in a Living Hell

"Now that Billy's agreed to see a therapist, it's a relief. This last year has been a living hell for all of us.

"When I got the call from the youth officer at the police station and it was the second time, I almost said, 'Let him stay there.' I'm running out of solutions. But how can you turn your back on your own son?

"The first time Billy was arrested, it was because he and his friends were pulled over for speeding and the officer found open bottles of beer in the car. Rick, the driver, was drunk.

"I knew Billy and his friends drank beer on weekends. You'd have to be pretty blind as a parent today not to know that this is what kids do. I was no perfect kid myself, and I freely admit this to Billy. I grew up in the sixties, and there were plenty of drugs around, and I guess I tried most of them. I don't want to be a hypocrite. I try to understand Billy and see his side. But I couldn't believe Billy was stupid enough to speed around with open liquor in the car after curfew.

"Billy has never been an easy child to raise. My wife says that he's ruining her life. She's always on him about one thing or another. Especially school. Billy ditches his classes, and we get calls all the time. He wants to quit and get a job. We won't allow it, even if it means we drag him out of bed every morning. It's tough. I've written so many notes excusing his tardiness to school on one pretext or another. Look, I know it's wrong, but in high school today they flunk kids for being late without an excuse. What are we supposed to do? We want him to graduate.

"There are times I'd just like to run away from all of this. I look at my life, and it seems there's been so much unhappiness in it. I've thought of leaving my wife many times. Our marriage was never all I had hoped it would be. I wonder if I'm going to die one day without ever knowing what it means to love and be loved and be happy. But I could never leave with Billy and all of his problems. I've resigned myself to staying until Billy's eighteen.

"After the car accident, we grounded Billy for two weeks. We tried to talk him into seeing a therapist, but he absolutely wouldn't go.

"Last week we got the second call. This time, it was Billy on the phone. 'Dad, I'm in jail. I need you to come and get me out.'

"This time, Billy, Rick, and some other kids had broken into the school. Billy had been caught walking out the back door carrying a computer. The other boys ran away.

"My first thought was that it figures Billy was carrying the goods. It was just like him to be that stupid and allow all the rest of them to have their hands free to run away. His first words in the car on the way home, were, 'You're going to get me a good lawyer, aren't you?' We got home and my wife was hysterical. Nobody slept that night. Finally, the next morning, Billy agreed to see a therapist.

"I don't know. Maybe something good can come out of all of this, yet. Even after all of this, I still believe Billy's a good kid. I don't even believe he wants to be involved in these things. I think he just wants to be accepted by the other kids so badly that he loses his judgment.

"I'm not sure how to cope with Billy and his problems anymore. Maybe I've done a rotten job as a parent. But how? I gave this kid everything. I pray that this is just a phase he's going through, and that he'll snap out of it and be the kid I remember before all of this happened."

Here again are the themes of codependency and lack of separation, and their result. One of the myths of parenthood is that if we're good parents, we should be willing to destroy ourselves if it might help our children. "If someone were aiming a gun at one of my children's heads, I'd stand in between" is a statement so many parents make that it's become a cliché.

But rarely are we defending our children from something as brutal as a firearm. Most often what we defend our children from are the consequences of their own self-destructive behavior.

All behavior has consequences. These consequences are tools that teach us. Billy, who ditched school and broke into buildings, might have learned from the consequences of his behavior if he had been allowed to. To Billy's father, however, the thought of his son spending a night in jail or standing trial without the best lawyer he could provide was tantamount to child neglect, and he couldn't allow it.

Many parents will rise up at this point, siding with Billy's father, saying that heartless and cruel measures such as allowing a child to spend a night in jail or obtain court-appointed counsel would make things worse, and what

Billy needs is help and more love and understanding. Until you meet parents who have done everything in their power, including spending thousands of dollars trying to cure the problems of their delinquent children, this illusion remains firm and dangerous.

When our children are in trouble with the law, drugs, or alcohol, our behavior follows a predictable pattern. First we deny the problem, as Billy's father did when he readily blamed Billy's friends and pictured Billy as helpless against their influence. Much of his denial was fueled by an unconscious need to justify his own adolescent behavior— drinking, drug use, or worse—by being too understanding and accepting of similar behavior in Billy.

Once we can no longer deny the problem, we accept that it exists. Too often, our acceptance is flavored with justifications and rationalizations.

Where many parents at this point would go for help themselves, and learn to deal more effectively with the problem from parents who have been there before him, the parent who loves too much takes a different tack. His guilt is enormous. He exerts all of his control, and enmeshes himself in the problem. It's all he thinks about. He feels compelled to solve it. He suffers. Nothing becomes too difficult to do if it will help the child. He begins to take over his child's responsibilities and separate him from the consequences of his behavior. He rescues the child over and over again, loving him and forgiving him even when he does the unforgivable. At the bottom of all of this is the belief that if he tries hard enough, he can make his child behave as he thinks he should, just because he wills it.

It's a difficult course to take but such a parent actually gets some gratification out of all the enormous self-sacrifice it takes to live day in and day out with a self-destructive person. Old movies come to mind of the misunderstood young offender in the courtroom, his tearful parents sitting in the front row, loving and supporting him no matter what he's done. Isn't this what it truly means to be a parent?

It's never that romantic in real life. We give all of our

love and support, but nothing changes. We try everything we know. Through it all, we shield ourselves from an important fact: Children do not stop their self-destructive behavior to please their parents or make them happy. They stop when the consequences of their behavior become unbearable to them.

There are reasons for Billy's problems, but they have nothing to do with his parents' lack of concern over his welfare or their efforts on his behalf. They have to do with the fact that he gets some gratification from acting out. Sometimes children unconsciously create serious problems and symptoms to deflect other problems in the family. Billy's father spoke of wanting to leave the marriage. Billy may have sensed that his parents were unhappy with each other. The thought of his parents getting divorced is scary for any child.

Teenagers, especially, will try to take care of their parents, preserve the family, and absorb their parents' pain. Some will sacrifice themselves to this end, and engage in all sorts of self-destructive behavior. They are saying, "I'll be a problem if it means the two of you will stay together to solve it."

The parent who loves too much focuses on the child's problems because it's natural to give his own troubles a backseat. He may usher the entire family into therapy, seeking ways to help the child. Months pass, but nothing changes. The therapist watches the child do everything he can do to stay "ill," to keep his problems at the forefront of family life. On an unconscious level, the child has decided, If I'm depressed, if I flunk all of these classes, if I never have any friends, if I keep gaining weight, my mother and father will have someone to take care of, someone to rescue. If I can't solve my own problems and I remain a child, my parents have someone to "baby."

There may be many other problems festering beneath the family's surface that are worthy of the parents' attention. The therapist may point this out. But the parent's own marital conflicts, depression, and emptiness are minimized.

Thousands of parents each year seek therapy for their

children, hoping that the therapist will be able to succeed where they have failed. When it's recommended that the parents themselves participate in therapy, anger and denial set in. But rarely is much accomplished when the child is labeled the "designated problem" and the parents refuse help in dealing with their own needs and feelings that impact on the relationship.

When we love too much, we don't always see that we also need help. Our needs are just as important, yet all we see is a child—our child—in trouble. We think that with enough love and attention, we will one day prevail. But while some problems our children have are amenable to love and understanding, there are serious problems that demand a different approach. Alcoholism, drug addiction, and delinquency are among them. Destructive behavior will continue if we never allow our youngster to realize the consequences of his own actions.

We need to look at why we keep rescuing our children. Is it because the consequences of their actions would be so awful for them? Or is it because we feel too guilty watching them endure the results of their own behavior? It's a symptom of our lack of emotional separation from our children that results in our feeling their pain, and we need to look at that squarely.

This is not to say that the second our child gets into trouble, we should abandon him. This message is for parents who have already tried months of love, attention, and understanding, and whose help and assistance has got them nowhere: We tend to think that if we expend enough energy, we can solve any problem. This is a myth. It's also a display of grandiosity on our part, which we need to give up before we can go on.

What can we do, when watching our children destroy their lives feels like a knife in our heart? Although it's the opposite of what we want to do, when our children are self-destructive, we love them best by admitting our own powerlessness over their behavior. We need to stop blaming ourselves. We can't be perfect. We will require great support to truly understand this, because every time our child hurts, we're going to want to run in and rescue him because we feel solely responsible.

If you can identify with this pattern, these are groups of parents who have been there before you and have also made the mistakes of loving their children too much and inadvertently shielding them from the lessons the consequences of their behavior would have taught them. These parents are found in Al-Anon, TOUGHLOVE, and more than twenty thousand parent support groups across the nation. Their lessons are simple once we open ourselves to them: Give up your self-will. Focus on managing your own feelings. Set firm limits that will allow you to live your own life. Give up the idea that you can control other people, even your own children. Take a stand, and share your guilt and anger with others who will understand you, support you, and help you manage these feelings. Realize that what your rescuing, caretaking behavior does is enable your children to continue the exact patterns of behavior that you're trying to prevent.

If this advice is hard to hear, it's because thinking of ourselves first, before our children, is the antithesis of loving too much. Detaching from our children's lives and problems is foreign to us. Focusing on ourselves is something we've avoided. And while love, understanding, and help are always a first step when we love someone, we must admit it when our efforts are in vain and go on from there.

If you've tried gentleness and forgiveness, rescuing and getting tough, counseling and treatment, threatening, crying, begging, and otherwise driving yourself crazy in an attempt to change the child you love so much, ask yourself these questions:

Am I willing to go for help, not to learn how to change my child but to understand and gain control of myself?

Does endlessly rescuing my children from the consequences of their behavior really mean that I'm a good parent? Should I rethink this definition?

Am I afraid to take a stand with my children for fear of losing their affection? How high a price am I willing to pay for this affection?

Seth L.: Parents Who Pay

"My wife always asks me why I keep shelling out money to my children. She thinks that after I finished paying alimony and child support to their mother years ago, it should have been enough.

"It's not that I can't say no. I can say no. If one of my children came to me and said that they wanted to buy a gram of cocaine or something, I could say no. But when they ask for something reasonable, I want to give it to them. I want to help.

"When my youngest daughter, Sheryl, decided to go back to graduate school and study acting at twenty-six, it wouldn't have been my choice of career for her. Still, I listened to her arguments, and I decided to give her the money. All I could hope for is that she'd finally find herself, and be happy.

"When she called from the university and told me the program was a competitive nightmare, and that no matter how hard she tried, she still wasn't good enough, it upset me. I had to do something. Anything. She was having migraine headaches; the band was practicing outside her room at six in the morning and she couldn't sleep, and all I could think of was, How can I help? I'm here and she's there. What can I do? How do I get her to a doctor? How do I solve this problem?

"I sent her money to go to a doctor. I told her that if she wanted to move out of the dorm, she could rent an apartment and I'd pay.

"This drove my wife crazy. She says I obsess about Sheryl's problems, and never think about anything else. She thinks I spoil her by giving her money. Well, what am I supposed to send my children when they call me for help? A crate of oranges?

"The divorce was harder on Sheryl than on any of the other kids. She was the youngest. I left my ex-wife for good reasons, but I gave up tucking my kids into bed every night. I gave up having any real control over how they were raised.

"I look at my kids, and I think that I haven't always been happy, and I want better lives for them. I can't help wanting them to have everything they want. When you see that your children have emotional problems, that's guilt-inducing, and you have to do something. If my money means that they can live a happier life, even if I have to go without something, then I give it to them. To be honest, I'm glad that I'm the one they come to when they need something. Maybe I pay just because I *can* pay. This is one thing I know I can do for them, and to me it's worth a fortune."

Today, it's estimated that 53 percent of all eighteen- to twenty-four-year-olds live with their parents and depend on them financially. Eleven percent of twenty-five- to thirty-four-year-olds live at home, and the figures are growing. Children who have had more education and opportunities than their parents ever had are returning to the nest, unable to function independently of their parents.

The question is, whose needs are really being met in this situation? Seth's story is a case in point. He willingly sacrificed for his children for a simple reason: He wanted to. A hangover of guilt over divorcing their mother provided potent motivation for him to give his children anything they asked for as compensation. "I'll make it up to you for my mistakes," was his message to them.

Was Seth giving too much when he sent his twenty-six-year-old daughter back to school, and used his money to solve the problems she encountered there? It would have been unreasonable for Seth to deny his daughter money for medical care. Providing her with financial support to go back to school may also have been a legitimate decision. But what makes all of this giving suspect is Sheryl's difficulties in school. Were Sheryl's problems at school due to a harsh, competitive environment? Or were they due to the fact that she was totally unequipped for experiencing failure or stress due to a lifetime of being rescued from it?

In Seth's case, his capacity to spend all of his waking

moments worrying about his daughter's troubles yet do so little about the swelling problem right under his nose at home is interesting. How long until his second wife's feelings about the financial support he continues to give his grown children erupt into irreconcilable differences? The hardest thing to realize is that behind all of our altruism toward our children can lurk an intense need to control them, keep them bound to us, so that we can deny the reality of our own circumstances and our own feelings. We wedge our children between ourselves and our spouse, forever fending off intimacy. We can use their problems to distract us from our own pain, or to assuage our guilt.

It can be hard to determine the difference between the times when our financial assistance is legitimately needed and should be granted, and when the outcome of it will be incompetent, irresponsible children who never leave us to take responsibility for themselves. It's a good bet that if we're indulging our children for our own satisfaction, we're over the line. If we use our money to rescue them from natural consequences of their actions, we're over the line. If we're giving money because it's easier than giving ourselves, we're over the line. If we're giving money to convince our children of our value to them, we're over the line. In each case, we're fostering dependency over independence.

We have to take a hard look at all of this financial assistance. Do we need to be needed in order to feel worthy? On some unconscious level, do we want our children to rely on us, even if this means they become unable to function without our help?

The problem with rescuing our children financially or otherwise is that they never learn to deal with inevitable stress in their lives. They end up fearing adulthood, and at the same time expecting too much from it. Rather than raising grateful, responsible children who are devoted to us, we often get rebellious, resentful children, rudderless in their careers, critical of our values, and hopelessly dependent on our support.

Sandra Z.: Grandparents Who
Love Too Much

"When Shawn was born, I thought it was the greatest thing that ever happened to me. He was the first grandchild, and so adorable with his head full of blond hair and blue eyes. I couldn't believe that from my daughter, Leah, this gorgeous child had come.

"Leah never should have gotten married. She certainly never should have had a child. She was too young, and she never had any common sense. I once found the baby with his diaper over his head, almost suffocating in his crib. She was watching a movie, and although the baby was crying so loudly that he was turning purple, she was waiting for a commercial to see what the problem was.

"Her husband, Bob, was another story. I never had any confidence in him to become a part of Shawn's life. When Shawn was born, he took one look and admitted, 'What do you do with babies?' Fatherhood was overwhelming to him.

"Neither of them should have gotten married. But when my daughter decides she wants to do something, there's little anyone can do to talk her out of it, and no one knows that better than I.

"Anyway, they had Shawn, and neither was able to cope with anything. It wasn't just my feelings about it—it was pretty much so. My husband and I worried about Shawn all of the time. Dan would call me from his office and say, 'Go there, watch them, make sure they have something to eat.'

"Leah welcomed me with open arms. Bob got married, but it was like he didn't get married. He wasn't home half the time, because he was out with his friends or playing basketball, and she was left alone with the baby. It was a constant exodus back and forth for me, bringing food, and making sure Shawn had what he needed. I didn't do it for Leah. I did it for Shawn.

"I was with Shawn every step of the way throughout his childhood. A day didn't go by that I wasn't over at their place, or that they didn't come to me. I sat with him when he had the measles. When he had to have his tonsils out, I was the one he woke up to, and it was my coat he threw up all over on the drive home from the hospital.

"I was the one who paid for Shawn's clothes, bought his toys, checked with his teachers about how he was doing in school. Leah spent her money on herself, and wouldn't step inside one of Shawn's schools. Often, I would be over at her house and she and Bob would be fighting, and I'd look at Shawn and think, What kind of life is this for him? My friends would tell me that I worried too much. After all, Shawn was healthy, and seemed happy. Still, I kept thinking, with the right environment, this kid could be outstanding.

"Naturally, Shawn and I were very close. When your grandchild looks at you and says, 'Grandma, I love you,' you go crazy. It's like nothing else in the world. It made everything worth it.

"I started to really worry about Shawn when he was in junior high. If you ask me, Leah and Bob's expectations of Shawn have always been much too low. When Shawn and I were alone, I tried to talk to him. I told him how important it is to be educated, to have goals. I didn't expect Shawn to be any great brain. My daughter wasn't too bright, and Bob's no genius, so I didn't expect their offspring to be Einstein. But I did expect him to keep up with the mainstream, and naturally to want to better himself. I tried to influence him in a way I knew his parents wouldn't. I took him to museums, taught him about music and art. But I was up against a lot of bad influences.

"Sometimes I was like a broken record: 'Shawn, start your homework. Call some friends and make plans for the weekend. Stand up straight. Don't look so bored all of the time.' It exhausted me. I was no teenager. But who was going to give Shawn any direction, if not me? What Shawn wanted to do, if left to his own devices, was to lie around in his room or play video games for hours.

"When he was a teenager, I started to feel shut out. Shawn used to come to me first, before other people, with his problems, and all at once he didn't do it anymore. He told his mother that I was too pushy; that I was always telling him everything that was wrong with him. Well, I have high goals, but they're really not too high for Shawn.

"When Shawn decided not to go to college, they didn't tell me. After I heard about it, I thought it was terrible, and I told Leah how disappointed I was in her for letting him make this decision on his own. She should have at least made him take his ACTs. She should have made him apply to college, in case he changed his mind. I almost hit the ceiling when Shawn stood there telling me that college wasn't relevant to him, and Leah backed him up.

"But I'm not his mother, so I couldn't do anything about it. Truthfully, they told me when it was too late for me to do anything about it. Shawn's excuse for not going to college was that he wanted to get a job. So what does he do? He gets jobs in gas stations, or busing tables in restaurants. I try to talk to him. I say, 'Better yourself, Shawn. You can handle more responsibility.' But he gets this stubborn look on his face, which reminds me of Leah.

"Although I keep trying to build him up and build him up, there's a limit to how much you can build up a person. You can't just look into his eyes and say, 'You're so wonderful,' when he comes over, looking like a slob, with a big chip on his shoulder. I keep telling him he should make something of himself before it's too late. He could still take college courses at night. He could learn accounting and have a decent future for himself. But whatever I say these days, he does the opposite.

"Last week Shawn walked in wearing an earring. I threw him out of my house, and told him never to come over again like that. He walked out the door, and I felt like I had killed a part of myself. What if he never comes over again? What if he hates me?

"Leah called that night and lectured me that I shouldn't talk to Shawn about what he wears, because he's expressing himself. But an earring? On a boy? Is this supposed to be Shawn's identity?

"The whole thing is breaking my heart. But what can I do? I'm only Shawn's grandmother. I thought the hardest job in the world was to be a parent, but to be a grandparent is even harder. You have no control. You see mistakes being made, and you're helpless to do anything about it. The intensity of the love you feel for the child is so great, yet your hands are tied. And knowing that you can have that grandchild removed from you completely, by that child's parents, you tread lighter than you want to, because you never want to risk that.

"Leah tells me to back off. 'You already had your shot at being a parent, with me, and you didn't do such a great job,' she says. Well, I guess that's the thanks I get."

Here was Sandra, so strong and responsible, yet unrewarded and misunderstood, driving herself crazy as her children and grandchildren became more adroit at circumventing her efforts with each passing day.

Why do we do it? Why, when our child-raising years should be over, do we seize as many parenting responsibilities for our grandchildren as our children will allow us? Why was Sandra so compelled to pick up the reins of child-raising once again? Was it really to protect her grandson from parents she felt were incompetent? Or was there more?

Sandra's need to devote so much of her energy to Shawn was born of love but fueled by guilt. So often, one special child in a family is "singled out" for an onslaught of obsessive love, concern, and attention. When grandparents love too much, it's often the offspring of the child they feel most that they've failed with. Knowing their child's weaknesses too well, they find in the birth of the grandchild a cause of great joy, but also great anxiety. The grandparent has little faith in his child's ability to be a parent. At the same time, all of the unmet expectations of what it means to raise children take a final curtain call. With the birth of a grandchild, everything seems possible once again.

Loving and protecting a grandchild from the "sins" of his parents can become an obsession, especially if we have the guilty feeling that we are somehow responsible for those "sins." Shawn's birth fanned the fire of Sandra's unmet expectations as a parent as well as her strong yearnings to be needed, loved, and vindicated.

To combat her guilt over Leah, whom she felt she had failed somehow, as well as her anxiety for Shawn's welfare, Sandra took control. The alternative was to leave Shawn, a defenseless baby, at the mercy of his parents' immature and unpredictable ways. This was unthinkable—like casting Shawn's fate to the wind.

There is no person on earth more tirelessly dependable than a grandparent who loves too much. There is no person more selflessly capable and willing to assume the responsibilities of others than this "experienced" parent who knows so much more now than he knew then. Sandra exhausted herself in order to give Shawn what she thought he needed, and to parent him in a way she was sure only she could do.

With all the energy Sandra put into raising her grandchild, it seems a mystery that Shawn ended up as irresponsible as the parents she tried to protect him from, yet this was predictable from the start. When we take over children's responsibilities, no matter how good our intentions, we take away their reasons to become responsible themselves. When we anxiously direct and manage them, believing that we, and we alone, know what's best, their ability to initiate and accomplish things through their own efforts is sacrificed. The self-esteem we try to bolster with constant lectures about how much we believe the child is capable of is diminished because no opportunity is given to increase it through independent accomplishment. Praising them, and at the same time denying them the room to develop pride in their own accomplishments, is something that we need to be wary of.

Sandra's attempt to control her family and make them become what she needed them to be had high costs for all involved. Leah reacted to her control by becoming helpless—an effective but passive-aggressive way of resisting her mother's attempts to control her life. She internalized her mother's anxiety over her motherhood, and depended on her more than was reasonable. When any of us depend completely on another, believing we're unable to do for ourselves, we grow to resent the person we depend on, even though we may need that person desperately. Leah resented her mother, as much as she needed her, and when her need diminished as Shawn grew up, she began to express it.

Shawn also reacted strongly to Sandra's control. He rebelled by avoiding her, aggressively walking into her house wearing an earring and acting in other ways he knew would deeply upset her. What Shawn feared was his grandmother's high expectations of him. Every time she looked at him and said, "You can be successful, you can do better, you can do more," he grew anxious. She was trying to tell him that she had tremendous faith in him. What Shawn heard was something else: "I want you to change; nothing you do is good enough; I'm disappointed in you."

In the middle of it all was Sandra, exhausted and frustrated from raising two generations of children, battling against their irresponsibility while at the same time helping to create it.

Control invites resistance. Instead of releasing control and allowing her children to make their own decisions as they grew up, Sandra increased it. Where her children once ran to her and depended on her, they began to fight for their freedom. The more they fought her, the more she enmeshed herself in their lives.

A host of grandparents may rise up at this point and say, "Yes, but you don't understand my situation. My grandchild really needs me. There are real problems here. I have to take control, no matter what the price."

It's difficult to give up control. As grandparents, we feel intense love for our grandchildren. Accepting our children's imperfections as parents without trying to help or exert our influence can seem impossible.

There are times when we should intercede. Obviously, if we sense the child is the object of abuse or neglect, it would be irresponsible to look the other way. However, when we're interceding over less crucial matters, such as parenting style or philosophy, then we run the risk of stepping over the line between grandparenting and parenting. It's a setup for creating a power-and-control game between the parents and the grandparents that follows a particular pattern: The parent, having felt controlled all of his life by the grandparent, uses his power over the child to pay the grandparent back. He makes passive-aggressive statements such as, "We're not coming over anymore if you ever say that again," or veiled hints that let the grandparent know where the true power over the grandchild lies. It's a manipulative, often cruel game, which leaves the grandparent feeling frustrated and helpless.

What can a grandparent do to avoid this trap? Instead of directing and controlling our grown children or grandchildren, we need to face our own fears. We must learn to manage our own anxieties. We must take a harder look at our own needs and how they may impact on the situation.

Loving grandchildren too much can be an unconscious way of attempting, one last time, to meet our needs and achieve an identity through the people we love. Parts of us are starved for love and praise we never got from raising our own children. Hungry for accomplishment and recognition that's denied us, we hope to see our dreams come true in someone else. However, if we're not careful, we'll crush this grandchild whom we love too much with unrealistically high expectations coupled with stifling overprotection. Sometimes, to love them more, we must love them less.

Alan A.: Parents Who Just Want to Be Good Enough

"There's something to me, as a parent, that is shocking: We're really not prepared for the rejection of us by our children.

"When your children grow up—and all of mine are in their thirties now—your desire to be a parent, to inject yourself into their lives in order to help them, doesn't change. What changes is their need of you. One day this beautiful child, who you have all for your own, is not your own anymore. He's off in a world of his own, doing things that you don't even know about, that he doesn't want to include you in on. That's a shock. To me, it was interpreted as rejection. No matter how much I thought I knew about being a parent, I wasn't prepared for it.

There is a difference in generations in terms of how we treated our parents and how our children treat us. I might not have a close relationship with my own parents, but I never abused them. I went out of my way to see that I wasn't hurting them in any way. I think about my children, and realize that we're so often used as a target for their frustrations.

"I think we were all victims of the Walton syndrome. We all want that beautiful picture of the family sitting around together and enjoying each other; the children respecting the parents; the parents getting the honor and respect of their children. It hasn't worked that way in our case.

"Christmas was a good example. Our children all came home, and while I was happy to have them come, I was just as happy to see them leave.

"My wife and son ended up in a huge argument that was so silly I can't even remember what it was about. I drove my son to the airport, and he said, 'Dad, I'm just not going to come home anymore. Mom's the only person in the whole world that makes me feel like this—like some stupid little kid. I keep telling myself that I won't let her get to me, but she always does.'

"I wonder how two people I love so much, and who I know love each other so much, can't get along. When I try to intervene, they both pull away from me.

"The twins were just as bad. They used our house like a hotel room, and I was surprised they even found time to sit down for Christmas dinner with us. When I asked them about their classes, or their boyfriends, they told me to stop worrying and stop prying. I think I asked out of habit, more than anything else, but it gets so that you never know what to say to your own children, without starting a fight.

"All of my children are thought of by me every day of my life: What are they doing? How is it going? And the worst question of all: How can I help? This is what has brought me into a lot of problems with my children—this 'How can I help?' attitude or drive. It somehow evolved itself into a mode of intrusion into their lives, of not letting them grow up, or take their knocks alone.

"I should have been able to figure out that if something became too stressful and difficult to deal with, and I could contribute in some way, that I had a strong enough relationship with my kids for them to pick up the phone and call me and say, 'Dad, I want to talk to you about something.' But I couldn't wait. I'd have to know what was going on in their lives. I pushed my way in more than once, and though I don't think I made anything worse, I couldn't always make things better.

"I've come to realize that, as a human being, your ability to help and your ability to accomplish things is limited. I can't change the relationship between my wife and our son. They are going to have to work it out for themselves. And I can't make the twins care more about the rest of the family. I can't make them confide in me if they don't want to.

"Maybe I'm finally giving up. I listen to my family fight at the dinner table, and I find myself thinking about my golf game the next day, or an investment I want to make. It's not that I'm indifferent. It's that I've lived through so many of these arguments. I've come to see that many problems resolve themselves over time. I've learned that it's suicide for me to keep worrying and trying to make something happen that perhaps was never meant to be. I think I've spent two thirds of my life as a parent, and there's still a third left. It's my time now.

"My wife and I have pushed ourselves to develop friendships and other interests we didn't have time for when we were raising the kids. It hasn't been easy. Nothing can really take the place of all of those years where everything revolved around the children and caring for them, worrying about them, driving them places, seeing to their needs. We weren't perfect parents by a long shot, even though we sure tried. But if my children come to me one day and say, 'Dad, you weren't a perfect father, but you were good enough,' it will be okay. I think I can live with that."

* * *

Alan's poignant remark—that he can live with simply being a "good enough" parent—is the foundation for recovering from a lifetime of overparenting. When Alan let go of the need to be a perfect parent—and with it, the need to create perfect children by controlling, rescuing, and intruding his will on them—it freed him from an obsession that had been both painful and ungratifying.

Not that this was easy for Alan, or any parent. There will be times when Alan will undoubtedly feel compelled to step back into old roles of pushing, rescuing, aiding, and advising. Sometimes this will be appropriate. Loosening the bonds of mutual dependency with our children does not mean we no longer love or help. It means we make a distinction between giving what's truly needed and giving too much. It means that we let go of the need to be a perfect parent, and just be a parent. We simply be ourselves, without trying to please everyone around us, or make our life's mission maneuvering our children in order to make them change and be closer to our expectations. We step out of the way and allow them to take the responsibility for their lives that will teach them the lessons they need to grow, more than anything we could do for them.

For Alan, this meant overcoming a fear that had haunted him since the day he became a parent: that he'd be a failure if he couldn't solve his children's problems. Facing our fears about what will happen if we stop controlling every element of our children's lives is always the biggest obstacle. It may seem contrary to everything we believe that it is not our job to solve our children's problems or manage their lives, and that our biggest task is to take care of ourselves. Fear or guilt can be formidable hurdles in the way of our allowing the people we love to suffer the natural and logical consequences of their actions, but it is the only way they can learn and grow.

At first we may feel very selfish, stepping back. But if we look at why we stepped in, in the first place, we'll get a better picture of where our selfishness really lies. Often we step in because we can't bear our own feelings when one of our children is unhappy. If they are in pain, we are in pain. We do many things for them that they could do for themselves, if they chose to, because our own feelings are so uncomfortable that they became unmanageable.

What we do we often do for our own sake, under the guise of helping another. We must realize that our children, especially our grown children, have skills and capacities for taking on responsibilities. What they may lack is the motivation or the need, and often they lack it because we are there, advising, managing, and giving.

For Alan, the realization that he was powerless over many of his children's problems, and that many could only be resolved naturally, over time, was the beginning of self-acceptance rather than self-defeat. Today, he loves his children no less. In fact, the love he gives them is in many ways more genuine and honest, because it is based less on guilt or a need to control. As he freed himself to pursue his own needs, he freed his children to pursue theirs.

Change is a process. There's a great deal of ambivalence about taking the steps we need to take in order to change old patterns. But soon what once felt normal and familiar begins to feel uncomfortable and unhealthy. This is the first way we know we're changing how we think and feel. And if the change we wish to make involves focusing more on our own lives, and less on our children's, we may feel bored and anxious now. Even if being enmeshed in their lives was a torment instead of a joy, without this constant focus we feel panic. We've spent our lives looking for happiness in our children. How do we settle down with ourselves?

The chapter that follows outlines a plan of action to help you get started.

CHAPTER 12

IF YOU'RE A PARENT
WHO LOVES TOO MUCH

"Where did we go wrong?"

You became a parent who loves too much for a reason. Your own mother and father may have been parents who loved too much. They served as a model for how you would one day react to your own children.

Or perhaps you were deprived as a child. Your physical or emotional needs weren't met, so you made a conscious decision that your children would never suffer in the way you did. Somehow, in your enthusiasm, you were pulled to the other extreme of overindulging your children, and now this worries you.

Maybe you feel guilty. As hard as you tried, you failed to become the perfect parent, and your children failed at becoming perfect kids. Their pain feeds your guilt. In an effort to assuage this guilt, you give and give.

Maybe you are a single parent or a parent with an unsatisfying marriage. Your children fill the emptiness you feel inside. They are what you live for. You know you should let go, but you fear it. Your life would seem empty.

Perhaps your overinvolvement began because you felt you had to compensate for the underinvolvement of your husband or wife in your children's lives. You try to make up for it by doing everything you can for them.

Sometimes we overparent to bolster our self-esteem: "I'm a good parent, see how much I do for my children."

We believe that the more involved we are, the better parents we are, and it makes us feel good about ourselves. We do not see the cost of our overinvolvement.

The cost is borne not only by our children, but by ourselves. Do you suffer from unrelenting anxiety over your kids? Are ulcers, headaches, insomnia, or high blood pressure something you've acquired along the way? After all you have given to your children, do you find that they are nonetheless plagued with problems and use you as a target for their frustration? Are your dreams of closeness with your grown children turning into a reality of tense get-togethers and avoidance?

Solutions are not often easy. Change is always met with resistance. No matter how much pain you may be in, it's still easier to stay the way you are, because it's comfortably familiar.

Changing any life pattern requires desire, persistence, and courage. If you see yourself as a parent who loves too much and wish to change, the following steps will be helpful.

Stop Trying to Be the Perfect Parent

It is no more possible for you to become the perfect parent than it is for your son or daughter to become the perfect child. Perfection is an illusion—and a perfect setup for failure.

When we're busy trying to be perfect, we also tend to expect perfection in others. We cannot truly meet the needs of a growing child if our high expectations won't allow us to accept the youngster's abilities without comparing them to our own or others.

The intense emotional involvement with our child will sometimes cause us to make mistakes. We must remember that the mistakes we make are more than compensated for by all the times we succeed as parents. We don't have to be perfect to raise our children well.

It's emotional common sense to strive instead to be a good enough parent.

Good enough parents provide for their children's needs without becoming enmeshed in every drama of their lives. They don't attempt to orchestrate their children's social lives, or fight battles for them. They encourage their child's internal strengths and qualities without becoming overly concerned with externals or the way their child compares with others. They provide a nonjudgmental atmosphere in which self-esteem is fostered, without anxiously judging the child who can't live up to rigid expectations. They realize that their children can't always match their expectations—and that they can't always match their children's. They understand that making mistakes is a part of the learning process—even for parents. Most of all, good enough parents encourage the child's independence, realizing that the child's emotional separation from them is a healthy step to maturity.

To begin to break your patterns of perfectionism, start with the following steps:

- Stop torturing yourself over the mistakes you make. Your children don't need you to be perfect. They are tremendously resilient. The bond between parent and child is instinctively strong. It will allow a few errors on both your parts.
- Stop anxiously brooding and conjuring up lists of things you should be doing to improve your child's life. Focus on relaxing and enjoying your children as they are.
- Be wary of the demands you may be making on your children because of your own need for their lives to be perfect. They don't expect this, and neither should you.

    Look at your "shoulds" for them. List them on a sheet of paper: "He should get an 'A' in math; she should make the Olympic team; he should earn a six-figure income; she should graduate at the top of her class."

    Ask yourself, "Why do I believe my child should do these things? Am I so sure that doing them would make my child happier? Am I less of a parent because my children won't make the same choices with their lives that I'd have them make if I were truly in control?''

As you answer these questions, you will open the door to conscious living. Awareness is the pathway to choice, and choice is the opportunity for change.

Learn to Accept and Validate Yourself Daily

If you're overinvolved with your children, there's a good chance that you're underinvolved with yourself. When we feel empty or insecure inside, we are compelled to meet our emotional needs through others. Often we attempt to meet these needs through our children. However, no one relationship in life can meet all of our needs.

Look back at your own relationship with your parents. Did you feel accepted for who you really were? Was it okay to be angry, sad, hurt, adventurous, or silly? Were you constantly told to calm down, speak only when spoken to?

Were your parents around to encourage and spend time with you, or were you often left alone? Was there constant conflict in your home? Did you withdraw out of fear?

Many of us received the message from our own parents that it is not okay to acknowledge and validate ourselves. This was true for Jim, a forty-year-old architect and father of three. "If my dad told me once, he told me a hundred times, 'Never brag about yourself. You'll bring on bad luck.' He was always negative about everything. I think he thought that if he allowed himself to be happy about anything, God would strike him down or something.''

What disturbs Jim most about himself is that he seems to have inherited this quality of his father's. "My kids call me Mr. Doom and Gloom. They don't want to talk to me about anything, because they say I get too bent out of shape. My wife says I'm always worrying and expecting the worst. She says the kids have the problems they have because I put too much pressure on them and I'm never satisfied with anything.''

For Jim, awareness was a beginning. It gave him the courage to challenge some of his beliefs. He began to see that acknowledging his own accomplishments and thinking more positively about himself and his life didn't mean he was being selfish or conceited. The more positive he became about himself, the less demanding he was able to be with his children.

Many of us learned in childhood that feeling important, complimenting ourselves, or displaying any evidence of self-satisfaction was wrong. What we can't give ourselves we have a hard time giving others. Worse, because we are so emotionally self-depriving, we look toward others to validate us to fill us up. An obvious place we look is toward our children. We may need them to be out conquering the world in order to feel better about ourselves. Or we may need them to stay dependent on us, in order to feel useful and needed.

The most important thing we can learn to do is to validate and accept ourselves. The more we love and validate ourselves, the less we will need to depend on our children's accomplishments to boost our self-esteem. When we accept ourselves, we are more at peace with ourselves, and this will have enormous benefits for our children.

Try the following steps:

- Make a list of ten qualities that you like about yourself. Look at this list at least once a day.
- Acknowledge yourself five times a day. This will probably be more difficult than it sounds, because your inner critic will be outraged. He will respond with all the reasons you're not good enough. For example, if you say, "I'm proud of the way I shared my feelings with Carol today," your inner critic may respond with, "She was probably thinking that I'm really stupid and a terrible mother."

    Or perhaps you acknowledge yourself with, "Good job on setting limits with Jimmy," and your critic chimes in with, "Yes, but now he hates you, and you've made him miserable." Be aware of your inner critic, and don't let him undo your efforts at learning to validate yourself.

• One way to combat a harsh inner critic is to practice affirmations. Affirmations are positive statements about yourself expressed in the present moment. For example, "I accept myself just the way I am" is a powerful affirmation. It essentially expresses a personal goal, yet is stated as if it is already true.

Affirmations are usually in direct opposition to current beliefs we already hold about ourselves. Most of the messages we hear in our heads are negative: "I'm not good enough," "I'm a lousy parent," "I don't deserve to be happy." As we start to repeat positive messages about ourselves, we can begin to challenge and change our inner thoughts.

Be persistent. Practice saying the following affirmations, and make up your own:

I am deserving of love and happiness in my life.

I freely accept all of my feelings; I am secure.

I let go of the past; I am at peace.

Reach Out to Others Who Can Help

To change patterns that are making you miserable and that push your children away rather than closer to you, you need support. When we're always the ones in charge and are overly concerned with helping others, we may miss the signs that tell us that it is our turn to be listened to, to be understood and helped.

Parents who love too much need to mourn their losses, share their hurt, and verbalize their anger and disappointment. We cannot heal what we don't allow ourselves to feel.

If we reach out, there are lots of resources available to us. Therapists or counselors are experienced in identifying unconscious patterns that stand in the way of our living more fulfilling lives. They can show us parts of ourselves that we are unable to see. Skilled in communicating with us in a manner that will help keep our defenses out of the way, they can help us create a vision for a better life.

In such a relationship, we are protected under the umbrella of confidentiality. We needn't worry about "looking good." Over time we build a trusting and honest relationship that allows us to unveil our true selves, perhaps for the first time. The process of telling "our story" is often the most liberating experience of our lives.

Often, the greatest personal growth we can achieve comes from working with people like ourselves, parents who know what it means to care about our children more than ourselves, and who have also become so absorbed in the problems of others that they have little energy left to identify or solve their own.

Groups of people working together toward change meet in an environment that spotlights the interplay between people. It re-creates a "family," and with it, the style of relating to others that was shaped for us in childhood. We'll replay whatever role we played in our families—the quiet one, the helper, the achiever, or the clown—when thrust into a group of people whose care, concern, and behavior recalls our family's.

Support groups are "families" with new rules: honesty, support, and constructive criticism. Manipulative games, deceit, and avoidance get confronted, but in a caring way. Expressing feelings is encouraged. Everyone is allowed to experience intimacy in relationships, take off masks of defense, and experience more of who they truly are.

There are hundreds of support groups in the world today that are appropriate for parents who are struggling with the challenge of family life: Al-Anon, Alcoholics Anonymous, Overeaters Anonymous, Parents Anonymous, TOUGHLOVE, Narcotics Anonymous, Adult Children of Alcoholics, and others. None of us has a "case" so exceptional that we won't find help and understanding in one of these groups if we reach out for it.

For parents who love too much, taking the first step and contacting one of these groups will be the hardest part. It will mean letting go of the notion that we can do it all ourselves.

We can't sometimes. It's hard to accept our imperfections, our inability to change others, especially those we created ourselves. But we need to go for help if our love shows every sign of becoming an unhealthy addiction. We need caring, constructive support to allow ourselves to let go.

If you see yourself as a candidate for help, yet feel embarrassed to seek such assistance, consider the following:

- Life is an endless process of exploration, learning, and discovery. You don't have to know it all. You don't have to have all of the solutions to everyone else's problems. You don't need to know all the solutions to your own.
- Attend a group seminar, anything from a public lecture on effective parenting to a private parents' support group. Remember, you can go and just sit and listen, without participating at all. You'll be surprised at how safe you can feel with people who have been there and know exactly what you feel.
- Call a friend and share your concerns. You will probably be surprised that your vulnerability will enhance your friendships as well as offer you needed support.

Develop Your Own Network of Support and Healthy Interests

Backing out of your children's affairs will be very difficult. You may feel empty and alone, without your role as "helper" and "problem solver." You may feel off balance and out of control. At times you may even feel as if you've lost a part of your identity. Your kids may pull you back to old patterns. In order to break out of this pattern of mutual dependency that hurts more in the long run than it helps, you will need other resources in your life.

Overinvolved parents see life through tunnel vision. The focus of their attention is almost always related to their children. They do not see that they have many other roles and options in their lives: "What? Take a vacation? With the kids along, it wouldn't really be a vacation, and I just couldn't leave them behind." "I'm too tired to play tennis. I haven't played since Joey was a baby, and I'd probably be awful."

The truth is that each of us is able to expand ourselves and meet our needs in many different ways, and our children aren't as needy for us as we'd like to imagine. Aside from the satisfaction we get from our parental role, we may also achieve satisfaction as a businessperson, a tennis player, a friend, an investor, an explorer, an entrepreneur, a member of a club, a bowler, a singer in a choir, a sculptor, or a writer. Our options are only limited by our desire, our imagination, and the excuses we make for not exercising them.

If you wish to become less involved in your children, become more involved in developing other roles in your life.

When we focus on our own needs, we are not abandoning others. Many devoted parents erroneously feel that the perfect parent should always be involved with the needs of his or her children, and that to take care of one's own needs is selfish. To be the best possible parent, however, we must take care of our own needs, too. Try the following:

- Make a list of all of the things that you once thought you'd do after your children were grown. If your children are still young, make a list of all the things you'd do if you didn't have children. Look at your list and ask, What is really holding me back today? Generally, it's a fear of the unknown. People who put all of their eggs in one basket do so because it makes them feel secure.
- Compile a list of what you need in a relationship. Many of us have no idea. Perhaps we never received what we needed as children and have felt undeserving our entire lives. Or perhaps we learned that a good parent is self-depriving. Maybe we give too much to our children as a way of avoiding dealing with our

own needs. No matter what the cause of this belief,
we need to start taking care of ourselves, too.

- Contact that old friend whom you were meaning to
connect with for so many years. Or find a new friend.
One of our most important needs is friendship.

As you start to realign this balance of needs, you
may feel guilty. Affirm to yourself, "The more I give
to myself, the more I have to give to others; the more
happiness I have inside, the more I can share; by
watching me give to myself, my children can learn to
give to themselves."

Deactivate Your Automatic Pilot

We react. Instead of taking time to think through a problem, we're compelled to take action. Controlled by the
drama of our children's lives, we're unconsciously hooked
into getting deeply involved. The "automatic pilot" goes
on, and we go through our paces: listening, worrying,
taking control, advising, begging, arguing, pushing, and
wringing our hands.

David is a man who's on "automatic pilot" when it
comes to his children. His daughter, Jeannie, came home
crying over something her swim-team coach said to her.
David headed for the school to punch out the jerk who
upset his little girl. What exactly did this jerk say to his
daughter to make her cry? David never asked.

David's son, David, Jr., was two hours late coming
home from work because he stopped with his coworkers
for a beer. David, Jr., is twenty-three. David, Sr., was
pacing the floor in a panic, thinking of a hundred terrible
things that might have happened to make his son miss
dinner, and was ready to call the police.

Frank, the baby, is struggling with his final paper for
history class. David is in the next room, as anxious as he.
After a matter of minutes, it's David in there, writing the
paper.

Like David, many of us respond intensely and quickly.
Too quickly. We use "crisis thinking" even when there is

no crisis. Ruled by our emotions, we are unable to use logic. We dive into the first solution that comes into our heads. We react, and the way we react is often not in our best interests or our children's.

What we fail to realize is that certain problems resolve themselves over time. Some of our children's problems are serious, and would benefit from our involvement. Others will resolve themselves naturally, over time, and there's no need for our concern. Yet we tend to look at all of our children's problems as if they were equal. Consider the following situations:

Our grown daughter calls us and cries over an argument with her husband. We lie awake all night, thinking of solutions, getting upset, feeling terrified for her safety, only to find that they kissed and made up the next morning. This happens twenty more times. What will it take for us to see that our daughter's problems with her husband are larger in our mind than in hers, and will resolve themselves over time?

Our little boy cries that all of the other kids hate him, he'll never go to school again. We call the teacher, the principal, think about moving to another town, and torture ourselves thinking about his rejection. The next day we approach him with the solutions we've sat up all night devising, and he looks at us in wonder: "Oh, everything's okay now. I didn't really mean it. I love school."

Our thirty-year-old daughter complains about her job. We give her names and numbers of people who will help her find a new job. We call all of our friends, and get more names. She never calls anyone. We think she's too humiliated to call. When we have a talk with her husband, he laughs it off and says, "Well, you know your daughter. She likes to complain, but she really loves it there."

As parents, we get confronted with an endless array of problems while raising our children. If we become wrapped up in every detail of our child's life, we are likely to create more problems then we attempt to solve.

Overreacting is a cornerstone of overparenting. The answer lies not in ignoring your children and their problems, but conquering your unrealistic fears. When you sense that your child is troubled, ask yourself, is your fear and anxiety based on reality? Or are you magnifying the situation because of your own internal fears and need to overprotect your children?

If you can begin to see how your "automatic pilot" is forcing you to crash land in your relationships, try the following:

- Begin to notice your "automatic pilot" in action. In what situations do you find yourself reacting to your children, rather than making objective, conscious choices? Make a list of your most reactive "trigger" points. Do you go crazy when your kids don't look good? Follow your rules? Act like adults? Meet your expectations?
- Instead of jumping into action, STOP! Take a few deep breaths and wait a few minutes. Think quietly. This time will allow you to cool your emotions and begin to get perspective on the situation. We rarely make our best decisions when we are acting out of fear, anxiety, or anger. Under stress we are most likely to magnify problems beyond what they really are. If we allow ourselves to calm down, we can best help our children and ourselves.
- If you are unable to calm down, call a support person instead of dealing immediately with your child. Choose a friend who understands the situation but who is not emotionally involved. Talk about your feelings and be open to feedback. Remember, when it comes to our children, we often lose our best judgment. We are just too close.
- Realize that as you stop reacting to your children, they may stop provoking you. Every interaction is a two-way street. Control invites resistance.
- Once a day, repeat the following words, borrowed from the famous serenity prayer of Alcoholics Anonymous: "God grant me the serenity to accept the things I cannot change, the courage to change the things I can, and the wisdom to know the difference."

Learn to Let Go of Control

You've given everything you have and more. You advise, protect, encourage, rescue, reassure, supervise, counsel, and see untapped strengths in your children that even they, in their wildest dreams, can't imagine. You'll do anything and everything to get your children on the right track. But the more you do, the more you are defeated. Nothing seems to work.

Ask yourself: Am I doing all of this in an effort to help and advise my children? Or could it be that I want to guide my children because I don't trust them to take the right path without my assistance? Consider Joan's story:

"It really bothers me that Carol's so shy. I've tried everything. I try and draw her out by asking her all sorts of questions about her day. I enrolled her in a public-speaking course, thinking it would help, but when she came home crying, I pulled her out. I tell her all the time how beautiful she is, how she has every reason to feel confident in herself. Nothing helps.

"It hurts me so much to see her alone on weekends. I've called some of the mothers of kids in her class and explained what's going on. They always make sure that their kids invite her to parties, but Carol doesn't even want to go.

"Desperate, I talked to our pediatrician. I thought maybe he could talk to her, or maybe there was a medication that could 'pick her up.'

" 'You've got to stop coddling her,' he told me.

" 'But if I let her do what she wants,' I argued, 'she'll never do anything. She'll sit in the house every weekend, by herself.'

"The doctor insisted that I was taking too much control. When he said Carol's shyness was a reaction to my pushing her, I was outraged. All I was trying to do was help her."

Over time, Joan learned to back off. "It was hell. The more I tried to let go, the more I came to see how over-involved I really was."

At first things appeared to get worse. Carol seemed quieter than ever. "Then the most amazing thing began to happen," Joan says. "She started to do things on her own. She started to talk more. In the next year, she began to make a few new friends—kids I really liked. And for the first time that I can remember, she actually came into my room just to discuss things with me. She's a very different kid today than she was a year ago. I'm not saying that she's Miss Popularity, but she's not half as shy as she used to be."

If you take charge of your children's problems, they are not encouraged to take responsibility for their lives. Letting go of control requires a combination of insight and action. Consider the following:

- Controlling our children is a setup for conflict and disappointment. Even with the best of intentions, it doesn't work. The bottom line is, people will do exactly what they want to do, and this is true for our children. They will behave in ways that appear to meet their needs. They will choose destructive ways to meet their needs if they can't find constructive ones. They will only change when *they* feel a need to change. True motivation only comes from within, and the only person you can ever change is yourself.

- Stop giving advice, focusing on all the negatives, obsessing and worrying, imposing your own viewpoint, and generally staying wrapped up in your child's daily affairs. You do not have to stop loving or caring, but you do need to stop controlling your children. Distinguish your child's responsibilities from yours. Start by noticing which of your child's obligations you automatically take on as your own. Do you return their library books? Do you clean up their rooms? Do you push them to make plans with their friends? Do you stand over them as they do their homework?

  If your children are grown, do you file their taxes for them? Pay their rent? Do you involve yourself in the daily affairs of their marriages? Do you play the role of therapist if they look a little tired?

Recognize that the fear that drives you to take over these responsibilities stems from the unconscious belief that your children cannot make it on their own. You want to ensure a safe outcome because it is so hard to see your children suffer. Yet paradoxically, the more you take over, the less you allow them to experience their own sense of competency.

Which responsibilities can you give back to them? Make an action plan. Have a meeting with your kids and define whose tasks are whose. This may open the lines of communication to a better relationship.

• Your strategies must change and adapt as your children grow up. The abilities of a toddler are far different from those of a grade-schooler. A six-year-old is usually able to clean himself, make his bed, and straighten his room. A twelve-year-old can take on the increased responsibility of watching a younger sibling, doing his homework alone, or cutting the lawn. Every year a child should take on more responsibility than in the previous year. Keep in mind that the ultimate goal of parenting is preparing the child for independence.

A Healthy Marriage Shapes a Healthy Family

Be honest about your marriage for a moment. Is it working? Does it meet your needs for closeness, affection, sexual fulfillment? Is your communication open and honest? Do you have fun together? Do you share secrets and dreams? Do you plan time alone with each other?

For many of us, these can be very discomforting questions. Too many marriages have turned into a lifestyle of mutual convenience and unspoken resentment. We accept indifference and neglect in the name of security. We try to keep it all together for the children.

We struggle through years of denial and quiet disillusionment waiting for the good part of marriage to come. Many times it never does. So we invest our hopes, dreams, time, and energy in our children to avoid feeling the emptiness of our marriages. It's easier to tackle their problems than our own.

Bringing children into an unhealthy marriage is like building a house on a shaky foundation. As the cracks begin to appear, the psychological costs become clear.

Children always sense marital problems. Often they react by developing their own problems, to distract their parents from their problems with each other. This solution creates more problems.

If you want healthy children, don't overlook the foundation. Work on your marriage.

How can you make your relationship better? Here are some guidelines that have worked for many people:

- Find out what your partner needs. Don't assume you know. Often what we think our partner needs is not really what he or she needs at all.

  Jean would agree. She surprised Jeff with a romantic vacation to Acapulco for his fortieth birthday. She thought he would be thrilled. However, Jeff's response was cool and indifferent.

  What went wrong? Jeff, who felt anxious about this particular birthday, would have welcomed his wife and children taking a low profile on it. All of the hoopla over the birthday trip only served to highlight an event he would rather have forgotten.

  Be careful not to project your own needs onto your partner. Check out your assumptions.
- Express what you need. Open communication is the best way to a healthy relationship. Many of us subscribe to the philosophy that if you have to ask, it doesn't count. As a consequence, we often live in a world of endless frustration and unmet needs. Remember, your spouse is not a mind-reader.

  Putting out your needs may be something you never learned in childhood. Perhaps you were too busy taking care of others. Or perhaps the few times you tried, you were disappointed and vowed never to be hurt again. As a result, you play out this pattern in your marriage, and hold your hurt and disappointment inside.

To get what you need often involves some degree of risk. If you can't do this with your spouse, whom can you hope to do it with?

Start with small things first. Ask for some time alone to talk. Or suggest a romantic night on the town. You may realize that your expected rejection was more about the past than the present.

- Don't analyze everything. Sometimes relationships become playgrounds for games of verbal volleyball. This game consists of overanalyzing the relationship, being the other person's psychologist, and scoring points off each other by continually "processing" the relationship and everything that happens in it.

Saying to someone, "Do you know why you do that?" and launching into your critique, alienates the other person and raises defenses. Stick with your own feelings. A simple "I get frustrated when you do that" is much more effective, and "Why do you do that?" followed by willingness to listen to the answer is what communication is all about.

- Share the responsibilities of raising your child. You'd be surprised at the numbers of parents that complain that their spouse is underinvolved with the children yet unconsciously set up such a situation. Deeply mistrusting their partners' ability to parent their child, they refuse to share any of the responsibilities. They undermine the other person's attempts at discipline, argue over methods of dealing with issues, and connive to get in the way whenever their partner is alone with their child.

What becomes suspect when partners argue constantly about how to raise the children is that one or the other cannot bear to give up any of the control. Again, the issue is control, rather than what's really best for the child.

Be wary of undermining your spouse's efforts to participate in raising your child. Make sure you both have responsibilities. Back each other up with support and acknowledgment.

- Plan for time together, away from your children. This is a necessity. The biggest complaint husbands have about their wives, post-baby, is that they feel neglected and secondary. Often it's true, because the demands of child care can be exhausting. Try spending a night at a hotel or motel every few months, away from the kids.

  There are always solutions if we commit ourselves to finding them. One woman whose husband complained that she was never sexual with him anymore after their second child was born solved the problem by turning to him in the morning and joking, "If you want me, you better be with me now, because by the end of the day, there's going to be nothing left!" Her husband was delighted with the compromise.

- If communication is blocked, seek marital counseling. Sometimes communication stops. People become stuck in old patterns, or behind walls of defenses. At this point, you need an objective third party to intervene. A good counselor can offer support, suggestions, and active steps to break through the barriers.

- If there is no hope of a meaningful life together, consider separation. There's no use telling yourself that if you and your spouse separate, your children will be happy about it. They will be upset. They may be angry. But does this mean you have to stay in a marriage that gives you no possibilities for happiness for the sake of your children?

  The way to approach making this decision is to be pragmatic. Consider the real factors—your children's ages and maturity, your economic situation, possibilities for flexible custody arrangements. What solutions can you arrive at to counterbalance all of the practical problems inherent in separation?

  If these practical problems seem insurmountable and you find yourself rejecting every option as impossible, consider whether what's really standing in the way is your fear for yourself and what it will mean to be on your own rather than fear for your children. Many people fool themselves into thinking that they are staying together for the sake of the children alone, rather than tackling these fears.

When marriages become unbearable, people separate. They find a way to solve the problems because they are motivated to do so. If you make this decision, you will hardly be alone. Millions of other mothers and fathers have been there before you, and you can rely on their experience if you reach out for it. This is not the time to be independent. This is the time to get the support and counsel of professionals, friends, and others who can help you during this difficult period.

Stop Giving In

Disciplining a child is difficult for most parents. For parents who love too much, it's even harder. When we are so devoted to our children, the very thought of setting limits and enforcing consequences brings guilt and pain.

Some parents who love too much substitute bribes for discipline. They dangle the carrots of toys, money, and privileges in their children's faces, hoping their children will return the favor by becoming accomplished and obedient. Such children look for the rewards in all of their good behavior: "I got an 'A,' where's my ten dollars?"

Others make a long list of rules on Monday that by Tuesday evening are not even remembered by anyone in the house, because no one could bring himself/herself to follow through and enforce them.

Because we feel our children are so special, we assume they deserve special treatment. Our children are the exception to most rules. We give them everything, and find a way to forgive them for anything.

At worst they become expert manipulators, expecting to whine or cry their way out of their problems and feeling entitled to favors from everybody. Many end up as little tyrants, never taking responsibility for their deeds and always feeling abused by everyone else.

Even at best, the child who never had to endure any

limits on his behavior fears adulthood and independence because he will never get the treatment he is used to from his parents.

A more effective way to teach our children is through the use of his or her direct experience.

Consider this scenario: Jack, the youngest son, comes home and says, "Mom, I need a favor. I missed school Tuesday, and I need you to write me a note saying I was sick."

His mother, who is more than ready to understand Jack's problems, says, "I thought you were in class. Tell me what happened."

Jack tells her that a bunch of guys decided to take the day off and would have thought he was a "geek" if he went to class. He gets very convincing in his arguments. "You want me to have friends, don't you? I'll have to stay after school for a week if they find out and I'll miss baseball practice. I probably won't get to play all summer if I miss practice."

If his mother loves Jack too much, she may think, What harm will it cause if I help my son this one time? He's usually such a good kid. I really would hate to see him get in trouble.

If Jack's mother joins in with his conspiracy, she gives Jack the following messages: Lying is okay; people will rescue you when you get into trouble; manipulation pays off, and there are no consequences for breaking rules that your parents can't remove for you.

However, if Jack's mother allows him to experience the natural consequences of his behavior, Jack might be unhappy, but she will be teaching him responsibility. Undoubtedly, he will learn a lot more from his week in detention than from his mother's rescue. He will think twice the next time he decides to break the rules.

Natural consequences are powerful educators. The child who refuses to eat his dinner will learn what it's like to be hungry. The child who leaves his toy in the street will experience the loss of his toy. A young adult who must find his own lawyer and foot his own bill in order to defend himself against a DWI arrest will learn the consequences of drinking and driving. These memories last a lifetime.

Uncover Your Unrealistic Expectations

No parent can be completely objective about his own child. Each of us is influenced by our own personal history, internal needs and cultural values. Essentially, we view the world through tinted glasses shaded by our own personal values and expectations. We are unable to see through the blind spots in our perspective.

Unconsciously, we superimpose our expectations on others. Then we get angry when others don't behave in accordance with our wishes.

Most vulnerable to these projected expectations are our own children. In order to bring our expectations of our children more in line with what is truly possible for them, we need to look at what underlies them:

Unfinished business from the past. Children can be a means to work through unresolved issues from our youth. Jack, a father of three, was unable to follow through on setting any limits for his children, until he realized that his actions were actually a rebellion against his tyrannical father, who punished him for even the smallest infractions. Through his "softness" with his children, Jack was unconsciously attempting to fill his own unmet needs for empathy, compassion, and love.

Our own needs. Many of our parental decisions are shaped by our own needs. If we feel unsuccessful in life, we may attempt to compensate by pushing our children to excessive achievement so that they reflect well on us. If we feel ignored in our adult relationships, we may become overinvolved with our children in an effort to fill our emptiness inside.

Take a look at your relationship with your children. Are your motivations coming from your child's needs or your own? Actively plan other ways of getting your needs met. When we use our children exclusively for our own needs, they will pay the price.

Comparisons to others. Parenting is so often filled with the anxiety of the comparison game. Susan finished fifty-seventh in her class. Betsy is the prettiest girl in her grade. Barry made third-string singles on the tennis team.

Cultural values strongly influence our expectations. Yet when we try to push our children beyond their current level of ability, we are giving them a strong message that they are not good enough. As a result, their self-esteem drops.

To avoid the comparison game, support your child's unique abilities. Encourage them within reasonable expectations. Remember, self-esteem is built from the inside, not the outside.

Lack of experience. Our society prepares us for the development of almost any skill except the most important one—parenting. As a result, most of us fly by the seat of our pants. Our inexperience and the anxiety it causes work against us. As a result, we overreact to even the smallest problems.

Now more than ever, there are tremendous resources for the new parent. A wealth of parenting books on an endless variety of topics fill the bookstores. Parenting classes and support groups are available at local colleges and adult-education centers. Individual and group counseling is more available and accepted than ever before. Taking advantage of these resources can help you become a more realistic and self-assured parent.

Learn to Communicate Effectively

Effective communication is clear, consistent, and honest. Words match actions, and feelings match words.

To communicate effectively with our children, we need to be open to our emotions and able to share the truth in a way that they can hear and understand. When we love our children too much, we often have difficulty communicating effectively with them. Because we're so absorbed in them, so devoted to making them happy and bent on changing them to our highest expectations, we unconsciously shape our words to manipulate and control them.

"I don't like Uncle Frank. He's mean."

"Don't be silly. Of course you like him. He's your uncle."

"But I don't want to go over to his house. I'm tired."

"You're not tired. You just took a nap."

Our children's true feelings make us nervous. We substitute what we want to hear, and tell them that this is what they think or feel. Why? Because if our children feel differently than we do, then it means that we're separate. That can be difficult for us to handle, and makes us feel out of control. We may feel we're losing them.

Communication breaks down when we try to control what we hear. Often when we appear to be listening, we really aren't. Instead, we're daydreaming, judging, speculating, or preparing a case that proves everything our child has just told us is wrong and here's why. Unconsciously, we're more concerned with fulfilling our own needs than those of our children.

Other times when we are talking to our children, we are sending out a host of mixed messages. We say we aren't angry, but our bodies give the clearer message that we're furious. We don't want them to know it, though, and would be shocked to realize how transparent we really are to them. Body language speaks louder than words.

Clean and honest communication is the hallmark of healthy relationships. It can be learned with a little practice. Researchers who have studied communication offer these tips:

Listen actively. This means let your child know you've really heard him. How? One way is to reflect his feeling back to him. When your child says, "I hate school and I'm never going back," you say, "It sounds like you're feeling frustrated and angry." Think how acknowledging this is compared to typical responses—like, "Oh, that's silly," or "You'll drop out over my dead body"—that shut down communication.

Paraphrasing—stating back what you've heard in your own words—also makes your child feel deeply heard and understood. Ask questions so that you really understand what your child has experienced before you jump in with feedback.

Show empathy. You don't have to agree with something your child has said in order to show some empathy. This can be very difficult for devoted parents who are torn when listening to their children's self-criticism, anger, or frustration. Instead of telling children why they shouldn't feel the way they do, which only ignites anger and unwillingness to share feelings with you, try saying, "I don't agree, but I can understand how you might feel that way."

Share feelings. Sometimes we think, Why should I have to explain myself to my children? They couldn't possibly understand, and besides, they should just do as I ask. But consider that if you never open up to your children, they will become much less likely to trust you and open up in return.

Use "I" Statements. Beginning sentences with "You," as in "You never do your chores," or "You never call me," connotes an accusation. It invites your children to defend themselves, and often incites an argument. More effective is to use "I" statements: "I get frustrated when you don't take the garbage out after you promised," and "I miss it when you don't call me." These statements are assertive without inflicting guilt. You're modeling the fact that everyone takes responsibility for his own feelings, and relationships become more honest and less manipulative.

Be wary of hidden agendas. Sometimes there are hidden agendas—things we want to prove to our children without coming out and saying them—behind our words. See if you can spot the hidden agendas in the following statements:

"Please don't yell at me. You know my stomach has been upset all day."

"I ironed your father's shirts, cleaned your bedroom, went to the store, returned your library books. How was your afternoon at the beach?"

The hidden agenda behind the first is to convince our children that we're too delicate or weak, and they should feel guilty exposing us to more stress. The agenda in the second is to say, "Look how much I suffer."

Hidden agendas are ways of attempting to get our needs met without asking for what we want directly. We may very well have learned to use them from our own parents. We can, however, avoid passing them on to future generations by learning to spot them, and finding more effective ways to get what we need without making others feel guilty or uncomfortable.

Don't Allow Your Children to Exploit You

Patience is, by far, the most prevalent trait of parents who allow their children to exploit them. It allows them to charge ahead, and take on a legion of teachers, principals, social workers, psychiatrists, nurses, doctors, policemen, lawyers, judges, and drug-abuse counselors, and keep trying to find ways to "help" when anyone else would have given up out of sheer exhaustion.

Unrelenting patience is sustained by denial. Many parents who love and give too much carry around a mental picture of their children as successful, accomplished, gifted, and stunningly beautiful that leaves little room for feedback from others—including the child himself. Anyone who dares to disturb this picture is the enemy.

Some realize their children's faults and imperfections. But instead of believing that their children have to change and adjust, they believe that the rest of the world should adapt and be more understanding.

Most fall somewhere in between. They're patient with their "problem" children because they fear that the harsh action they long to take may be the wrong one. They doubt their intuition. They fall back when they need to take a stand. Hoping that someday the child will return to their guidance, they wait for better days with a patience that's scary.

While waiting, some parents accept the unthinkable. They live with angry and violent children who break and destroy everything in their wake. They answer the doorbell to find the juvenile officer, a crowd of stoned teenagers looking for a place to party, or the bill collector parked on their doorstep. They rush off to work, exhausted and feverish because they can't risk losing their jobs, and barely get a wave good-bye from the thirty-year-old child they support, who lies on the couch, primed for another day of soap operas and sitcoms.

If you can identify with this kind of patient acceptance of the unacceptable, your first step will be altering your bottom-line belief that if you try hard enough, your child will become all you want him to be. Stop thinking that if you have loved more, so many things would have been different. You have already loved too much. Your job is to detach.

June, a forty-eight-year-old mother of three, would agree. "Susie was in every kind of trouble in high school. She totaled my car. She mouthed off to her teachers and cut her classes. She lied to me all of the time. I would come home and smell marijuana smoke in the house. I thought that was the worst thing she could ever do to me, until the afternoon I came home from work early with the flu and found her in bed—my bed, mind you—with a man I'd never laid eyes on. Susie stared at me, defiantly as if it was my fault for interrupting her.

"What did I do? I took her for birth-control pills. I brought her pamphlets about drug abuse. I bought a new car. I made excuses for her at school, and listened, begged, and prayed. In two years, I spent ten thousand dollars on therapists, doctors, and tutors."

"It was a woman at work who first told me about being an enabler. She had a husband in AA, went to Al-Anon meetings, and told me about a saying they have: 'Let go and let God.' But it seemed impossible to do. Susie was my child. This woman's husband was an adult. I thought that made it very different at the time."

Growing depression and helplessness over Susie's deterioration drove June to a therapist of her own, one who specialized in treating codependents. "It took months for me to realize that it really wasn't my job to find solutions to Susie's problems. I'd given her everything, driven myself crazy with worry, and nothing helped. The therapist said, 'Give up all of that self-will. You can't control it all. Focus on what *you* need.' She gave me the support I needed to take a stand with Susie.''

June and her therapist wrote a contract together for Susie to sign. Susie would go to school each day. She would not have boyfriends over when her mother wasn't home. She would not smoke marijuana in the house. She was to be home at curfew. If she wanted to see a therapist, her mother would pay, but Susie would pay for any appointments she missed and arrange her own transportation.

When June approached Susie with the contract, she was more direct with her feelings than she had ever been. She told Susie, "You can destroy your life, but you're not going to destroy mine. I don't want strange boys in my house or in my bed because it scares me and sickens me. I want you in school because I'm humiliated dealing with truant officers and principals when I'm at work. I want you in at curfew because I don't want to be up all night worrying about you, and exhausted all of the next day. I've given up trying to tell you what all this is doing to you. You're seventeen. Make your own choices, but don't exploit me.''

More important than the contract was the change in June's attitude. "I stopped eavesdropping on Susie's phone conversations, and searching her bedroom for signs that she was on drugs. I stopped paying so much attention to every expression on her face. I'd want to, but I'd say, 'Let go and let God' over and over again, like a mantra.

"I used to believe Susie had these problems because she was unhappy, and that I was somehow the cause of her unhappiness. Susie knew this on some level, and used it to her advantage. Today, I realize something. All of us have problems. Susie had no more stress in her life than anyone else does. She chose self-destructive ways of dealing with her problems because there were no consequences and I was always so patient and willing to think that everything was my fault. I was always there to pick up the pieces. Well, I forced myself to acknowledge that Susie's problems were beyond my ability to help. She needed to see the consequences. I stopped doing anything for her that I knew she could do for herself if she wanted to, even if it meant I had to go into my bedroom, shut the door, and cry.''

What June did is called detaching. In her book *Code-pendent No More*, Melody Beattie writes, ''Detachment is based on the premises that each person is responsible for himself, that we can't solve problems that aren't ours to solve, and that worrying doesn't help. We adopt a policy of keeping our hands off other people's responsibilities and tend to our own instead. If people have created some disasters for themselves, we allow them to face their own proverbial music. We allow people to be who they are. We give them the freedom to be responsible and grow. And we give ourselves that same freedom.''

June learned this lesson with a lot of effort and even more soul-searching. She looks back at those days and concludes, ''Susie didn't become the perfect daughter after I took a stand with her. She has values, morals, and ambitions of her own, and the hardest thing for me to accept is that I don't have control over what she thinks and feels. But she follows our contract to the letter. I don't have the kind of relationship with my daughter that I once dreamed of. But sometimes I get a little glimpse of a young woman who may not make the choices I would, but who I really like. She's making some good choices, like her recent decision to get a part-time job. I have to be happy with small things like this. And because no one changes overnight, I have to bite my tongue hard when I want to suggest that she do even more.''

You can't truly detach until you give up your expectations. But your expectations may be the single thing that allows you to accept it when your children exploit you. If the idea of detaching immobilizes you, consider the following:

• Many of us find detaching difficult because we're convinced that our ''problem children'' on drugs, in jail, out of school, out on the streets, *need* us. What they need is a sense of responsibility for their own lives. If you have a grown child whose problems are severe, and all of your efforts to help have been in vain, recognize an essential truth: Your loving concern, affection, or authority are pretty meager weapons when you're battling a child in the grip of drugs, alcohol, gangs, street values, or eating disorders.

• Quit searching yourself for the cause. Quit enumerating all of the things you could have done differently. The key is allowing the behavior to become less your problem and more their problem, no matter how harsh that sounds.

• Quit bailing your children out. When you try to force your solutions on your children, you are practicing codependency and you will rack up the results of it— a young adult enabled to practice destructive behavior by someone who rescues him from the consequences of it. Instead of looking for new sources of help for your child when all have failed, look for sources of help for yourself.

One Step at a Time!

This step is borrowed from Alcoholics Anonymous— groups of people committed to changing unhealthy, addictive behaviors.

Any kind of personal growth is usually viewed as two steps forward and one step backward. To expect change overnight is a setup for failure. Seeing change in your personality style is like watching your hair grow. Nothing seems to be happening until you are forced to go to the hairstylist. If you keep this simple thought in mind, you will spare yourself the anguish and frustration of unrealistic expectations of yourself.

The road to change is paved by small successes. For example, if you find you are overinvolved with your daughter's academic life, and worried because it isn't everything you would like it to be, do not expect to withdraw completely. Hold back on one area. If you habitually ask her if she's done her homework every night, then take not mentioning this for one week as your final step. Let her take control in this area, and acknowledge yourself for your personal success.

If you find yourself obsessed with your son's social life, try for one evening not asking him about his plans for Friday and Saturday night. He may actually volunteer the information if you let him. Even if he doesn't, your hovering over him won't guarantee an exciting and gratifying social life. Let go a step at a time.

If you are working on becoming less critical of your children's friends, do not expect change overnight. Set a realistic goal of withholding two critical comments a day. You've probably made these same statements a hundred times already with no result.

Be patient with yourself. When we are feeling most stuck, we are often on the verge of a breakthrough. Just the fact that you are reading this book means you are working on yourself. Have faith, and take one step at a time.

Remember, you could be accused of a lot worse things in life than loving your kids too much. You have opened many doors and provided your children with lots of wonderful opportunities. If along the way your children ended up with some emotional problems, they are not alone. Let go of the guilt; it won't help. It's not too late to change. Life is a process, and mistakes are an opportunity for growth.

CHAPTER 13

SURVIVING PARENTS WHO LOVE TOO MUCH

"What do I do now?"

"Wouldn't it be easier to just relocate to Australia
or something?"

—Mark, age 25

Surviving parents who love too much doesn't mean you
have to lose your compassion or love for your parents. We
can loosen the bond that ties us to our parents and still
maintain a vital and loving relationship with them. What
this will require is focusing on changing ourselves, rather
than hoping to change them. It will mean embracing the
challenges and possibilities of independence and separateness.

To change, you have to *get started*. Taking action is the
key. Here is a twelve-point start-up plan that can help start
you on the path to a freer and more fulfilling life.

Learn to Feel Again

If you want to heal, you have to feel. Look at feelings as
something you can count on to interpret life for you and
give you accurate information about yourself, rather than
something you have to hide, repress, or change.

Adult children who were overparented tend to have a habitual way of dealing with their feelings. They pretend. Shamed by their parents for having feelings different from theirs, they kiss and hug people they feel indifferent to, exclaim over gifts they hate, and laugh at jokes that aren't funny, and smile through their anger.

Part of this is due to a childhood where such dishonesty was encouraged as "politeness" and "looking good." Part is due to parents who modeled the repression of feelings. Such people don't know what they feel, have no idea how to go about expressing their emotions, or fear that they'll be overwhelmed by their own emotions, should they let them out of their cage even for a moment.

One's way of dealing with feelings can be changed. It's been demonstrated that group therapy—people working actively together and supporting each other on common issues—can transform people who have spent a lifetime rigidly controlling their feelings into people who are comfortable with a full range of emotions.

When Gail, a special-education teacher, listened to two women in her group yell at each other at the top of their lungs, she cowered in the corner, feeling embarrassed and anxious. Later, when everyone in the group went out for a snack, as they did every week, she saw the two women talking and laughing with each other as if nothing serious had happened. "I learned something that night. They had gotten their feelings out, and they were done with them. Their relationship survived. In some ways, I think they were even closer for having been so honest. In my home, an outburst like that would have been good for two weeks of my mother's sulking, a stern lecture from my father, a week of my feeling ashamed, and a month of us all analyzing why it happened in the first place.

"One day a woman in the group provoked me, and I was the one screaming. Afterwards, the woman I yelled at hugged me. It was the single most incredible moment of my life. Now I've given up being the kind of mechanical zombie I used to be, afraid to get angry and ashamed about feeling hurt. I look at my feelings as evidence that I'm alive.''

Why is group therapy so effective in helping people learn to be emotionally honest with themselves and others? While most types of therapy bring ego defenses—rationalizations, intellectualizations, denial—into conscious focus so that we can learn to let go of them, groups are very active in their approach. In a group, you'll have obnoxious people, controlling people, victims, people-pleasers—a full range of human beings who become your ''family'' and who sometimes knock heads. You react to these people. Perhaps your father was defensive, and Joe, the guy in the group who sits in the corner with his arms crossed over his chest, is also defensive. You will have an emotional reaction to him. He'll plug you in.

If you're so removed from your feelings that you have no reactions to anyone, a good therapist may provoke you to have feelings. ''What are you feeling?'' is the most commonly asked question in groups.

You'll work through your feelings. In an effective group, you'll get support and understanding as you express your feelings honestly, and learn how to get this from people in the world.

Most important for the child who was loved too much, you'll become able to feel comfortable with being imperfect. You'll work through generalized feelings of shame that result from feeling that you're ''bad'' because you were never good enough to meet your parents' high expectations. You'll learn to turn this generalized shame into specific feelings, based on specific incidents. You'll learn that you can still love yourself, without loving everything you do. You'll learn to distinguish between your self-concept and your actions. You can make a mistake and still be a good person. You can get angry and feel hurt without fear that others will abandon you.

Don't believe that when you start feeling, all you'll feel is bad. When we refuse to feel the ''lows'' in life, we prevent ourselves from feeling the ''highs.'' Adult children who were loved too much are people who are constantly in control. They can no more throw their heads back and scream with laughter than cry out loud when they've been hurt. They exist in the middle of a wide spectrum of feelings, forgoing the joy to avoid the pain.

A primary goal of therapy is to get people to feel feelings that have been too repressed for too long, so that they can heal and have a full emotional life, free of "unfinished business." Joy is one of these feelings. Hurt and anger are others.

Further steps that will help in this process include the following:

- Focus on getting out of your "head." People who were loved too much have a tendency to be overly intellectual. Stop analyzing everything. Applying too much logic to human relationships is counterproductive. People act illogically, because their emotions are often ambiguous. We really can't control what we feel, or always make sense of it. Our feelings aren't good or bad; they just *are.*
- Take risks. Dare to be honest. Be current with your feelings; don't stockpile them until you finally explode. You needn't attack others. You needn't play the "victim" and blame them for all you've suffered. But you can learn to state what you feel honestly, and set the foundation for a full emotional life.
- Be vulnerable with your parents. This will include telling them when you're angry, and telling them when you're hurt. Learn to express anger and hurt effectively with them. Anger needn't be hostile or violent. It needn't be an attack. Hurt doesn't have to be expressed in a tearful, hysterical outburst. Expressing your feelings effectively means making a statement of what you feel—why you're upset, why you're angry, and what you need. Remember, the goal isn't to change your parents, or anyone else by expressing these feelings. It's to release the feelings, so that you can go on.

Save "Looking Good" for Times
When It Will Do Some Good

Dispassionate self-sufficiency may be just the thing a prospective boss is looking for. But friends and lovers find it hard to be close to us if we're all hard edges.

The ability to be vulnerable with others is the hallmark of a person who is unafraid of intimacy. Vulnerability allows us to accept others as they are, just as we accept ourselves.

An aversion to appearing vulnerable to others is one of the most common reasons adult children who were overparented "look good" on the outside, but feel lonely and empty inside. It can be a hard habit to kick, especially if being loved was contingent on putting our achievements out where our parents could see them. Massing our strengths and accomplishment into a perfect "package" in order to impress others and make them love us becomes a habit.

Consider Rosemary, who romanced Dan by preparing impeccable gourmet dinners, over which she enumerated her accomplishments and supplied a litany of advice on how he could jump-start his career with a VP title at his next review.

One night he said, "Rose, can't you just relax? I'm not here for career counseling."

Rosemary admits that she was angry and hurt at first. "Then I realized what I was doing. I was auditioning for the role of 'wife.' By showing him how smart and accomplished I could be—'putting my best foot forward,' as my father always used to say—I thought he'd see the light and want me to be with him forever. But I was so frantic about it that Dan was really turned off.

"When I stopped trying to impress him and spoke, honestly, about some of the times I wasn't so sure of myself or felt confused and empty, I found out that he wasn't my father. He wasn't disappointed in me, and he didn't need me to be perfect. It was okay not to have it all together all of the time. In fact, we felt closer to each other."

"Looking good" is not a show of self-confidence. It's a defense—a mask that hides who we truly are and what we really feel—founded on internalized, perfectionist demands of our parents. Others see it as aloof detachment, or an anxious need to impress.

How do we exchange "looking good" for something more honest? Some therapists have helped people ease out of the compulsion to "look good" all of the time by giving them a special "assignment": Spend a week making one mistake a day. Be late for a meeting. Spill your glass of water in a restaurant. Wear a wrinkled blouse to work, or an awful tie. Oversleep. In other words, mess up.

After a week, the person has to report to the therapist on his mistakes. If the mistakes weren't risky enough, he has to go back and make some more.

People who were overparented are terrified of this assignment. It goes totally against the grain of everything they know. The first time they attempt it, they feel an enormous block, like an invisible concrete wall. What if they're laughed at, ridiculed, rejected, and humiliated? As one man put it, "I'd be a BAD PERSON. All my life I've been terrified of being a BAD PERSON."

There is nothing as liberating as being ordinary and normal and letting go of the need to be perfect. The purpose of this assignment is not to teach people that it's wonderful to make mistakes, but that there's an enormous range of choices they can make and still be accepted. "Looking good" is only one of those choices. People can be imperfect, make mistakes, and survive without being abandoned or humiliated. The fear is much greater than the reality.

Overcoming the fear of making mistakes in front of other people enhances spontaneity. The goal is not to convince others of your inadequacy. It's to be able to take risks; to be able to relax defenses and go with what you truly feel.

We can always pull out the mask when we need it. But it's tremendously self-limiting to be governed by rigid, perfectionist boundaries. Monitoring our "looking good" behavior and replacing those responses with more open and easier ones can allow us to experience the joy of being accepted for all we really are.

What does the end of a lifetime of "looking good" look like? George, an advertising executive, discovered the freedom of no longer needing to be perfect during a sailing lesson on a Sunfish in Martinique. "The instructor barely spoke English, and handed me the helm after about five minutes. I had no idea what I was supposed to do. The sheets got tangled up immediately. The boat started bobbing, the sail swung around, and all I could hear was the instructor yelling something that sounded like 'Zubu! Zubu!' The next thing I knew, we were in the water. I could hear my friends on shore, baying like hyenas.

"Six months ago, I would have wanted to die. But trying to get the silly boat back up in the water, I thought, This is my vacation. Who cares how I look? So I'm not a great sailor. What difference does it make?

"I sailed to shore, waving to my friends, and fell down on the sand laughing like an idiot. I never felt so good. My friends bought me a T-shirt that said 'Captain' and I thought it was great."

To give up a lifetime of "looking good," as George did, you have to give up your illusion that the only way you'll be accepted is if you're out there doing, achieving, and convincing everyone that you're perfect. These three steps will help:

- Make a small mistake in front of someone you trust. Notice what you feel. Notice what the other person does. Does he reject and abandon you, as you fear? Or does he barely notice your mistake? Begin to realize that other people are more focused on themselves than on your behavior. Your concern that you'll be rejected if you aren't perfect is a fear you've built up that has little basis in reality. Apply some "reality testing" to those assumptions by loosening up and noticing that nothing devastating happens.
- Make a list of five secrets that you feel you could never reveal to anyone else. Next, look at your list and pretend it was written by a coworker or friend

whom you admire. Do these secrets make you despise this person? Or do they make you want to shrug your shoulders and say, "So what?"

- Make a list of five things you've never shared with your parents. What do you expect will happen if you do? How realistic are these answers? To test them out, try sharing one of these things with your parents. One woman who thought her mother would be appalled if she shared her decision to spend three thousand dollars on a fur coat was stunned when her mother smiled and told her, "I'm glad—it's something I always wanted you to have." Although not every child gets results like this, our fear of our parents' disapproval loses its power over us when we find out that we can survive it.

Stop Giving Your Parents Ammunition

People who come to terms with their overly devoted parents learn to weigh their words. They don't compulsively share every detail of their lives with their parents. They allow themselves some privacy.

People who are ambivalent about true separation from their parents' smothering love and control unconsciously plug their parents into nervous overconcern by dropping little "bombs" of information around them, like, "I'm dating a married man," or "My husband hasn't made love to me in a month," or "I'm a thousand dollars over my credit limit," or "Nothing's wrong; I just haven't been able to eat a thing all week."

After dropping one of these "bombs" and hooking their parents into shock and anxiety, they complain, "My parents worry about me so much, it's ridiculous. They make such a big deal out of everything I do. Why can't they just leave me alone?"

We need to look at our motivation for telling them these things. We already know, from experience, what they're going to say. Why are we compelled to tell them these things that only upset them?

Sometimes saying, "I wish my parents would just accept me, stop telling me what to do, and not make such a big deal out of everything," really means, "Why can't I tell them I'm doing cocaine, having sex with men ten years younger than I am, and going deeper into debt—and still get their approval?"

We want to do it our way. But we want to do it with our parents' full consent because we're still bound to them.

People who habitually pour out tales of their dangerous episodes into carelessness, irresponsibility, and self-destruction do so because they're frightened of their own decisions. Unconsciously, they reason that they aren't fully responsible for their actions if their parents approve of them, or at least don't castigate them openly for their actions.

Or perhaps they share all sorts of sordid details so that their parents can punish them. This would help assuage their guilt.

If you're constantly giving your parents ammunition by sharing far more of your life than is reasonable for an independent adult, consider this: Telling our parents everything says to them, "Take care of me! I'm not ready to be independent. I'm not ready to be separate from you." No wonder they find it difficult to take us at our word when we say we want our freedom.

If we aren't comfortable with the things we are doing, we shouldn't be doing them. Compulsive, intimate confidences about things our parents would prefer not to hear only perpetuate self-defeating dependency and the belief that there are no consequences to our actions that our parents can't fix.

There's a time for honesty, and a time for privacy. If we complain about being loved too much, it's often because we prefer it to the risk of being on our own and taking full responsibility for our decisions. An aversion to holding back details about our lives from our parents in the name of "honesty" or "closeness" is one of the most common reasons for allowing overparenting to continue in adulthood. Blow-by-blow accounts of our sex lives, troubled economic situations, or problems at work hook our parents into familiar roles of giving too much, caring too much, getting overinvolved, and finally becoming enmeshed.

To be independent is to give up this kind of enmeshment. These steps will help:

- Realize your participation in the overparenting that goes on in your family. How often do you share a confidence with your parents, secretly seeking their approval, and end up feeling punished, controlled, or misunderstood? How often could you have predicted this outcome before you opened your mouth to speak?

  Only you can give your parents the ammunition. Realize that when you tell your parents everything and expect superhuman understanding for and sanction of your worst vices, you are also giving them the idea that you're not responsible or mature enough to handle your life.

- Prune the number of confidences you share with your parents. Do you share the details of your arguments with your spouse, his progress in therapy, his prowess in bed? Begin keeping the details to yourself. Do you pick up the phone to call your parents four times a day? Limit yourself to two calls. Do you have a compulsion to share the particulars of the wild Friday night you had drinking in bars? Share it with a friend, instead. Notice how you feel afterward. Use your anxiety as a clue that you're weaning yourself from dependency on your parents' approval, and are that much closer to learning to approve of yourself.

- Each time you find yourself anxiously spilling everything to your parents, stop and ask, Why am I doing this? Do I want to be punished? Am I uncomfortable with what I've done? Am I seeking their approval to bolster my confidence rather than making a decision to change my behavior? Do I expect my parents to fix the problem and take me off the hook? Do I need my parents to worry about me in order to feel that they love me? Is there a healthier way I can ask for their love?

Limiting what you share with your parents isn't dishonesty or deceit. It's mature acceptance of an adult's right to privacy.

Give Up the Battle Over Who Was Right

Men and women who are emotionally separated from their parents give up the battle over who is right. They declare a truce with their parents where both parties can agree to disagree, and go about their respective lives.

People still clutching to childhood dependency unconsciously perpetuate the battle by becoming embroiled in the same frustrating arguments and power plays over and over again.

The aching ambition to finally convince controlling parents that we're right and they're wrong can lead to major gaffes. When Roberta, a manufacturer's representative, quit her job to move to Europe to be with her boyfriend—a man her parents heartily disapproved of—she knew almost from the moment the plane landed that she'd made a mistake. He wasn't there to meet her, and it was an omen for the way the rest of their relationship would go. Roberta would pace the floor of his studio apartment, waiting for him, and he'd be somewhere else, with hardly a thought about her.

"Jack was everything that my parents told me to avoid, which, I know now, made him real attractive to me. Here I was in Paris, with no job, and no way, without citizenship, to get a job, bored and lonely, but still holding on to the idea that life with Jack could be great, just because I wanted to prove that my parents were wrong about him.

"In the end I wired them for money to come home. All of the 'I-told-you-so's' I had to listen to for months were humiliating."

Our parents aren't always right. They're also not always wrong, which can be harder to swallow. The problem isn't their opinions of everything we do as much as our being driven to rebel against their control at any cost in order to prove something to them.

Although it can be difficult to end the nonproductive cycle of control versus rebellion, we can start by dealing with the real issue: painful, unexpressed resentment. When Roberta's therapist asked her to bring in a list of resentments she felt toward her parents, she brought in six typed pages. As they read over the list together, and Roberta repeated statements like, "You think you know everything," and "You think everyone else is an idiot," she began laughing so hard that tears ran down her face. "I'm not one for making lists, but reading all of this made me picture my parents, like two little Napoleons, shaking their fingers at me because I didn't live up to their standards of who I should be and how I should act.

"You don't always see that your parents can be immature at times, and you resent them because they aren't everything you need them to be. Worse, in so many ways, I was becoming more and more like my parents. I had to be right all of the time. I wouldn't listen to anyone else, either."

Roberta began to see her parents as they were—two people desperately hanging on to their opinions and judgments, frightened that if anyone went against them and succeeded, it somehow made them less than they were. In Roberta's family, being "right" was tantamount to having self-worth. Roberta had inherited this belief, which was the foundation for the unending battle. When she began to see her parents' opinions for what they were—feedback that she could accept or reject, rather than an evaluation of her self-worth—she stopped needing to convince them that she was right by senselessly rebelling against them.

Many people fight against the necessity of dealing with their resentment of their parents, even though it can be a foundation of a lifetime of rebellion. They say, "You can't blame your parents for everything; you have to be responsible for your own life." This would be great, if they meant it honestly. Unfortunately, the statement too often comes from people who have raging migraine headaches, ulcers, ragged, chewed-up cuticles, and deep circles under their eyes, all stemming from painful, pent-up resentments. Although the mask they wear says, "Everything's resolved, my difficulties with my parents don't affect my life,'' what they really fear is reprisal for their own feelings of resentment.

The objective of dealing with your resentment is to get to the point where you can forgive the past. But, many of us feel we should be at the point of forgiveness right away.

You can't jump to the finish line. "My parents did the best they could" may be true but it can also be an excuse for never doing any work on your relationship with them. The result will be carrying the repressed conflict over into your other relationships, especially those with your own children, because you'll always need to be right, and have the last word.

We can senselessly rebel to prove a point. Or we can choose to see our parents as human beings—people who have the same needs for validation and acknowledgment as we do. We can begin to see our need to be right for what it is: a need for validation and acknowledgment.

There are much healthier ways to achieve these things, other than being embroiled in endless power struggles with our parents because we need them to tell us that we're right. You don't have to struggle with your parents as if your freedom to be who you are and make your own choices is something only they can grant you. These steps will help you end the battle:

- People who get off of this treadmill realize something: No one—not even our parents, whose approval means so much—can control us if we don't allow it. Take a hard look at your own investment in the control/rebellion cycle: It allows you to be reactive, rather than active. As one woman put it, "My whole life has been one big 'Fuck you' to my parents. Even though I thought I was breaking away from them by rebelling, I was sinking deeper into it, because their opinions were still controlling me."

  Mindless rebellion is as much evidence of our capitulation to our parents' control over us as nonthinking submission to anything that earns their approval or acceptance.

- If you submit to your parents' control because you feel too guilty rebelling against them, consider that you may have a huge stake in seeing your parents as powerful. It makes you feel more secure. You can, however, become secure in yourself, by controlling your own life rather than reacting to your parents' wishes.
- Deal directly with your resentment. Write a letter to your parents about how much you resent their constant control. You don't have to mail it, but just letting your feelings out can free you emotionally to give up the old battle.
- If your parents constantly dictate to you to the extent that you become enraged, realize that you may be looking at two people who are well into middle age who have a very needy little child inside of them. It isn't the mature side of your parents that causes them to try to rule over your behavior. It isn't their grown-up wisdom that makes them unable to tolerate anything but your acceptance of their dictates. It's a needy child who wants love, respect, and acknowledgment, but attempts to achieve it in a way that results in anger and disrespect. Remove yourself from the timeworn battle with a firm "We are different people, and I respect who you are, but I want you to also respect who I am." Wait out the silent tantrums without responding to them in kind. Realize that meeting your parents' needs is not your sole responsibility.

Don't Take More Than You're Willing to Pay For

Overparenting and the tremendous amount of gifts and attention that come with it have their price. Forgetting that the bill's going to come can lead to major problems.

When Ray's parents separated, he took his father's side. One semester away from completing law school, he was only too happy to move into his father's apartment in the city, where he could enjoy a huge allowance, get free food and maid service, share his list of longstanding grievances against his mother, and dream of his eventual position in his father's law firm.

When Ray passed the bar, he took a trip to Hawaii, all expenses paid by his father. On his return, his father met him at the airport and said, "I've got a great first case for you, Ray. I want you to represent me in my divorce suit against your mother."

Ray almost fell to the floor in shock. He'd never considered his father asking for such a thing. How could he face his mother in the courtroom? His refusal resulted in threats of not being allowed into his father's law firm, and a host of other consequences equally as devastating.

Not many people's "bill for services rendered" is as extreme as Ray's. But, our "bill" may contain charges to call our parents every day; never get angry; live within a mile of our parents' home; come every Sunday night for dinner; call brothers and sisters we have little to say to; marry someone our parents approve of; feel guilty when we don't do as they want us to do, etc. In other words, we may be restricted and limited in our choices because we "owe."

To gain control of our own lives and separate from our parents, we may have to separate from our parents' money. Giving up the lifetime allowance can be difficult, but we can never be truly independent as long as we take more than we give.

How do we disentangle ourselves, especially when we enjoy it so much? Ellen, a thirty-four-year-old executive secretary, took the money her parents gave her each month and bought clothes, makeup, and tickets to the theater, which she loved, yet she grew increasingly uncomfortable about her ongoing allowance as she grew older. "The hard part was going to them, to get the check. I'd go to my parents' house, and stay for an hour. As I was getting up to leave, my mother and father would look at each other, and my father would walk into the den, where he kept his checkbook. They'd walk me to the door, my father would hug me, and then he'd hand me the check. I'd want to say, 'I didn't come here just for this,' but I couldn't choke the words out. This was something none of us ever talked about, this unspoken agreement that they'd keep giving me three hundred dollars every month.

"I could see that my mother thought it should stop. But I could also see that they both had a lot of pride in the fact that they could do this for me. We went through this same scenario scores of times—my mother trying to hide her disappointment in me, my father silently defending me—until I knew that my embarrassment about taking their money was worse than having to do without it.

"The man I was involved with at the time was shocked when I told him I was still taking money from my parents. After all, my salary was nothing to be ashamed of. I felt like I had to defend myself, and it was a clue that I wasn't really comfortable with the whole situation anymore. My strongest defense was that they had more money than they'd ever need, but he called this a rationalization. Inside, I knew it had to end, and that my parents would never be the ones to end it.

"I gave myself sixty days. The next time I saw them, I said, 'After next month, I won't need the check anymore. I think I can make it without your help.' "

Cutting herself off from her parents' money was considerably harder than Ellen thought it would be. "I started compulsively worrying about money, dining on an apple and a can of tuna fish every night, cutting coupons out of newspapers, and pinching pennies like crazy. I'd get my bills and be depressed and anxious. It was over a year until I could finally relax and realize that I could cover my expenses, live within my budget, and even feel good about it. It's a lesson most people learn in their twenties, but my long-term dependence on my parents made it harder."

The money we take from our parents may mean more to us than dollars and cents that pay our bills. It may mean security. It may mean protection. That's what makes giving it up more difficult than it needs to be. But it always means the continuation of childhood.

If you depend on your parents for money, then you depend on your parents. When you relinquish responsibility for your finances to someone else, you relinquish a very important part of your control over your life. When we say we can't cut ourselves off from our parents' money, what we often mean is that we can't afford our own independence, which is scary.

Only you can decide how much debt to your parents you're comfortable taking on. Anxiety, guilt, embarrassment, or resentment are clues that the level of debt you've taken on is too high. Try the following:

- Give yourself a deadline for the time you will stop taking money from your parents. Six months will give you enough time to prepare yourself for a reduced income and financial independence. Confide this deadline in someone you trust, who will remind you of it.
- Learn as much as you can about managing money. A lack of financial savvy can be a clue that we're reluctant to take on adult responsibilities.

    Looking in your checkbook right now, do you see an accurate list of checks and balances, or a hodgepodge of figures you can barely read?

    Do you view money realistically? Or does it make you so anxious that your reaction to it is always extreme, i.e., self-depriving, compulsive, and rigid, because you live in fear of a rainy day, or are you so scatterbrained that you have no idea of the difference between your income and your expenses?

    Your answers to these questions may mean that financial independence is scary to you. But financial independence is a threshold of adulthood. Parents who love too much may use money to keep their children dependent. It's a hook that we take advantage of.
- Realize that there are debts we incur even if we never take a dime from our parents. If we rely on their connections, depend on them to baby-sit, borrow their vacation home, bring them our laundry, we incur debt. Make a list of the different kinds of debt you take on. How do you repay? Does what you're demanded to do or be in return exceed the value of what you've taken? Your independence may be too steep a price to pay.

Your Parents Are Stronger
Than You Give Them Credit For

The illusion that meeting our parents' needs is our responsibility, when it isn't, can be disastrous. Grace, a computer systems analyst, was miserable and torn when her boyfriend of over a year told her he'd had a great offer of a solid opportunity at a Los Angeles–based corporation and was going to take it. He wanted Grace to move there with him, and hinted at the possibility of marriage.

"I couldn't do it," Grace said. "I was the only one in my family still living in the same town as my parents. They were getting older, my father was sick a lot, and it was the worst possible time for me to leave them. I couldn't just go off to L.A. and desert them."

A year later, Grace was inconsolable when she heard that her ex-boyfriend, with whom she was still very much in love, was getting married to someone else. But that wasn't the worst. When her parents calmly announced that they were moving to a retirement community in Arizona, she could only look at them both, so stunned that she was bereft of speech.

Today, a much wiser Grace acknowledges that her sense of responsibility for her parents was misguided. "Loving your parents doesn't mean that you are obligated to put your life on hold. My mistake was assuming that this is what they expected from me. I never even discussed moving to L.A. with them, because I was afraid of hurting them. Now, I think although they might not have been overjoyed about it, they would have wanted me to do what I needed to do."

We think that if we separate from our parents, it will kill them. We feel a misguided sense of responsibility for protecting them, or for making up for all they never had.

Interestingly, children who were loved too much consistently describe their parents as weak, helpless, lonely, depressed, unhappy, and living empty lives. These same parents are often vital, active people, who run their households, operate their businesses, plan vacations, handle their finances, and otherwise function smoothly. True, they're depressed at times. True, they feel lonely once in a while. They have bad days. But don't we all?

Our parents are stronger than we give them credit for. The misperceptions of their strength that lead us to be overly protective of them go both ways. Our parents view us as constantly in need of their advice and protection, while we see them as desperately needing us.

If each of us feels we are taken advantage of, our relationship is a bitter one. At worst, it's rife with mutual resentment and dependence. We come to each other's rescue, advise and help each other on our problems. We lose sight of where our individual boundaries begin and end. As we switch back and forth, one moment the giver, one moment the receiver, there are barely enough emotional resources between us to solve anything. The problems persist. On and on we go, fighting each other for control and becoming infuriated when nothing we dislike in each other changes.

Consider this: Seeing others as unable to live without us makes us feel important. We may have an investment in seeing our parents as very vulnerable and dependent on us because it gives us a feeling of power. They may have the same investment in us.

Each of us shares a fear of separation. We may have great reluctance to acknowledge that our parents don't really need us as much as we think they do, because then we're faced with a worrisome fear underneath: It may be we who won't be able to make it without them.

The following tips can help you make a more realistic assessment of your parents and your relationship with them:

- Realize that all of us feel lonely, depressed, frightened, and hopeless at times. We all have problems. You cannot ''cure'' your parents of these feelings. Their happiness is not your responsibility, just as yours is not theirs.

- For a week or two, keep a daily diary of how often you tell "little white lies" to your parents because you feel the truth would hurt them. How often do you "look good" for them, so that they won't worry about you? If you find you're consistently interpreting your behavior as something that your parents must be protected from, question your assumptions. Risk monitoring these responses and replace them with more honest ones. Your parents will survive.

- Reconsider your guilt. The person who constantly feels guilty because he doesn't *do* enough for his parents, or can't make them happy, is sometimes really disappointed that he can't say or be whatever it takes to make his parents love him in the way he's always fantasized being loved. If this is true for you, realize that your parents love you as much as they can, in the way that they are able to. You may never be able to get exactly what you need from them. You may never be able to fulfill their expectations. They may always be more concerned with your "looking good" than with what you truly feel. You can only change yourself and the way that you react.

  Going to the same "empty well" over and over again hoping to finally draw water is both pointless and painful. Accept that your parents have their limitations.

- Persistent guilt over the way we treat our parents may be a signal that we're not comfortable with our actions and should change. It can also be a symptom of enmeshment. Some families have rules that no one has a right to be different, or have opinions or a lifestyle that contrasts with the status quo. Everyone feels guilty if he or she violates these rules. Family members may move thousands of miles away but still never really leave home.

  John Bradshaw, in his book *On the Family*, writes that "Leaving home means separating from our family system. It means giving up the idealizations and the fantasy of being bonded to our parents. Only by leaving and becoming separate can we have the choice of having a relationship with our parents. Relationship demands separation and detachment.''

In a healthy relationship, there are boundaries between individuals. Take a closer look at the guilt you feel and ask, ''Am I really deserting my parents by going after my own goals? Or is it too scary to desert the part of myself that still needs my parents to define who I am and how I should act?

• Stop using the fact that your parents will eventually die as an excuse for not separating your needs and goals from their own. One man said, ''I argue with my parents, shout at them, and walk out of their house. But even if I'm right, I can't let myself stay angry at them too long. I think, They're in their sixties now. They could die tomorrow. I'll end up with eternal guilt!''

This belief that we have to acquiesce to our parents because they might die and our last words to them will have been angry ones is really stretching it. It reflects a childish belief that there is some vindictive force in the universe that will get us if we ''misbehave.'' It also indicates an unconscious and erroneous belief that our anger will kill our parents.

You can be angry at people, disappoint them, be inadequate in front of them, go against their wishes, and frustrate them, and all of you will still survive. The goal is not to hang on to our anger at our parents. It's to give up our excuses for never allowing ourselves to be who we are around them.

While there are opinions and details of our lives that are better kept to ourselves, this doesn't mean we have to become a totally different person than we are every time we encounter our parents. Only when we can experience their anger and disappointment in us without having to react to it by placating, lying, or changing who we are can we realize that we are masters of our own fate.

Take Risks

Action pays off. The only way we gain competence is through experience.

Overparenting dramatically affects our ability to take initiative. Initiative assumes risk. Risks make us feel vulnerable, because risks were something our parents consistently tried to protect us from.

A child's initiative is something that can be threatening to a parent who loves too much, and who has such a deep need to control. Initiative means, "I can think and do for myself." Unknowingly, a parent who loves too much stifles it, replacing such thoughts with, "You need me, and you'll fail without me."

Such a childhood creates entitled adults—people who expect, unconsciously, that others will automatically take the initiative and give them love, affection, and material things without anything being expected in return.

Ken, a twenty-six-year-old commercial artist, laughs when he admits that he ended up in marital therapy over a running toilet and parched houseplants. "I agreed to see a therapist not because I wanted to change, but because I wanted Sue to change. I bought her the house of her dreams, and every time I looked at her I thought, She never had it so good. It cost a fortune, and what did I get? A woman who waited there, every night, with a list of things that had to be fixed, groceries that had to be bought, and chores that had to be done.

"The fight we had when the toilet broke got ugly. I expected her to get it fixed. She said she didn't have time to find a plumber, because she got busy at work. I went wild thinking of another night of the pots and pans.

"Sue bitched that it wasn't her fault. She wanted to know why I didn't take any responsibility. She said I didn't care about the house; I expected her to wait on me; I was so helpless I couldn't even water the plants. Well, what was I supposed to know about toilets or houseplants?

"I was sick of her and her organized little lists. I admitted that I thought the house was her responsibility. She said I was spoiled and lazy, but I said that I bought her the damn house she wanted, and there were other women who would have been grateful for it.''

Ken and his wife entered therapy with a long list of complaints about each other, each hoping that the therapist would take his or her side and straighten the other person out. What they learned was that what they had was a ''perfect'' match. Sue was controlling and domineering, as a result of being raised by two alcoholic parents who depended on her to take charge, raise her brother and sister, and clear away any mess they made. She spent a lifetime secretly choking on her resentments, hoping that if she gave enough to someone else, she'd finally get her turn to be needy and would be taken care of.

Ken was used to having his needs anticipated by parents who doted on him, and he expected to be taken care of. A history of being rescued from his responsibilities and foisting them on his parents left him afraid to risk fending for himself. To take any initiative in his relationship with Sue was a risk. He adopted the role of ''helpless'' and got annoyed when she required his help.

Sue and Ken did an age-old waltz together, stepping to a tune of mutual need and resentment. In therapy they poured out their resentment.

The therapist's advice? Take risks. Step out of old roles. Sue should give Ken responsibility. She should start by letting Ken take charge of something as simple as watering the plants. They might die, but that was a risk she'd have to take if she was going to stop taking control and rescuing him from responsibilities while complaining about his irresponsibility.

Ken should learn how to fix the broken toilet. He should stop thinking that he was going to fix it wrong, break it, ruin it, or embarrass himself. He should give it a shot, and then call a plumber if he couldn't fix it. He should stop depending on Sue, who might have had the motivation to get it fixed, but who had no more skills than he in plumbing.

The toilet got fixed, the plants got watered, and Sue and

Ken stopped dancing together. They risked stepping out of familiar roles because they knew the old roles they clung to eventually meant the end of their relationship. Ken, who had been loved so much that he never learned self-competence, began to depend on himself. Sue, who had been loved so little that she never trusted anyone to truly give to her, learned to take what others would give her if she let go of controlling them.

Overparenting may produce an adult who is bored, unable to take initiative, and unable to risk. If you, like Ken, grow queasy at the thought of taking a risk, and take comfort in being a bystander rather than an initiator, try the following steps:

- Set your goal at taking one risk a day. Try something as simple as buying a new shirt without asking anyone else how it looks on you, take a stab at fixing a broken piece of furniture, or call a friend you haven't spoken to in a long time. After a while, doing these things will seem simpler as your experience grows.
- Next time you hear yourself say, "I can't do this," catch yourself. Instead of giving up, try it two more times.
- Take a closer look at what you mean when you say you're bored. Boredom is often a defense against anxiety. Are you bored in a meeting? Ask if what you really feel is too inadequate to participate or assert yourself and get things back on track. Are you bored by your lover? Ask yourself if you're really anxious about having an intimate relationship. Are you bored when other people talk? Ask yourself if you're anxious because you don't have control over what's being said.

  The antidote to boredom is participation. Given your history, being active may make you much more anxious than lying back and watching from the sidelines. Make your goal to increase your participation in the events going on around you by 50 percent, and watch your anxiety dissipate.

It Takes More Than Luck

People who were loved too much often believe in magic.

Jeff, a thirty-two-year-old public-relations account executive, set up a meeting with his boss after three months in his new position. He complained of being bored, unchallenged by his work and left out of the more vital projects and client presentations. "I'm being underused," he explained. "I could be a lot more valuable to you doing something more important than writing news releases that anyone could do."

His boss listened in stony silence, and then replied, "You have a stack of news releases on your desk right now that should have gone out yesterday, but you're the first one out of here at five o'clock. How can I give you more responsibility when you don't even do the job you have now? When I looked over the report I asked you to write for a client and then asked you to make some corrections on, you gave it back to me exactly the way it was before I asked for the corrections. What I think is that you're in over your head already."

Jeff left his boss's office puzzled and resentful. Instead of the promotion he'd been expecting, he was on probation.

Years later, a more seasoned Jeff acknowledges his mistake. "I used to think that I was smarter than my coworkers, my boss, and even the president of the company. I thought all I needed to do was tell people about all of my 'gifts,' and I'd soar like a meteor right to the top. I thought I was above paying dues, and that magically I'd be spared them all. Well, believe it or not, people aren't that interested in how bright you are. You can be smarter than everyone else, but it doesn't really matter. They're more interested in whether or not you've paid your dues, learned to be a team player, and can follow through on the assignments no one else wants and do them well. I read what they say in magazines about people leaping, untried and unproven, straight to the top. That's luck and magic.

Reality is people allowing you to handle the big stuff after you prove yourself on the little stuff.''

An aversion to paying dues is a common hallmark of the adult child who was overparented, and for good reason. Jeff admits that he listened all his years to a familiar litany—his mother saying, ''You're so special; so brilliant; so talented; so much better than everyone else.'' This perception that he was especially gifted—overblown by parents who loved him too much—led to a secret conviction of entitlement or superiority. He should start at the top. All he needed was a lucky break.

Superiority and inferiority are flip sides of the same coin. The need to puff ourselves up comes from self-esteem based on other people's admiration of us rather than true belief in ourselves. Feelings of superiority rarely drive us to the top.

Researchers have found that successful people share certain characteristics:

- Realism. People who believe that nothing terrible can happen take unreasonable risks. Those who imagine the worst that could happen, and don't view themselves as magically protected from it, prepare for it.
- Reliability. People who succeed do what they say they are going to do. The can be counted on. They don't just talk a good game—they play one.
- Proactivity. The person who is ''proactive'' plans carefully, initiates action, and anticipates what will be needed. The ''reactive'' is blown by every wind. When something happens, he reacts too quickly and impulsively, without fully exploring the implications of his actions. Since he rarely makes anything happen but waits for others to react, he remains dependent on other people to shape his life.
- Perseverance. Dedicated and fully committed, the successful person believe he can overcome obstacles and setbacks, not through luck, but through work. He views personal setbacks as a fact of life, and mistakes as correctable with a solid plan of action. People who

are often defeated are perfectionistic to a fault, and
feel they've lost it all after a single defeat.
• A healthy skepticism of chance or external forces controlling their fate. Successful people believe that they
shape their own destiny. People who believe that their
fate lies in the hands of something outside of them
feel they can do little, if anything, to control what
happens to them, and often give up.

Everything we learned about succeeding as we grew up
may be in complete contrast to these behaviors. Our parents believed we would succeed just because we were special to them.

Fortunately, these qualities are acquired rather than
inherited. Although a lifetime of being loved too much
may have stunted the development of these behaviors, you
can still learn them at any age. Habits of thinking and
action can be changed. Start by doing the following:

• Match your drive to succeed with the kind of action
that encourages success. If we set our goals high but
make little effort, abandon careful planning, fold at
the first obstacle, and cast off our share of the "grunt
work" whenever possible, we'll fail to reach many of
our aspirations.
• Presuming that the work we do is beneath us is evidence of "looking good" behavior. We may be more
concerned with grabbing status and power in order to
"show well" than the quest for real achievement.
   Don't put the cart before the horse. Curb your impatience. In our families, we rarely had to wait for
what we wanted. Outside our families, we may have
to bide our time. But if you perform and persist with
total commitment, opportunities for growth and more
responsibility will follow.
• See failures as an opportunity for growth and change.
If you received a poor evaluation at work, or failed to
get a raise you feel you deserve, look at it as feedback. Why have others failed to recognize your
strengths?

Rather than getting emotionally involved, or seeing yourself as "bad," look at your organization as a scientist would look at an experiment. In other words, detach emotionally and use your intelligence. Would slightly altering your behavior achieve your goal, rather than seriously alter the integrity of the "experiment"? Have you considered all of the things in the environment that are impacting on the "experiment"? One woman who lost an account, and the commission that came with it, alternately blamed her coworkers, her boss, her secretary, and was bemused when she read in a trade magazine that the company was going bankrupt and had cut her services to save on costs.

• Successful people bounce back. They don't waste time wallowing in mistakes. Instead of defensively holding the position "They're wrong and I'm right," stick to your goal and consider what can still be done to achieve it. Quit worrying that you have disappointed your parents, your spouse, or your own idealized self. What makes failure seem so awful is the way you perceive it.

The way you view failure is something that was taught to you, perhaps by parents who feared it themselves. Your response to it can be automatic: "I'm bad; I've made a fool of myself; What's the use?"

Psychologists use a tool called cognitive restructuring to modify these responses with something more positive. Cognitive restructuring involves looking at all the elements in the environment that impact on events. If we've trained our minds to always blame ourselves—or to never blame ourselves—we look closely at other possibilities for what occurs. We realize that we don't have all of the responsibility, but that we share it. We open ourselves to new ways of viewing circumstances instead of letting our minds run in rigid cause-and-effect relationships that we've never really challenged.

One man who applied cognitive restructuring to a sales career where he dealt daily with rejection said, "I now see 'No' as an opportunity. It doesn't scare me, or make me feel ashamed for asking. It makes me work harder, and evaluate what happened and why. I've learned to look at rejection in a whole different way—much less personally.''

Stop Taking Yourself So Seriously

If you want to feel more alive, you have to stop taking yourself so seriously and scanning other people's faces anxiously for a judgment.

If you were overparented, you've borne the weight of your parents' high expectations for so long that you may fail to notice it. You've internalized these expectations. You exhaust yourself in trying to meet them, or give up, figuring, "What's the use?"

You may wish, more than anything, that you could just relax and be who you are. Yet you can't give in to this feeling because who you are never seems good enough.

Adult children who were overparented lost their childhoods in the quest to be the "good," silent, thin, talented, intelligent, sensitive boy or girl their parents would be proud of. Instead of being free, they're constantly obsessed with being in control.

Some therapists give people who have lost their childhoods an assignment: Be a child for a couple of weeks, and allow yourself to feel the joy of being silly and immature in an environment that will allow it.

When Anita, a thirty-four-year-old store manager, drew this assignment and was handed a coloring book and a box of crayons, she thought, This is really stupid. But used to doing what other people asked her to do, she started to draw. She looked at the silly pictures of cartoon characters and started to giggle. It seemed so crazy—an adult, coloring in a coloring book—and yet she realized she was getting a kick out of it.

The next thing she knew, she was letting herself act like a kid. During the next week, she spent an afternoon at the park, swinging on the swing. She bought a couple of Nancy Drew mysteries, and a Slinky.

Like Anita, we all have a child inside of us. There are different elements of this child that we may never have allowed to come to life: the needy child, the playful child, the wild child, and others. Allowing ourselves to be this child can be something that frees us.

This may seem like a contradiction. We're so "immature" at times as it is. We don't follow through on things. We have an infantile belief that everything will turn out okay for us. We have a childish dependency on people who appear stronger than we are. Why should we go back, further into childhood, when it seems like the one thing we really need to grow away from?

Sometimes the only way out of something is through it. If we were never allowed a real childhood, we may have to go backward and experience it.

Most of us have a faulty view of what constitutes childish behavior. Our parents filled us with so many rules about what was "appropriate" that we have the erroneous impression that children are "seen and not heard," mini-sized adults.

But from watching young children play, we can learn a lot about what it means to be free to be ourselves—without being restricted by other people's opinions or idealizations of how we should be. Children are creative risk-takers, unconcerned with the rules of society and the judgment of others. They are spontaneous and free emotionally, open to adventure and creativity.

When we lose our childhood, we lose a very important part of ourselves. To recapture some of it, try the following:

- Buy yourself a toy. Some Play-Doh, an Etch a Sketch, a teddy bear, a model, blocks, a coloring book—anything will do, as long as it's new and you're buying it for yourself. (No fair borrowing one from your children.) Play with it. Better yet, play with it wrong. Color outside the lines. Make a mess with the Play-Doh. Build something that doesn't look like anything anyone's ever seen before. Indulge the child inside you.

- Realize that there's a difference between being a child and being immature. There's a distinction between being carefree and being careless. Walking into work late for the fifth time in a week and expecting other people to believe your latest excuse is immature and naïve. Shirking all of your responsibilities and foisting them on others is carelessness. Either path will trap you rather than set you free.
- Children are honest and industrious, until they learn that dishonesty can manipulate others and that irresponsibility causes others to rescue them and take care of them. Cultivate the playfulness inside of you, not the recklessness.

Be Wary of Humming the Same Words to Different Music

Psychiatrists call it transference: an unconscious expectation that people will relate to us in the same manner as our parents or other important people in our past did.

Imposing these suspicions about how others will react to us on people who are not—and don't wish to be—our parents causes us to distort them, and resort to old patterns of communication and behavior in dealing with them. Julie discovered the perils of transferring her expectations of her mother onto her husband early in her marriage. "I poured out my whole sad story to a marriage counselor: the way Alex never wanted to go to the places I wanted to go to, never paid attention to me, never helped me when I had a problem. I ranted and raved for three weeks, frustrated because he'd never answer when I'd ask, 'What should I do? Do you think I'm right? What would you do?'

"The third session, I said, 'I'm quitting. I'm not going to spend sixty bucks telling you all of this if you can't even come up with a solution. Why won't you answer me?'

"He said what concerned him was that I didn't have an answer myself; that I didn't present him with any alternatives I'd thought about.

"I grabbed my coat to walk out, yelling that if I knew what to do, I wouldn't be there in the first place. It infuriated me that he didn't even try to stop me. When I accused him of being the most indifferent man I'd ever met, he said, 'You keep asking, "What should I do?," and getting angry that I won't tell you. But my answering that question isn't the solution. The fact that you keep asking it is part of the problem.'

"I sat back down, and he explained what he meant. 'You've told me that your mother is understanding, your father is sympathetic, but your husband is never understanding or sympathetic to what you need. He doesn't want to do the things you want to do when you want to do them. He won't help you every time you need it or give you the same type of understanding your parents give you every time you have a problem. Neither will I, and it's making you angry. The issue seems to be that when you want something and others can't give you what you want when you want it, you become very uncomfortable. That's what happens with your husband. I wouldn't be surprised if it happened with many people in your life. But leaving or staying in therapy is your choice. I'm not your mother or father. I don't need to cure you. I don't need to make you happy. I'm here to help you help yourself.' "

Julie sat down and recalled a lifetime of looking to others for the answer—a pattern that had seriously hampered the development of her self-esteem and competence and left her dependent on others, frustrated when they wouldn't come through for her.

Many of us can identify with Julie. We expect others to become our parents. We expect them to smother us, be disappointed in us, control us, praise us, expect too much from us, do for us, take care of us—love us too much.

It's very human to try to re-create situations that are comfortable for us, but the constant replay can play havoc with our relationships because it places others in a double bind. If they become our caretakers, the result is our failure to achieve feelings of competence and self-esteem from doing things for ourselves. Eventually, the people we're involved with come to resent us. They wait their turn for love and understanding, and never get it.

When others won't cater to us, it creates an imbalance between our expectations and reality, and we resent them for not "being good enough to us," because we're entitled to it. Often we end up sad, frustrated, and full of contempt.

The first step in breaking out of old routines is to be aware of them. This does not mean blaming and punishing ourselves. It's not our fault that our parents loved us too much. It's not our fault if they anticipated and fulfilled our needs to the extent that we never really knew frustration or were immobilized by it until now. We did nothing to cause our parents' overindulgence and intense devotion. We simply *were,* and to fulfill their own needs, they responded to us as they did.

We can make a decision to stop transferring old patterns onto new relationships, where they get in the way. We can acquire new ways of sharing ourselves with others. If we want to change our relationships, we need to change how we relate. The following guidelines can be helpful:

• Take a closer look at the assumptions you make about your relationships with others. Consider how you may be reacting to people on the basis of these assumptions, rather than on what these people do or say. For example, if you fear that all women are manipulative and controlling because this was your childhood experience, you may project this onto all women in your life and not allow yourself to get close enough to them to see that this isn't true. Or if you believe you can't trust people to keep secrets because your parents spread the details of your life all over town, you can be with the most trustworthy person in the world and not trust him.

The only way to combat this is to be open to experience other people, without prejudging them. Ask yourself if you judge others too quickly, stereotyping them and placing them into ready categories in your mind. Listen more openly. Check out your assumptions. Give people a second chance and a third chance.

- Realize that your past experience has left you insatiable for affection and attention. Too much of this in childhood can make you an approval addict, and you may feel that you never get enough. Before you accuse others of being cold to you, neglectful, or too needy, ask yourself if what you crave is more than your share. Are you participating actively in your relationships, returning what you get? Or are you searching for another parent who will love you too much?

- For a couple of weeks, adopt the role of a sociologist, studying how people react to you and others. Be open to all variables with the detachment characteristic of a scientific observer. This will require that you spend time with groups of people and push yourself to go different places. Watch for the times when you experience other people's reactions in new ways that don't meet your old expectations. As one man said, "The first time I saw conflict handled in a healthy way, with no tears, recriminations, or manipulations, it blew my mind."

- Some of us, for whom re-creating old patterns is the number-one difficulty, will benefit much from therapy. A good therapist will interpret patterns of transference over time. As we play out old roles with the therapist—a natural part of the therapeutic process—and get different responses, we will realign our expectations of others to a more realistic frame.

Come Clean with Your Parents

Breakdowns can be breakthroughs. Marie, a thirty-two-year-old account supervisor, was in the middle of an explanation of why she was leaving her company and going out on her own when she was interrupted by her father: "It's too risky. You'll never get enough clients. What about your health insurance and benefits? Your pension? Stick it out and don't be a fool."

"I completely lost it," Marie admits, "and got really angry at him. I tried to explain, but he wouldn't listen. He raised his voice, and I raised mine. I yelled about how much I hated my job, and how I was going to do what I wanted to do no matter what he said. He stood up, shook his finger at me, and said, 'Don't you ever talk to me that way! I'm still your father!' I walked out, slamming the door behind me."

Marie, who had spent the last year and a half working on her assertiveness and self-confidence, still found herself feeling like a guilty child for exploding at her father. "I'd learned that it's not a healthy relationship when one person is allowed to say whatever he wants and the other person represses himself. My new assertiveness was a plus in all of my other relationships. But with my father, it led to the biggest fight we ever had."

Marie's problem wasn't her assertiveness. It was that she had never come clean with her parents. The real issue wasn't whether her father agreed with her decision to quiet her job. It was her feeling that he never trusted her or supported her when she badly needed it, and treated her as a child, incapable of weighing the consequences of her actions.

For Marie, the argument that could have ended in a permanent rift with her father ended up being a breakthrough. She went over to see him, prepared to talk about issues. "If he had slammed the door in my face, I would have written him a letter. It was that important to me to explain how I felt, to not just apologize and continue some kind of superficial relationship where I'd have to lie or give in.

"Maybe it was because we'd never had such a blowup before that my father was shocked into listening to me. I explained how much it meant to me to be independent and to be able to make my own decisions. I told him how much it hurt me when he played the devil's advocate every time I wanted to change something in my life. All my life I'd listened to him, and it had made me terrified of change. Now, I had to work hard against my own tendency to stay stuck in a lot of situations that were comfortable but not good for me.

"I don't know if this kind of honesty would work for everyone, but I do know that my father and I really talked to each other that day. And although I didn't get his seal of approval for quitting my job, I did get the sense that he understood why I had to do it."

Coming clean with our parents doesn't mean that we tally up all the ways they've hurt us in the past, overprotected us, and expected too much, and demand retribution. It means developing our skills in communicating with them. This requires being vulnerable, assertive, and honest about our feelings. It means ending the approval-seeking and substituting sincerity.

This will not be easy. Some of us will meet with a lot of resistance when we adopt a policy of being honest with our parents. Our parents may sulk and remind us of all they've done for us. They may be angry and resentful. But our goal isn't to change them. It's to change the way we relate to them and alter the consequences of a lifetime of being loved and given too much. The challenge is to assume our own personal power and control over our lives. We accomplish this by demanding less and giving more of ourselves. We cannot turn off the voices of our parents, but we can learn to listen to them more realistically.

You may think that all of this sounds good in general, but that coming clean with your parents would never work for you. Breaking free of emotional bonds is scary, and your reluctance to alter patterns of communication with your parents is a symptom of your discomfort in loosening these bonds. The following tips will help:

- Get the support of others whose problems are similar. Hundreds of emotional support groups are available nationwide. In these groups, you'll be able to practice more effective communication skills. You'll get acceptance and support. Most important, you'll learn to share your feelings and to stop being a victim of your relationships.

- Accept your parents as they are. They may always attempt to overprotect you. They may always expect more of you than is reasonable. They may always attempt to control you. The only person you can change is yourself. You must give up your unrealistic expectations of your parents, and the hope that they will change and love you exactly the way you want to be loved.

  You needn't change your parents to gain control of your life. Today, your life is up to you, regardless of your parents' contribution to your outlook. You can define yourself. You are no longer powerless. You can grow and change. You needn't rely on your parents' judgments or approval. You can learn to affirm yourself and rely on yourself.

- Listen closely to yourself the next time you visit with your parents. How often do you hold back your real feelings and thoughts from them because you want their approval? What would happen to you if you didn't get it?

  Many of us have fallen into the trap of what psychologists call "catastrophic expectations." We think that if we're honest with our parents, they'll disapprove of what we say or do, reject us completely, or be so hurt that they'll never recover. We assume living outside our parents' approval will cause them to stop loving us.

  Do you stop loving your parents when they act in ways you disapprove of? Neither will they stop loving you. There are few bonds in life as strong as that between parent and child. Children of parents who love too much can rest assured that it would take much more than independence of thought and action to break this bond.

- Coming clean with your parents does not mean blaming them for everything that is wrong in your life. Blaming others places the responsibility for your choices on them rather than on yourself. Instead of saying, "My mother makes me feel guilty," or "My father treats me like a child," take responsibility for your own feelings and substitute, "I allow myself to feel guilty," and "I allow myself to be treated like a child."

- Coming clean with your parents may mean setting limits with them. You have the right not to discuss certain topics. You have the right to ask that they phone before dropping over. You have the right to choose your own job, friends, home, recreational activities, lifestyle, etc., without listening to constant criticism. You have the right to say, "I've heard what you have to say about this; I hear that you don't like it, and let's agree to disagree."
- Coming clean with your parents may mean giving up old roles that are no longer suitable. Loving your parents doesn't mean you have to be their little baby. It doesn't mean you have to be the family medal winner. Examine the role you've taken in your family. Is it "the Needy One," "the Perfect One," "the Rebellious One," "the Victim," "the Prince," "the Grateful One"?

  Examine whether the role you play fulfills you and makes you happy. Does it create distance in your relationships? Does it sabotage your self-esteem? What role would you really like to play? Make a decision about whether there will be more value in changing, and if there is, get all the help and support you need to accomplish it.

Change is an easy thing to decide and a tough thing to do. It's the day-to-day challenge of it that makes people give up.

Don't be too hard on yourself if old ways look good to you at times. Expect this. Worry only if you fall into them too often.

Our early experiences are important, but they don't have to be decisive. We make the choice. We can recognize our past and continue it, or understand it and change our future. The decision is ours.

SUGGESTED READING

Basch, Michael Franz. *Understanding Psychotherapy*. New York: Basic Books, 1988.

Beattie, Melody. *Codependent No More*. New York: Harper and Row, 1987.

Bloomfield, Harold. *Making Peace with Your Parents*. New York: Ballantine Books, 1983.

Bradshaw, John. *Bradshaw on: The Family*. Deerfield Beach, Fla.: Health Communications Inc., 1988.

Branden, Nathaniel. *What Love Asks of Us*. New York: Bantam Books, 1983.

Dowling, Colette. *Perfect Women*. New York: Summit Books, 1988.

Dyer, Wayne. *Pulling Your Own Strings*. New York: Harper and Row, 1978.

Friday, Nancy. *My Mother/My Self*. New York: Delacorte Press, 1977.

Halpern, Howard. *How to Break Your Addiction to a Person*. New York: McGraw-Hill, 1982.

Hollis, Judi. *Fat Is a Family Affair*. San Francisco: Harper/Hazelden, 1985.

Jampolsky, Gerald. *Love Is Letting Go of Fear*. New York: Bantam Books, 1979.

Jernberg, Ann M. *Theraplay*. San Francisco: Jossey-Bass, 1979.

Johnson, Craig. *The Etiology and Treatment of Bulimia Nervosa: A Biopsychological Perspective*. New York: Basic Books, 1987.

Miller, Alice. *The Drama of the Gifted Child*. New York: Basic Books, 1981.

Minuchin, Salvador. *Psychosomatic Families: Anorexia Nervosa in Context*. Cambridge, Mass.: Harvard University Press, 1978.

Norwood, Robin. *Women Who Love Too Much*. New York: Simon and Schuster, 1985.

Peck, M. Scott. *The Road Less Traveled*. New York: Simon and Schuster, 1978.

Viorst, Judith. *Necessary Losses*. New York: Fawcett Crest, 1986.

BREAKING FREE

The newsletter for families who love too much

Are you a parent who loves too much and has difficulty letting go? Are you an adult child who can't break free? This newsletter is for you!

Each issue contains:

- *Tools and techniques*. Practical advice for combatting your inner critic, building your personal power, letting go of control, developing intimate relationships, and breaking out of the overparenting cycle.

- *Current research*. Up-to-date information on codependency and its treatment to support you as you recover.

- *The Family Scrapbook*. True experiences of people who love too much and the solutions they've found.

- *The latest listings*. What's new in seminars, books, tapes, and videos for parents and adult children.

- *Questions and Answers*. Selected letters from readers.

Breaking Free, written by Laurie Ashner and Mitch Meyerson, is available only by subscription. To subscribe or obtain information on national seminars, workshops or services write:

> Mitch Meyerson/Laurie Ashner
> P.O. Box 10610
> Chicago, IL 60610–0610

INDEX

AND BABY MAKES THREE...

CHILDBIRTH & MARRIAGE

The Transition to Parenthood
75201-8/$10.95 US/$12.95 CAN

from the best-selling author of

PREGNANCY & CHILDBIRTH

·Revised Edition
75946-2/$10.95 US/$12.95 CAN

TRACY HOTCHNER

A comprehensive guide for new parents confronting the realities of trying to keep a happy, healthy marriage while raising a happy, healthy child.